EVERY NIGHT IN EVERY HOME

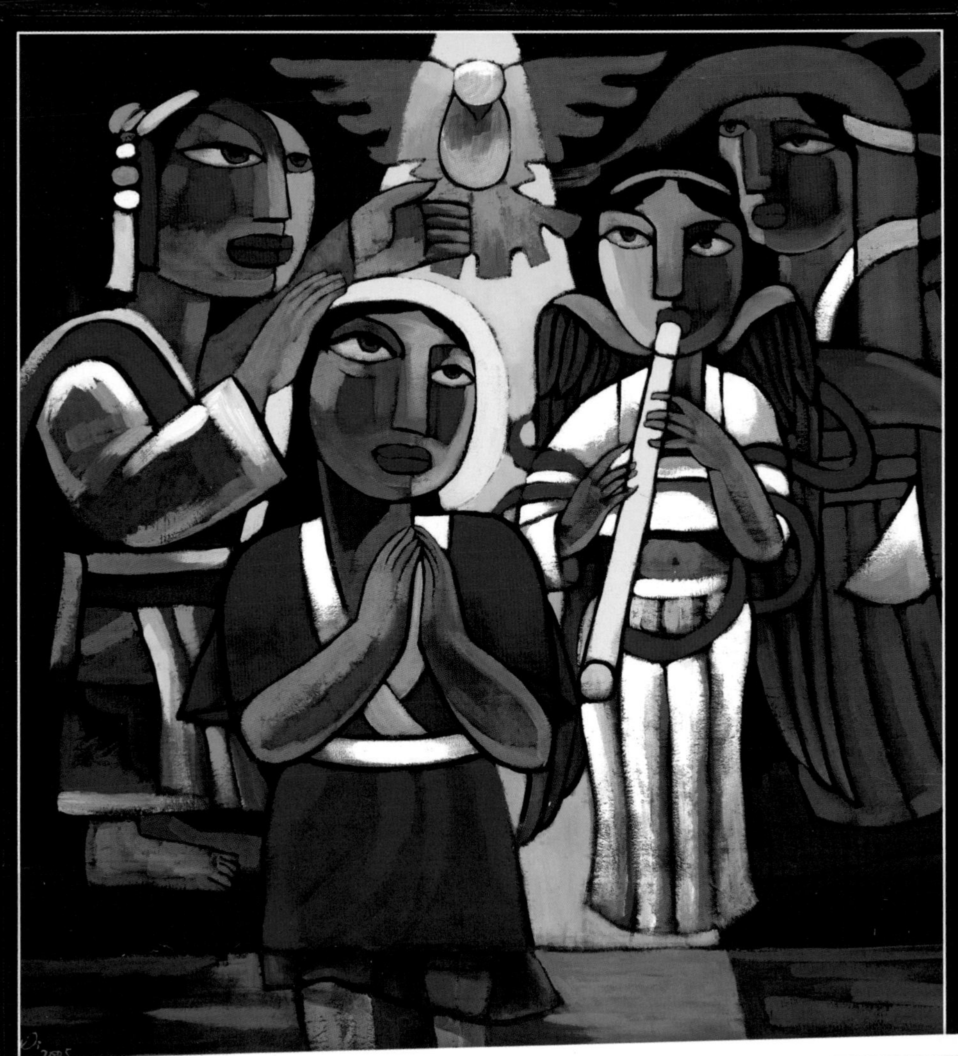

LIVING LUTHERAN

YEARBOOK & HOME JOURNAL

L. Precht

Living Lutheran

2nd Edition

P.O. Box 2307, Stillwater, MN, 55082

Toll Free Phone: 1-888-55FAITH, In Minnesota (651) 430-0762, Fax (651) 430-2377

Written and Compiled by Rich Melheim,
Nancy Gauche & the Faith Inkubators Writing Guild
Original Paintings and Theme Art by Dr. He Qi *(www.heqigallery.com)*
Verbatim Bible Songs for all of the quoted verses by the Faith Inkubators Music Guild
Book Design by Lookout Design *(www.lookoutdesign.com)* and Faith Inkubators
Luther Comic Book Art by Sherwin Schwartzrock *(www.blackrockgraphics.com)*
Cartoons by the Occasionally Most Reverend Rich Melheim
Cartoon Inking by the Sometimes Reverent Erin DeBoer-Moran
International Director of H2H Ministries Monty Lysne
Quotations from the FINK Quotelopedia

90 lessons corresponding to the themes from the Living Journals, PowerPoint™ presentations supporting each lesson, music for each Bible verse, and a myriad of additional resources are included in a membership to the Head to the Heart confirmation system. You can learn more about the system at *www.faithink.com*

CIP

ISBN 0-9785621-0-0

Table of Contents

Faith incubation every night in every home.

Faith Inkubators Mission Statement

Wouldn't it be fun to be able to look back on every single day of your adolescent journey and know what you were thinking?

This Living journal is designed to do just that. It can't do the work for you, but if you take a few minutes tonight and every night, you hold in your hands a tool that will help you see what you were going through, what you were thinking, what your friends were up to, and how God helped you along the way—every day—on your journey to becoming an adult.

The Living Journal

It may not seem like a big deal right now, but the next few years are going to be filled with life-altering changes. Your friends, your body, your school, your family, your shoe size and your brains—all of these are in transition. And transitions can cause CHAOS.

The symbol for CHAOS (left) means both challenge and opportunity. The years ahead are going to be filled with both. That's a guarantee. Wouldn't it be fun—and valuable—to have a record of it all? You can if you want to. It's in your hands.

Right Now.

During each week of your Faith Journey, we are honored to feature the artwork of Dr. He Qi.

www.heqigallery.com

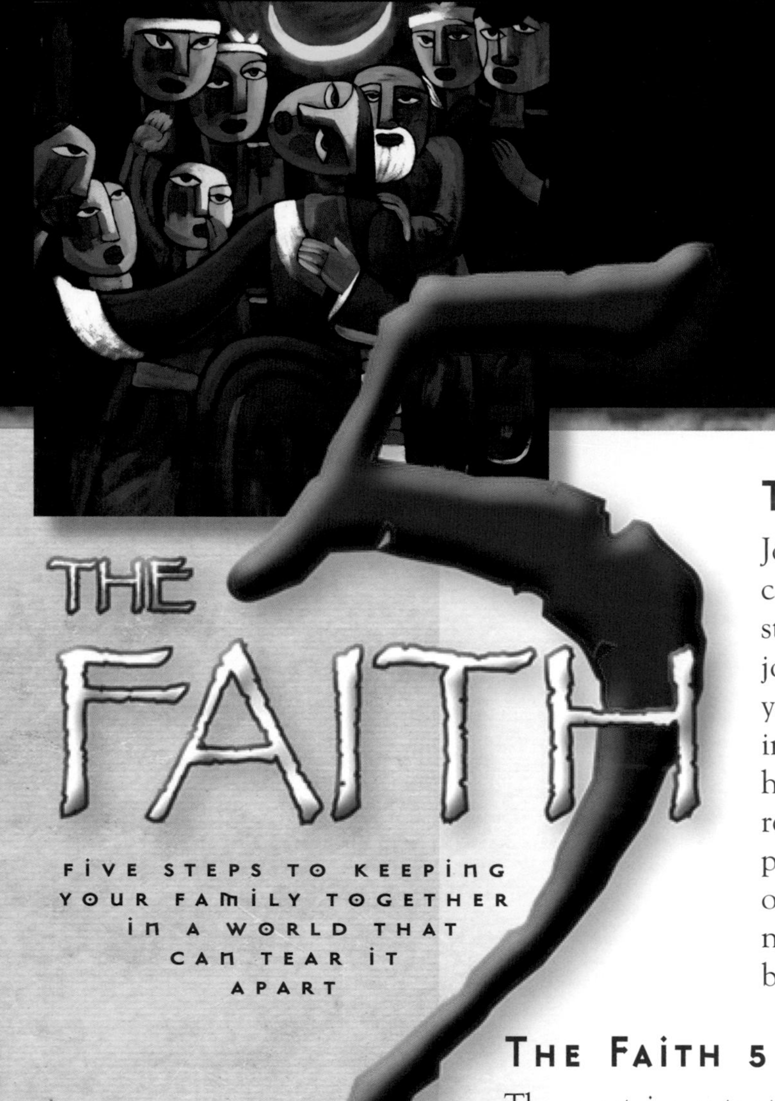

THE
FAITH
FIVE STEPS TO KEEPING YOUR FAMILY TOGETHER IN A WORLD THAT CAN TEAR IT APART

The Nightly Journal

Journaling is a great tool to help keep family communication open as you grow in your understanding of life, yourself, and God. This living journal—designed around the big themes of your young life—will help you clarify thoughts, gain insight into problems, and train yourself to see how and where God is active in your life. Simply record a sentence or two each night on the lines provided. If you use this tool regularly, you will one day be able to look back on your faith journey and see where you have been, who you have become, and where God has taken you.

The Faith 5 (Faith Acts In The Home)

The most important part of all this happens at home in a simple five-step process called the FAITH 5. Here's how it works: Whoever is going to bed first in your house calls "FAITH 5" or "Huddle Up!" Everyone must drop what they're doing, turn off the television and computer, put down their homework, and gather in a room of the convener's choice. Take turns going through these five simple steps:

1. **SHARE** highs & lows of the day (your best and worst experiences)

2. **READ** the verse of the week from your Bible

3. **TALK** about how this week's key verse relates to your highs & lows

4. **PRAY** for your highs & lows, for your family, and for the world

5. **BLESS** one another using the weekly blessing provided

FINK (fîngk)-n. 1. *Slang* term for Faith Inkubators (circa 1993), a fun-loving Christian education systems think tank and international learning organization committed to creating family-centered ministry models, training, and resources that help parents incubate faith every night in every home and have a blast while doing it.

FINKLinks Online

There are a pile of surprises and fun new theme-related resources awaiting you online each night to enrich your FAITH 5 JOURNAL experience. You can play the FINK*mania* Quiz Bowl live with family and friends. Listen to and learn the week's key Bible verse in song (NRSV verbatim) and purchase it if you wish to carry it along with you all week. Three complete devotional pages are online free for those wishing to dig deeper into each week's theme and verse. Simply go to *www.faithink.com* and enter the FINK*link* code listed for each specific theme.

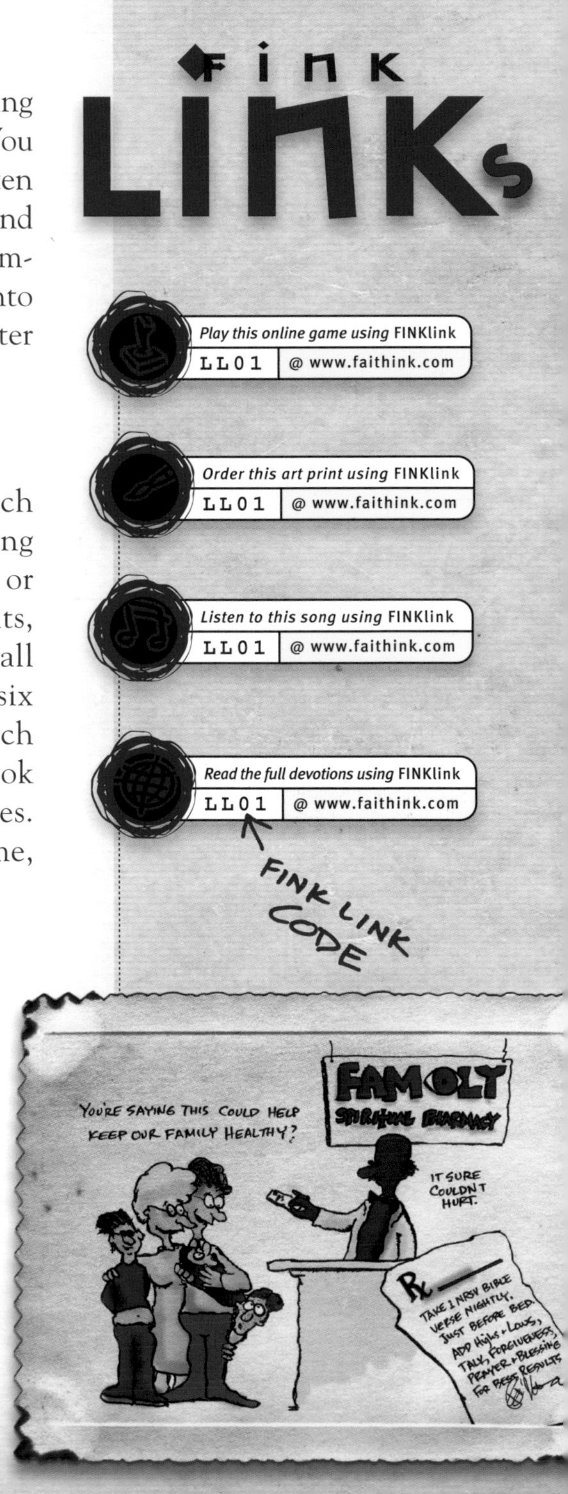

At Church

For churches using Head to the Heart confirmation curriculum, each theme in this book is designed to connect what you are learning at church with your nightly family conversations. First, a pastor or teaching team unveils the week's theme in art, song, cartoons, skits, and PowerPoint slides at church. Next comes FAITH 5 time in small groups, where 4-6 youth and a Small Group Guide use the first six pages of each lesson to review all they have covered. Once the church has helped kick off a theme, youth "bring it on home" using this book to share the FAITH 5 and these thematic resources with their families. This journal provides two week's worth of Bible verses for each theme, plus space to record highs, lows and prayers.

Beginning of the Year

Use the next few pages for pictures of each member of your small group, along with a photo of your small group Guide when they were your age. Record and share the information requested as a way to get to know your new friends. Then hop to the last page of this book and play OPERATION SPYGLASS to get to know the journal. Add photos of small group events on the last pages of the book as the year goes by. At the end of the year, take one last picture of your small group and use the final pages to summarize where you've been. You may look back on this book one day and see just how much fun it was to go through the CHAOS with such awesome friends and your awesome God!

A Moment in TIME

This Book Belongs To:

Take a moment to personalize this book. Include information about your family, friends and confirmation small group.

Name

Age & Grade

Today's Date

Phone

Email/IM

Birthdate

Baptism Day

My family includes (names and ages):

My three best friends are:

My favorite food is:

My favorite band is:

My favorite activities are:

This is Me

This is My Family

Looking Ahead

Confirmation Day

Drivers' Licence Day

Graduation Day

When I grow up, I can hardly wait to:

One great thing I'd like to do with my life for the world is:

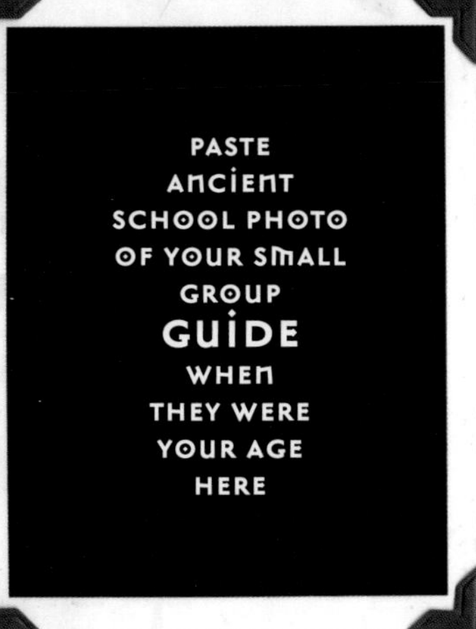

Name

Phone

Email/IM

Birthday

One thing about me:

My Small Group Guide

Name

Phone

Email/IM

Birthday

One thing about me:

My Small Group Friend

Name

Phone

Email/IM

Birthday

One thing about me:

Another Friend

Name

Phone

Email/IM

Birthday

One thing about me:

One More Friend

Name

Phone

Email/IM

Birthday

One thing about me:

Yet Another Friend

PASTE
SCHOOL
PHOTO
HERE

Name

Phone

Email/IM

Birthday

One thing about me:

Even One More Friend

MARTIN LUTHER

AND THE SMALL CATECHISM

1. THE STORMY MONK
2. THE PROTESTING PROFESSOR
3. TROUBLE, TROUBLE, TROUBLE
4. HERETIC'S TRIAL
5. MARTIN LUTHER: A LEGACY
6. TEN COMMANDMENTS OVERVIEW
7. LORD'S PRAYER OVERVIEW
8. APOSTLES' CREED OVERVIEW
9. THE SACRAMENT OF BAPTISM
10. THE SACRAMENT OF COMMUNION

The Stormy Monk

"By the tender mercy of our God, the dawn from on high will break upon us, to give light to those who sit in darkness and in the shadow of death, to guide our feet into the way of peace."

– Luke 1:78-79

Listen to this verse using FINKlink
LL01 @ www.faithink.com

Christopher Columbus had just returned from an amazing voyage around the world to a place he thought was India. The "fact" the earth was flat was possibly no fact at all.

As the 16th century dawned, everything was being challenged and changed. Astronomers like Copernicus and Galileo were exploring orbits and questioning our earth's place in the universe. A new middle class was rising in Europe, upsetting the old feudal system and empowering common people to demand human rights, property, and a larger say in government. Information technology was booming. Gutenberg's printing press and a new postal service spanning Europe sent ideas, books, pamphlets, and political cartoons flying out of print shops and across the world as fast as the ink could dry. Peter Henlein's invention of the pocket watch was making everyone more aware of time. (Everyone who could afford it, that is.) Science, technology, and economics were changing, churning and challenging old ways of thinking. The world was on the brink of transformation. The church would not be far behind.

It's the end of the world as we know it, and I feel fine.

REM

The End of the World as We Know It

In Europe, millions were dying from the Black Plague. Many believed this was a sign that God's judgment would bring the world to an end at midnight on December 31, 1499. The western Christian church, ruled by the Pope in Rome, was the supreme power of its day. The church crowned kings and dethroned them. It dictated rules for society, art, and culture. People who questioned its authority would be cautioned, then threatened, then silenced, imprisoned, or tortured until they confessed their sins. If they continued in their rebellion, they faced being banned from all commerce and could be kicked out of the church. If they still continued in their errors, rebels who defied the church could be burned at the stake. (Nice thing for a church to do?) The masses and the church were on a collision course with change.

That is where our story begins.

Young Luther

Hans and Margaretha Luther had just left the farm. Hans was working in the mining business near Eisleben, Germany, the year baby Martin was born. As the boy grew, Father Hans noticed his second child could argue with the best of them. With a good education, perhaps Martin would become a successful lawyer and take care of his parents in their old age. At age four and a half, young Martin was packed up and sent off to Latin school to start his formal education. (Children at this school spoke Latin even on the playground!) Nothing but the best for their promising son and future retirement plan.

Order this art print using **FINKlink**

LL01 @ www.faithink.com

Images in Art

- What do you see in today's cartoon art on the previous page?
- Where are you in this work of art?
- How do the image and the verse apply to your life today?

1436

Guttenberg Invents Printing Press

Black Plague ravages Europe (Rats!)

November 10, 1483

Martin Luther is born to Hans and Margaretha

1488

Luther starts Latin school (smart kid!)

1492

Columbus discovers America (10,000 years after Native Americans and 500 years after Norwegians)

1500

Century turns, world churns, some expect Jesus to show up and end it all

The Storm Within

Young Martin was a smart but restless child. He grew up in a strict family where he was often whipped for the smallest offenses. Once his mother beat him bloody for stealing a nut! The boy was tormented by a picture of God as a stern, angry judge he couldn't escape. To him, God was the Creator who first created him imperfect, then demanded perfection. How fair is that? No matter how hard he tried, he felt unworthy of God's love. He knew he wasn't good enough to earn heaven. To him, God was the judge, jury, and executioner, waiting to send him to hell if he messed up. How could he love a God like that? How could he find peace with himself, with his hopeless condition, and with God?

The Enlightening Lightning

Strangely enough, it was a storm in the sky that would end the storm in his soul. On July 2, 1505, young Martin was on his way home from college for spring break when he was caught in a storm that changed his life. A bolt of lightning struck a nearby tree. Was God out to fry him? Luther dove to his knees in the mud and prayed to the patron saint of miners, "Help me, St. Anne, and I shall become a monk!" The storm passed. He returned home and promptly told his parents he would be leaving law studies to join a monastery. Father Hans was furious! Martin wouldn't be taking care of his parents in their old age after all! Instead, he was off to the Black Cloister in Erfurt to search for peace with God.

The Vows

On the day he was accepted into the order of monks, Martin stripped to his skivvies and lay himself down on the cold stone floor over the bones of the monastery's founder. There he renounced all worldly passions and took the vows of celibacy, poverty, and obedience to the church. Maybe now, by leaving all earthly temptations behind, he could finally earn God's approval and find peace.

The Stormy Monk

At the monastery, Luther outdid all of the other brothers in acts of service, prayer, study, and piety. He disciplined and punished his body, wore out his supervising priest with constant confession, and volunteered for the lowest, dirtiest jobs. He was bound and determined to show God that he deserved God's love. It didn't work. No matter how hard he tried, he still felt no peace in his soul. In 1509, Luther said his first mass and became a priest of the church. He was assigned to serve as campus pastor and teach at Wittenberg University.

The Eternal City

In 1510, Luther made a pilgrimage to Rome on monastery business. There, in the center of the western Christian world, he visited many religious shrines hoping to amass brownie points on his heavenly record. Every holy site boasted a piece of Christ's cross, St. Peter's knucklebone, or a holy grail of some kind. At one shrine called Pilate's Steps, it was said you could free dead relatives from purgatory by crawling on your knees and praying upon each stone. Luther felt sorry his parents weren't dead at that time—he could have freed them from purgatory! The stormy monk thought his pilgrimage would be a holy highlight. Instead, he found priests living openly corrupt, drunken, immoral lives. The shrines were money-making tourist traps. He returned home disillusioned, confused, and angry with the church. What did he do with this anger? He went on a quest to find a God of love. That quest would one day change the world.

Next Time: The Protesting Professor

Next Time: The Protesting Professor

Time Traveler 1505

Imagine traveling back in time to medieval days. Imagine flying over Europe, down into the forests of Germany. The sky is black with clouds as you descend. Rain drenches you as you settle onto the ground. A muddy road appears and a lone horse-drawn wagon is making its way through the muck.

Suddenly, you are sitting on the wagon seat, rain pouring all around. Your clothes smell wet and musty. Your skin is cold and clammy. Next to you sits a young man, maybe twenty years old. He is drenched, cold, and very frightened. He whispers prayers, muttering. Suddenly—BOOM!—a lightning bolt cracks with a deafening noise in the tree right next to the cart. The horse bolts. You are thrown from the wagon into the mud. BOOM! Another blast explodes into a nearby tree. You dive for cover behind a rock wall. The young man cries out in fear, "St. Anne, spare me!" BOOM! Another flash hits a nearby tree, splinters flying everywhere. The branches burst into flames. Your nostrils fill with bitter smoke and your hair with ashes. Howling winds rip at your clothing. Again the man cries out, "St. Anne, spare my life! Only spare my life, and I will devote it entirely to God! I will become a monk!" You know this man. It is young Martin Luther. The storm has caught him, and you with him. He now cries to God, bargaining for his life. You push yourself into the stone wall, sensing panic in his eyes. A storm rages in his soul, even as the storm rages around you. Will it never end?

Then, as quickly as it came upon you, the winds die down and the rain stops. Inky clouds give way to a brilliant sun breaking through, drenching the land with warmth. The young man relaxes and leans his head against the stone wall. Together you heave a sigh of relief. The arch of a grand rainbow stretches across the afternoon countryside in front of you. You stand and stretch the kinks of fear from your tense muscles. You brush debris from wet hair and clothing. A few years from now Martin Luther will write about this day as the pivotal day of his life—the day God got hold of him. Later he will translate the entire Bible, inspire generations of Christians with his writings, and launch the greatest reformation in the history of the church.

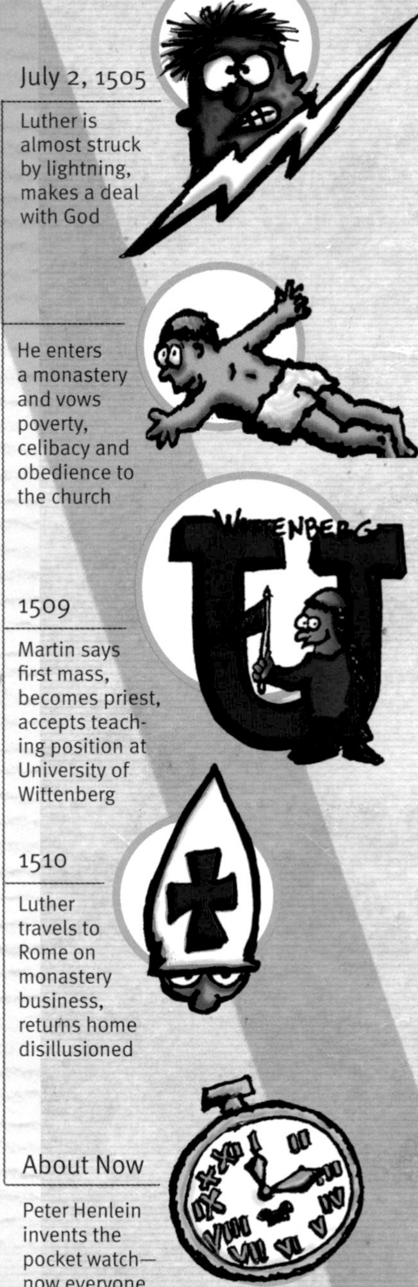

July 2, 1505
Luther is almost struck by lightning, makes a deal with God
He enters a monastery and vows poverty, celibacy and obedience to the church
WITTENBERG
1509
Martin says first mass, becomes priest, accepts teaching position at University of Wittenberg
1510
Luther travels to Rome on monastery business, returns home disillusioned
About Now
Peter Henlein invents the pocket watch—now everyone is late for everything

Restlessness and discontent are the first necessities of progress.

Thomas A. Edison

So What Does This Mean?

Erfurt was a bustling university city with 2000 students when Luther entered college in 1501. He saw his first Bible in a library there in 1503. Do the math. How old was he?

Bible Time

Read and highlight Luke 1:78-79 in your Bible, writing "The Way of Peace—see Romans 1:17" in the margin. What does this verse have to do with Martin Luther's search for peace with God?

Catechism Encounter

Flip through Luther's Small Catechism, looking for words that describe God. Write five of them here:

Questions to Ponder

1. Have you ever tried to make a deal with God? What happened?

2. How do you picture God? As a friend? A parent? A judge? An unknowable far-off being? A cosmic force? A Santa Claus who is watching to see if you are bad or good?

3. On what do you base your picture of God?

Small Group

share, read, talk, pray, bless

1. **SHARE** your highs and lows of the week one-on-one with another person. Listen carefully and record your friend's thoughts in the space below. Then return to small group and share your friend's highs and lows.

   my highs + lows this week were:

   ....

   my friend's highs + lows this week were:

   ....

2. **READ** and highlight the theme verse in your Bibles. Circle key words and learn the verse in song if time permits.

3. **TALK** about how today's verse relates to your highs and lows. Review the art for today, the Quiz Bowl questions, the terms, and the cartoons. Then write a sentence on each of the following:

   one new thing i learned today:

   ....

   one thing i already knew that is worth repeating:

   ....

   one thing i would like to know more about:

   ....

4. **PRAY** for one another, praising and thanking God for your highs, and asking God to be with you in your lows. Include your friend's highs and lows in your prayers.

   a praising prayer: ....

   a thanking prayer: ....

   an asking prayer: ....

5. **BLESS** one another using the blessing of the week. (right) Mark each person with the sign of the cross as you bless them.

this week's blessing

(NAME), may the storm of God ignite in your soul. Amen.

THE FAITH 5

JOURNAL

WEEK 1

Read the full devotions using FINKlink
LL01 @ www.faithink.com

DAY 1

TODAY'S BIBLE VERSE:

LUKE 1:78-79

By the tender mercy of our God, the dawn from on high will break upon us, to give light to those who sit in darkness and in the shadow of death, to guide our feet into the way of peace.

MY HIGH TODAY WAS:

MY LOW TODAY WAS:

MY PRAYER TODAY IS:

DAY 2

TODAY'S BIBLE VERSE:

PSALM 7:1-2

O Lord my God, in you I take refuge; save me from all my pursuers, and deliver me, or like a lion they will tear me apart; they will drag me away, with no one to rescue.

MY HIGH TODAY WAS:

MY LOW TODAY WAS:

MY PRAYER TODAY IS:

DAY 3

TODAY'S BIBLE VERSE:

PSALM 14:2

The Lord looks down from heaven on humankind to see if there are any who are wise, who seek after God.

MY HIGH TODAY WAS:

MY LOW TODAY WAS:

MY PRAYER TODAY IS:

my HIGH today was:

my LOW today was:

my PRAYER today is:

DAY 4

today's bible verse:

Psalm 18:2

The Lord is my rock, my fortress, and my deliverer, my God, my rock in whom I take refuge, my shield, and the horn of my salvation, my stronghold.

my HIGH today was:

my LOW today was:

my PRAYER today is:

DAY 5

today's bible verse:

Psalm 23:4

Even though I walk through the darkest valley, I fear no evil; for you are with me...

my HIGH today was:

my LOW today was:

my PRAYER today is:

DAY 6

today's bible verse:

Psalm 25:5

Lead me in your truth, and teach me, for you are the God of my salvation; for you I wait all day long.

SILENTIUM

my HIGHEST HIGH this week was:

my LOWEST LOW this week was:

my PRAYER for next week is:

DAY 7

this week's blessing

(NAME), MAY THE STORM OF GOD IGNITE IN YOUR SOUL. AMEN.

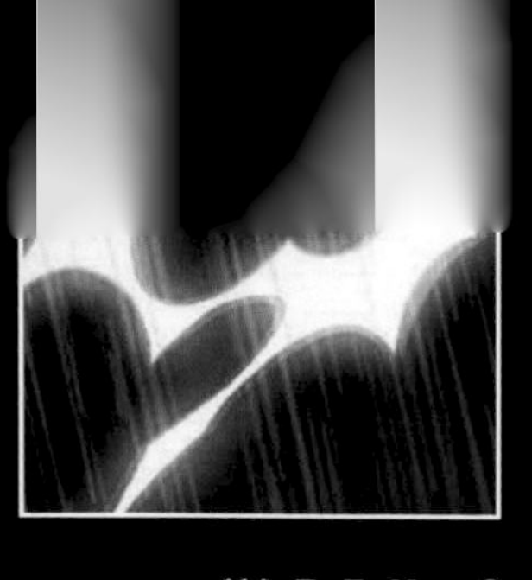

WEEK 2

FAITH JOURNAL

Read the full devotions using FINKlink
LL01 @ www.faithink.com

DAY 1

TODAY'S BIBLE VERSE:

Psalm 27:1

The Lord is my light and my salvation; whom shall I fear?

MY HIGH TODAY WAS:

MY LOW TODAY WAS:

MY PRAYER TODAY IS:

DAY 2

TODAY'S BIBLE VERSE:

Psalm 34:10

The young lions suffer want and hunger, but those who seek the Lord lack no good thing.

MY HIGH TODAY WAS:

MY LOW TODAY WAS:

MY PRAYER TODAY IS:

DAY 3

TODAY'S BIBLE VERSE:

Psalm 46:1-2

God is our refuge and strength, a very present help in trouble. Therefore we will not fear, though the earth should change, though the mountains shake...

MY HIGH TODAY WAS:

MY LOW TODAY WAS:

MY PRAYER TODAY IS:

1. SHARE HIGHS & LOWS OF THE DAY.

2. READ AND HIGHLIGHT THE VERSE OF THE DAY IN YOUR BIBLES.

3. TALK ABOUT HOW TODAY'S VERSE RELATES TO YOUR HIGHS & LOWS.

4. PRAY FOR YOUR HIGHS & LOWS, FOR YOUR FAMILY AND FOR THE WORLD.

5. BLESS ONE ANOTHER USING THIS WEEK'S BLESSING (ON THE PREVIOUS PAGE).

DAY 4

TODAY'S BIBLE VERSE:

Psalm 99:1

The Lord is king; let the peoples tremble! He sits enthroned upon the cherubim; let the earth quake!

my HIGH today was: ....

my LOW today was: ....

my PRAYER today is: ....

....

DAY 5

TODAY'S BIBLE VERSE:

Psalm 107:28-29a

They cried to the Lord in their trouble, and he brought them out from their distress; he made the storm be still…

my HIGH today was: ....

my LOW today was: ....

my PRAYER today is: ....

....

DAY 6

TODAY'S BIBLE VERSE:

Psalm 130:1-2a

Out of the depths I cry to you, O Lord. Lord, hear my voice!

my HIGH today was: ....

my LOW today was: ....

my PRAYER today is: ....

....

S | M | T | W | TH | F | S

THEME IN REVIEW

CHRIST IS NO LAW GIVER, BUT A LIFE GIVER.

MARTIN LUTHER

FAMOUS MOMENTS IN HISTORY
JULY 1505: LUTHER PREPARES TO RETURN TO HIS LAW STUDIES FOLLOWING SUMMER VACATION...
YOU'D MAKE A GOOD LAWYER. STUDY HARD. YOU'LL MAKE BIG BUCKS AND WE'LL BE RICH & FAMOUS!
SUCH A GOOD BOY
SUDDENLY A STORM COMES OUT OF NOWHERE. A BOLT OF LIGHTNING HITS THE GROUND NEAR LUTHER. THINKING GOD IS OUT TO FRY HIM, HE MAKES A DEAL WITH ST. ANNE, THE PATRON SAINT OF MINERS.
SAVE ME AND I'LL BECOME A MONK

A MONK? ACH! WHERE DID WE GO WRONG?
NOW NO ONE WILL REMEMBER THE NAME LUTHER!
TO BE CONTINUED...

DAY 7

MY FAVORITE VERSE FROM THE THEME WAS:

LOOKING BACK ON THESE TWO WEEKS, MY HIGHEST HIGH WAS:

MY LOWEST LOW THESE PAST WEEKS WAS:

ONE WAY GOD ANSWERED MY PRAYERS WAS:

ONE WAY GOD MIGHT USE ME AS A SACRED AGENT TO ANSWER THESE PRAYERS:

FAMILY COVENANT

We have shared *Highs & Lows* this week, read and highlighted the verses assigned in our Bible talked about our lives, prayed for one another's highs and lows, and blessed one another.

Parent's Signature *Teen's Signature* *Date*

THE FINKMANIA QUIZ BOWL

Question 1:

The reformer Martin Luther was born in:

(A) Eisleben, Germany, in 1483,
(B) Selma, Alabama, in 1929,
(C) Eisleben, Alabama, in 1483,
(D) The back of a '56 Chevy

Question 2:

When Columbus discovered America, Luther was:

(A) 9,
(B) 99,
(C) Both A & B,
(D) Older than our pastor but not as good looking

Question 3:

Luther decided to become a monk when:

(A) He saw a group of monks and liked their cool hair,
(B) Monk recruiters promised free college tuition,
(C) His girlfriend became a nun and he wanted to live in the monastery across the street,
(D) He almost got zapped by lightning and thought God was out to get him

Question 4:

When Luther told his parents he was going to become a monk, they were:

(A) Angry they wasted all that money on his college education,
(B) Angry he was wasting his life and talents,
(C) Concerned he wouldn't be able to take care of them in their old age,
(D) All of the above

Question 5:

At the monastery, Luther was:

(A) Always late for chapel but his penitence was real,
(B) Always late for everything, except for every meal,
(C) A slacker, trying to get by with the minimal work,
(D) A teacher's pet, trying to surpass all other monks in prayer, study, and piety so God might possibly love him

Question 6:

On the day he became a monk, Luther lay bare-chested on the cold stone monastery church floor and made sacred vows of:

(A) Poverty,
(B) Poverty and celibacy,
(C) Poverty, celibacy, and obedience to the church,
(D) Silence, but a lot of good that did!

Question 7:

After monk school, Luther went to Rome on church business and:

(A) Climbed 26 stairs on his knees, wishing his parents were dead so he could get them out of purgatory,
(B) Was shocked to see drunken priests and church corruption
(C) Both A & B,
(D) Knocked off a papal knick-knack store

Question 8:

How old was Martin Luther when he saw his first Bible?:

(A) 2,
(B) 12,
(C) 20,
(D) Older than our pastor at the turn of the last millenium

Question 9:

Luther thought his trip to Rome would be a high-light, instead it became:

(A) A good excuse for him to hate Italian food,
(B) The source of his new tourism show on the *Travel Channel*,
(C) The beginning of disillusionment with the church,
(D) The reason he never left his house again. Ever.

FINKmania Final Question:

Luke 1:78-79, the verse of the week, tells us:

(A) God wants to break lights over our heads and feed us peas,
(B) God wants to break light into our lives and guide us into the way of peace,
(C) God knows lighting design,
(D) God is super-interested in our feet

Play this online game using **FINKlink**
LL01 @ www.faithink.com

THE WEAKEST FINK

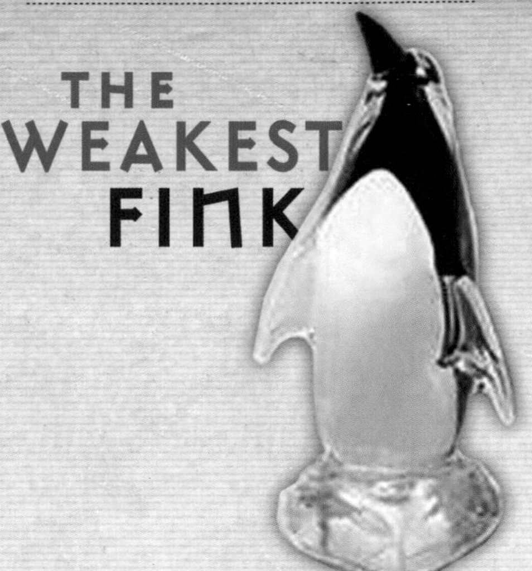

Cautious, careful people, always casting about to preserve their reputations... can never effect a reform.

Susan B. Anthony

TERMS

Write a definition below.

Black Plague

....

....

Eisleben, Germany

....

....

Luther, Martin (1483-1546)

....

....

Monastery

....

....

Pope

....

....

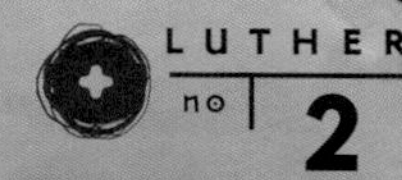

The Protesting Professor

"The one who is righteous shall live by faith..."

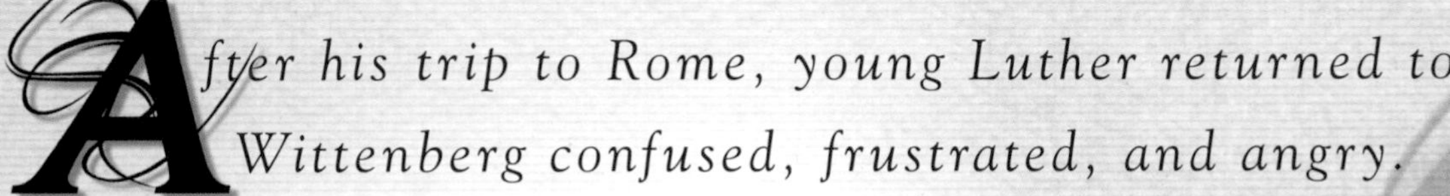

After his trip to Rome, young Luther returned to Wittenberg confused, frustrated, and angry.

The young monk was confused. He thought a trip to the Holy City would finally bring him peace with God. However, he found no peace there. He was frustrated and angry. The city was filled with drunken priests, trinket salesmen, and corruption at the highest levels. Upon his return, Luther was assigned to teach classes on the books of Psalms and Romans at the university. He was also placed in charge of groups of monks and asked to preach in area churches. Was he happy with these new duties? No. Brother Martin, now a doctor and professor of the church, still felt unworthy of God's love. The teaching job made him uneasy. He was supposed to be lecturing theology students about the gracious love of God, yet he hadn't experienced that love himself. How could he do anything but hate a God who created him imperfect, then demanded perfection? Luther was trapped, obsessed, and angry. Deep inside he knew no peace.

The Black Tower

One night in 1513, Martin was studying in the Black Tower of Wittenberg University. As he searched the scriptures trying to find peace with God, he stumbled upon a verse that hit him like another lightning bolt: Romans 1:17. This verse claimed God's righteousness came to sinners by faith, apart from good works. It quoted an Old Testament verse, Habakkuk 2:4b, "The righteous shall live by faith." When Martin read this, everything changed. All his life he was trying to do good works in order to earn God's love and favor. This verse claimed a right relationship with God comes through faith. Could it be he had been looking in the wrong place to find his peace? Could it be all of his futile striving to be holy and perfect was a wasted effort? Could he now live by faith—not in his own righteousness—but in the righteousness of God? Luther later wrote he was "born anew" at this moment.

The Fuse Is Lit

This simple verse, Romans 1:17, lit the fuse on a reformation soon to explode across Europe. The stormy monk finally found his peace, but would soon unleash a storm of his own on the church. The righteousness of God was not a standard to achieve. God's righteousness was a gift from God to be accepted by undeserving sinners through faith. Luther's responsibility was not to meet the impossible demands of perfection. His responsibility was his ability to respond - through the power of the Holy Spirit - to a God who had already done it all for him in Christ. He would accept this gift, go as a beggar clinging to the cross of Jesus, and live in faith that Christ's righteousness would become his own—by grace through faith!

Dear Lord God,
Give us your guidance that we may rightly understand your word, and more than that, do it. O most blessed Lord Jesus Christ, see to it that our search after knowledge leads us to glorify you alone. If not, let us not know a single letter. Give only what we, poor sinners, need to glorify you. Amen.

– Luther's Prayer for Guidance

Order this art print using FINKlink
LL02
@ www.faithink.com

Images in Art

- What do you see in today's cartoon art on the previous page?
- Where are you in this work of art?
- How do the image and the verse apply to your life today?

Psalms
Romans
1510
Back from Rome, Luther is assigned to teach the books of Psalms and Romans at Wittenberg U
1513
Black Tower experience—Luther finds peace with God by grace through faith
HABAKK 2:4b
1516
Tetzel arrives in Germany selling indulgences—Reformation fuse is lit
LUTHER
THE POPE VATICAN
1516
1st European Postal Service—information now flies at the speed of horse
Oct. 31, 1517
LUTHER NAILS THE 95 THESES TO WITTENBERG CHAPEL DOOR
October 31, 1517
Luther Nails 95 Theses—Reformation begins

Pope Leo's Indulgence Sale

Pope Leo X, the leader of the Roman Catholic Church, needed money to build a magnificent new worship center for the world, St. Peter's Basilica. He sent emissaries all around the empire to raise funds by selling certificates called indulgences. In those days, the church had two teachings which came in handy for raising money. First, it was thought and taught that the saints had done so many good works during their lives, they had reserve bank accounts of good works (merits). It was also thought and taught that a place called purgatory existed where dead souls went to be "purged" of their sins before entering heaven. Now, if saints had extra merits and dead people needed extra merits, why not make a deal? Why not ask relatives of the dead to purchase those merits from the church? The dead would be released. The living would be relieved. The church would be funded. Sounds reasonable, doesn't it?

Tetzel the Pitchman

Into this scene came Friar Johann Tetzel, the slickest indulgence salesman of them all, with bells ringing, choirs singing, and the best show in town. When Luther heard Tetzel was offering to forgive even the worst sinners for a price, he was outraged. Luther knew the only merits that counted came freely from Christ, not from doing good works or buying a piece of paper from the church. Giving money to the church couldn't and wouldn't buy an hour out of any purgatory that may or may not exist. The poor Germans of his town were being pressured to pay the church for a free gift. To Luther, this was immoral. Jesus—not the church—owned forgiveness. Jesus—not the church—would give it to any sinner who came in true confession. The book of Romans (which Luther was teaching at the time) made this crystal clear: Grace, faith, and salvation were God's gifts alone to give. No one owned them. No one could sell them.

The Wittenberg Door

Dr. Luther didn't find just one problem with the wholesale sale of indulgences and other abuses of the church. He found 95! As legend has it, on All Hallows Eve (Halloween) day, October 31, 1517, the protesting professor walked over to the community bulletin board—the door of the Castle Church—and nailed his 95 objections up for students and faculty to debate. Luther also sent copies of these "95 Theses" to his boss, the archbishop. The archbishop, who was getting a kick-back from the indulgence sale, was angry and immediately forwarded Luther's complaints to the pope. Martin had written his arguments in Latin, hoping to simply initiate a scholarly debate at his university. He hadn't intended it to go any further. His students had other ideas. They had Gutenberg's printing press and the new European postal system at their disposal. Before Luther knew what had happened, his 95 Theses had been translated and spread across Germany in ten days. Within three weeks, this unknown monk's complaints had been translated into a dozen other languages and were flying across the empire.

Next Time: Trouble, Trouble, Trouble

Bible Time

Luther's first teaching job included lecturing on the books of Psalms and Romans. By the time of his "Tower Experience" those books were deeply ingrained in his mind. Read and highlight the verse of the week, Romans 1:17, and write "Reformation Fuse" in the margin of your Bible. Next, find Habakkuk 2:4b and write "Reformation Fuse: See Romans 1:17" in the margin. Now page through the Psalms. Find and highlight three other verses you think might have given Luther comfort and faith in a God of love:

Choice 1:

Choice 2:

Choice 3:

Now turn to Romans 5:3-4 and 8:31-38. Highlight these verses and mark "see Romans 1:17" in the margins. Find and highlight three other verses in Romans that might have been comforting to Luther:

Choice 1:

Choice 2:

Choice 3:

Flip to the back of your Bible and write "Words of Comfort and Hope" on a blank back page. Copy your chosen Psalms and Romans references under the title. Keep these chosen verses close throughout your life. There may be a day when they come in handy if you are feeling threatened, defeated, or attacked. God's word may speak powerfully to you at those moments, just as it spoke to Martin Luther.

So What Does This Mean?

As soon as the coin in the coffer rings, the soul from purgatory springs.

Friar Johann Tetzel's indulgence sale slogan

Catechism Encounter

Open your Small Catechism to Luther's explanation of the Third Article of the Apostles' Creed. What does the Holy Spirit have to do with life-changing events like Luther's Wittenberg Tower experience?

Questions to Ponder

1. What do you do when your conscience tells you one thing and your friends tell you something else?

2. What are three things going on in the world today you think are clearly wrong and against God's will? What would it take for you to protest these wrongs? Will you do it?

3. What was Martin Luther's problem with the indulgence salesman Johann Tetzel?

Small Group

Share, Read, Talk, Pray, Bless

1. **SHARE** your highs and lows of the week one-on-one with another person. Listen carefully and record your friend's thoughts in the space below. Then return to small group and share your friend's highs and lows.

   MY HIGHS + LOWS THIS WEEK WERE:

   MY FRIEND'S HIGHS + LOWS THIS WEEK WERE:

2. **READ** and highlight the theme verse in your Bibles. Circle key words and learn the verse in song if time permits.

3. **TALK** about how today's verse relates to your highs and lows. Review the art for today, the Quiz Bowl questions, the terms, and the cartoons. Then write a sentence on each of the following:

   ONE NEW THING I LEARNED TODAY:

   ONE THING I ALREADY KNEW THAT IS WORTH REPEATING:

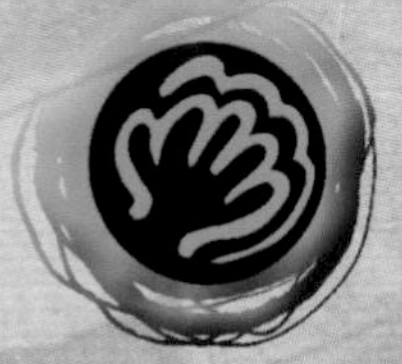

   ONE THING I WOULD LIKE TO KNOW MORE ABOUT:

4. **PRAY** for one another, praising and thanking God for your highs, and asking God to be with you in your lows. Include your friend's highs and lows in your prayers.

   A PRAISING PRAYER:

   A THANKING PRAYER:

   AN ASKING PRAYER:

5. **BLESS** one another using the blessing of the week. (right) Mark each person with the sign of the cross as you bless them.

THIS WEEK'S BLESSING

(NAME), MAY GOD GIVE YOU EYES THAT SEE CLEARLY AND A HEART THAT STANDS BOLDLY FOR THE TRUTH. AMEN.

THE FAITH 5

Read the full devotions using FINKlink

LL02 @ www.faithink.com

WEEK 1

JOURNAL

DAY 1

TODAY'S BIBLE VERSE:

Romans 1:17

The one who is righteous shall live by faith.

MY HIGH TODAY WAS:

MY LOW TODAY WAS:

MY PRAYER TODAY IS:

DAY 2

TODAY'S BIBLE VERSE:

Romans 3:10

There is no one who is righteous, not even one...

MY HIGH TODAY WAS:

MY LOW TODAY WAS:

MY PRAYER TODAY IS:

DAY 3

TODAY'S BIBLE VERSE:

Romans 3:20

For no human being will be justified in his sight by deeds prescribed by the law.

MY HIGH TODAY WAS:

MY LOW TODAY WAS:

MY PRAYER TODAY IS:

my HIGH today was:

my LOW today was:

my PRAYER today is:

DAY 4

today's bible verse:

Romans 3:21-22a

But now, apart from law, the righteousness of God has been disclosed, and is attested by the law and the prophets, the righteousness of God through faith in Jesus Christ for all who believe.

my HIGH today was:

my LOW today was:

my PRAYER today is:

DAY 5

today's bible verse:

Romans 3:22b-23

For there is no distinction, since all have sinned and fall short of the glory of God.

my HIGH today was:

my LOW today was:

my PRAYER today is:

DAY 6

today's bible verse:

Romans 3:24

They are now justified by his grace as a gift, through the redemption that is in Christ.

my HIGHEST HIGH this week was:

my LOWEST LOW this week was:

my PRAYER for next week is:

DAY 7

this week's blessing

(NAME), may God give you eyes that see clearly and a heart that stands boldly for the truth. Amen.

WEEK 2

THE FAITH5

JOURNAL

Read the full devotions using FINKlink
LL02 @ www.faithink.com

DAY 1

TODAY'S BIBLE VERSE:

Romans 4:3

For what does the scripture say? "Abraham believed God, and it was reckoned to him as righteousness."

MY HIGH TODAY WAS:

MY LOW TODAY WAS:

MY PRAYER TODAY IS:

DAY 2

TODAY'S BIBLE VERSE:

Romans 4:13

The promise that he would inherit the world did not come to Abraham or to his descendants through the law but through the righteousness of faith.

MY HIGH TODAY WAS:

MY LOW TODAY WAS:

MY PRAYER TODAY IS:

DAY 3

TODAY'S BIBLE VERSE:

Romans 5:1-2

Therefore, since we are justified by faith, we have peace with God through our Lord Jesus Christ, through whom we have obtained access to this grace in which we stand.

MY HIGH TODAY WAS:

MY LOW TODAY WAS:

MY PRAYER TODAY IS:

2. READ and highlight the verse of the day in your bibles.

3. TALK about how today's verse relates to your highs & lows.

4. PRAY for your highs & lows, for your family and for the world.

5. BLESS one another using this week's blessing (on the previous page).

my HIGH today was:

my LOW today was:

my PRAYER today is:

DAY 4

today's bible verse:

Romans 5:3-5a

Suffering produces endurance, and endurance produces character, and character produces hope, and hope does not disappoint us...

my HIGH today was:

my LOW today was:

my PRAYER today is:

DAY 5

today's bible verse:

Romans 5:18

Therefore just as one man's trespass led to condemnation for all, so one man's act of righteousness leads to justification and life for all.

my HIGH today was:

my LOW today was:

my PRAYER today is:

DAY 6

today's bible verse:

Romans 8:1

There is therefore now no condemnation for those who are in Christ Jesus.

S | M | T | W | TH | F | S

THEME in REVIEW

WHY DON'T YOU STAND UP LIKE A WOMAN AND TELL THE TRUTH?

CORRIE AQUINO TO PHILLIPINO DICTATOR MARCOS

DAY 7

MY FAVORITE VERSE FROM THE THEME WAS:

....

....

....

....

....

....

....

....

....

FAMOUS MOMENTS IN HISTORY:
TETZEL COMES TO WITTENBERG SELLING
INDULGENCES

LUTHER REACTS

YOU CAN'T SELL FORGIVENESS! IT'S A FREE GIFT!

OH NO? WATCH ME MONK BOY!

AS SOON AS THE COIN IN THE MONEY BOX RINGS THE SOUL FROM PURGATORY SPRINGS!

OCT. 31, 1517 LUTHER NAILS THE 95 THESES TO WITTENBERG CHAPEL DOOR

YOU THINK ANYBODY WILL PAY ATTENTION TO A NOTE TACKED TO A CHURCH DOOR?

I GUESS WE WILL SEE, WON'T WE?

LOOKING BACK ON THESE TWO WEEKS, MY HIGHEST HIGH WAS:

....

MY LOWEST LOW THESE PAST WEEKS WAS:

....

ONE WAY GOD ANSWERED MY PRAYERS WAS:

....

ONE WAY GOD MIGHT USE ME AS A SACRED AGENT TO ANSWER THESE PRAYERS:

....

....

FAMILY COVENANT

We have shared *Highs & Lows* this week, read and highlighted the verses assigned in our Bible, talked about our lives, prayed for one another's highs and lows, and blessed one another.

....	....	....
Parent's Signature	*Teen's Signature*	*Date*

THE FINKMANIA QUIZ BOWL

Question 1:

When he returned from his trip to Rome, Luther was assigned to teach the following courses at the University of Wittenberg:

(A) Old Testament and Church History,
(B) Psalms and Romans,
(C) The Seven Deadly Sins and Some That Aren't So Deadly,
(D) Pottery and Small Engine Repair

Question 2:

Duke Frederick, Luther's friend and protector, boasted the largest collection of what commodity that could rescue you from 1443 years in purgatory if you paid to see and adore them?

(A) Holy grails,
(B) Holy relics,
(C) Holy roller blades,
(D) Girlfriends

Question 3:

What Bible verse changed Luther's life forever?

(A) Romans 1:17, "The one who is righteous shall live by faith,"
(B) Ephesians 2:8, "For by grace you have been saved through faith,"
(C) Psalm 23:1, "The Lord is my shepherd, I shall not want,"
(D) Psalm 50:9, "I will take no bull from your house"

Question 4:

What did Pope Leo X do to raise cash for the new St. Peter's cathedral?:

(A) Install a jacuzzi in the Pope Suite of the Vatican to attract rich German tourists,
(B) Open a fast food chain called "Pope-eyes,"
(C) Offer rides in the Pope-mobile,
(D) Send people out to sell forgiveness of sins

Question 5:

An "Indulgence" was a document from the pope guaranteeing:

(A) Forgiveness of sins you already committed,
(B) Forgiveness of sins you might one day commit,
(C) Forgiveness of sins for your dear departed relatives in purgatory,
(D) All of the above and a rather clever fund raising idea

Question 6:

Johann Tetzel's actual sales pitch was:

(A) "Indulgences: Buy or fry!"
(B) "Indulgences: They're not just for living folks anymore!"
(C) "As soon as the coin in the money box rings, the soul from purgatory springs!"
(D) "As soon as the coin in the money box rings, I'm rich and you're stupid!"

Question 7:

Luther responded by:

(A) Nailing 95 Theses (statements against corruption) to the Castle Church door on Oct. 31, 1517,
(B) Nailing 95 Reeses Pieces to the Castle Church door on Oct. 31, 1517,
(C) Nailing 95 fleeces to the door on Oct. 31, 1517,
(D) Staple-gunning Johan Tetzel's mouth shut

Question 8:

Luther hoped his 95 Theses would:

(A) Create the Protestant Reformation,
(B) Create a debate on campus,
(C) Create a name for himself and a fat publishing contract,
(D) Create a new religion

Question 9:

Indulgences:

(A) Are not found in the Bible,
(B) Are not found in the Bible,
(C) Are not found in the Bible,
(D) All of the above, but can still be purchased today at the Vatican Gift Shop just outside St. Peter's Cathedral in Rome

FINKmania Final Question:

Romans 1:17, "The one who is righteous shall live by faith" means:

(A) If you want to be righteous, live next door to a girl named Faith,
(B) Everyone has fallen short of perfection, except pastors and Oprah,
(C) Those right in God's sight live by faith in Christ's righteousness on their behalf,
(D) Jesus loves getting gifts

Play this online game using FINKlink
LL02 | @ www.faithink.com

THE WEAKEST FINK

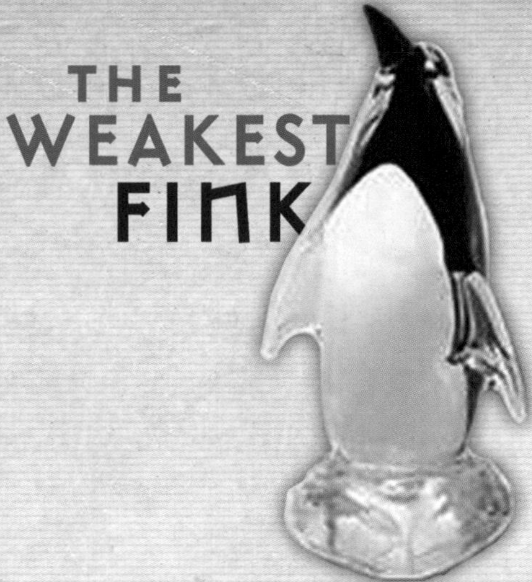

The Medevil era ended and the modern era began with a 95 point sermon.

Leonard Sweet

TERMS

WRITE A DEFINITION BELOW.

Black Tower

....

....

Indulgences

....

....

Ninety-Five Theses

....

....

Purgatory

....

....

Righteousness

....

....

FAITH INKUBATORS

Trouble, Trouble, Trouble

"Take courage, all you people of the land, says the Lord; work, for I am with you, says the Lord of hosts, according to the promise that I made you when you came out of Egypt. My spirit abides among you; do not fear."

— Haggai 2:4-5

Listen to this verse using FINKlink
LL03 | @ www.faithink.com

A problem of major league proportion had now been delivered to Rome, compliments of a minor league player.

The church's power, authority, and purses were being threatened by an insignificant monk from the sticks. What were they to do about this annoyance? In 1518, Dr. Luther was called to a series of Diets (inquiries) to answer for his arrogance. First, Martin's own Augustinian brothers took his case and tried to settle it "in house." Many younger priests listened and agreed with their brother's argument against indulgences. Many older priests didn't and sent private letters to the pope condemning him. Luther wrote: "I have great hope that this true theology, rejected by opinionated old men, will pass over to the younger generation."

The Wise Guy Frederick

Luther was now given six weeks to appear in Rome for a fair trial where he could state his case and then be fairly burned at the stake. In stepped Luther's patron and protector, Duke Frederick the Wise of Saxony. Many of Frederick's advisers were Luther fans. They saw an opportunity to gain political freedom from Rome and advised Frederick to politely tell the pope, "German matters should be settled on German soil." Rome quickly dispatched the powerful Cardinal Cajetan to settle the matter. Cajetan—shown on the Timeline as a fool in an unflattering political cartoon of the day—treated Luther like an ignorant little brother. Things got hot when Luther wouldn't confess his errors. He wanted to be shown his errors in Scripture. Cajetan became angry and threw the rude German out. In 1519, another diet was called. One hundred of Luther's students marched to the event carrying spears to protect their teacher. The famous Professor Eck was sent to debate Luther, but he acted more like a judge than a debater. "Are you the only one who knows anything?" sneered Dr. Eck. "Except for you, is all the church in error?"

Revolution in the Making

German knights looking for national identity rallied to Luther's defense. German civic leaders, tired of being exploited, taxed, and treated like second-class citizens by Rome, joined in. All had been waiting for a voice to say aloud what they were thinking. In Luther they found that voice: a voice of loud, strong, sometimes obnoxious bare truth. Along with these political opportunists, sincere Christians who believed indulgences to be wrong joined in from pulpits and classrooms—all ready to stand up and say, "Enough!"

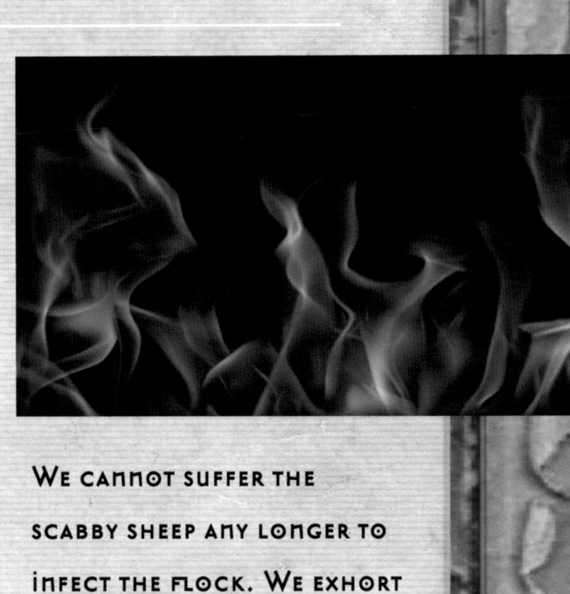

WE CANNOT SUFFER THE SCABBY SHEEP ANY LONGER TO INFECT THE FLOCK. WE EXHORT YOU TO INDUCE HIM (LUTHER) TO RETURN TO SANITY AND RECEIVE OUR CLEMENCY. IF HE PERSISTS IN HIS MADNESS, TAKE HIM CAPTIVE.

– Pope Leo X, in his letter to Frederick the Wise, July 4, 1520

Images in Art

- What do you see in today's cartoon art on the previous page?
- Where are you in this work of art?
- How do the image and the verse apply to your life today?

1518

A series of inquiries are held to question Luther

The Duke

Frederick the Wise steps in to protect his favorite professor

1519

Cardinal Cajetan tells Luther to recant (back down)

Professor Eck tells Luther to recant (back down)

Political cartoonists have a blast making fun of Luther & the pope

1520

Papal letter (bull) condemns Luther as a heretic and kicks him out of the church

Bonfire

Dr. Luther burns the bull

Wittenberg swelled with students from Switzerland, Scotland, France and Czech areas, all thrilled to be in the place where one monk was changing the world. Luther's writings became bolder. In a small best-selling pamphlet, *On the Babylonian Captivity of the Church*, the protesting professor charged religious leaders with enslaving the people of God. The sacraments—particularly baptism and communion—were free gifts. The church did not own them, and it did not own the people! Luther went further. He began to teach that the office of pope was the Antichrist because it was going against the clear truth of the Bible.

Pamphlet Wars & Political Cartoons

The debate, intended as a university conversation, was now becoming a hot topic at dining room tables across Germany. It spread to Rome, France, Spain, Switzerland and England. All 600 copies of the 95 Theses printed in France and Spain sold out immediately. Political cartoonists and satirists had a field day. One anti-Catholic drawing showed the pope as an ass playing bagpipes. On the anti-Protestant side, one cartoon depicted Luther as a seven-headed monster. Another had Luther literally bowling the pope over. Another showed the Devil playing a bag pipe and blowing his music out the monk's nose. Luther kept two printers busy around the clock. Religious debate took on even deeper political overtones. Peasants looking for someone to champion their rights rallied behind the brave German monk's cause. In his pamphlet, *Address to the German Nobility*, Luther claimed everyone was equal before God. Kings, serfs, priests and laborers were all nobility. They all had rights and deserved respect. This was the "Emancipation Proclamation" of its day. Some would say it was the beginning of our modern human rights movement. With this kind of revolutionary talk, the masses wouldn't remain oppressed much longer.

The Bull and the Bonfire

This was the last straw. In the summer of 1520, Pope Leo published a letter kicking Luther out of the church and calling on all true Christians to hunt him down and turn him over. This Papal Bull (summons) called Luther a "loose boar" in God's vineyard and a "scabby sheep infecting God's flock." It placed Luther under arrest. The only problem was, Luther wasn't in Rome. He was safely under Frederick's care, and the wise Duke wasn't about to let the most popular professor of his newly famous university fry. Luther showed the letter to his students one night during a bonfire at the city gate. They were in the process of burning papal writings, smearing mud on them, and dumping them into the river. His students urged their professor to throw his letter into the flames. This would be an act of open defiance and rebellion—a complete break with the church. "Burn it! Burn it!" they cried. Luther held it high, made a speech, said a prayer and tossed the letter to the flames.

The Protestant Reformation was underway.

Next Time: Heretic's Trial

A Protestant Action

Luther's life may have ended much sooner if it weren't for the actions of his protector, Frederick the Wise. There are victims of political oppression all over the world in need of protection. They may have no voice against the abuses of their own governments. You, however, may have the power to free a prisoner of conscience, stop torture, or prevent executions. Go to *www.amnesty.org* online and choose an endangered person. Organize a letter campaign in your church on a prisoner's behalf. Every appeal counts. A simple letter could stop someone from being tortured. A hundred letters from your friends and church could save a life. Send respectfully worded letters to:

The President of the United States

1600 Pennsylvania Ave.

NW Washington, DC 20500

The Honorable___________

United States Senate

Washington, DC 20510

The Honorable___________

US House of Representatives

Washington, DC 20515

Bible Time

Read and highlight Haggai 2:4-5, writing "Take Courage" in the margin. What does this verse have to do with Luther, protest, and you?

Luther's Prayer for Guidance

Dear Lord God, give us your guidance that we may rightly understand your word, and more than that, do it. O most blessed Lord Jesus Christ, see to it that our search after knowledge leads us to glorify you alone. If not, let us not know a single letter. Give only what we, poor sinners, need to glorify you. Amen.

So What Does This Mean?

JUSTIFIED? IT MEANS WHEN I'M TRUSTING IN JESUS, GOD SEES ME JUST AS IF I'D NEVER SINNED.
Melheim

Catechism Encounter

Open your Small Catechism to Luther's explanation of the First Commandment. What does this Commandment and explanation have to do with Luther's dangerous stand?

Questions to Ponder

1. Have you ever taken a stand to defend someone in trouble? Why did you do it? What happened? Why would anyone risk their life to stand up for another person or a belief?

2. What are three things you see happening in the world today that you know are clearly against God's will?

A.

B.

C.

3. What can you do to speak out for God and challenge or change the things you listed above?

A.

B.

C.

Getting into hot water helps keep you clean.

– G. K. Chesterton

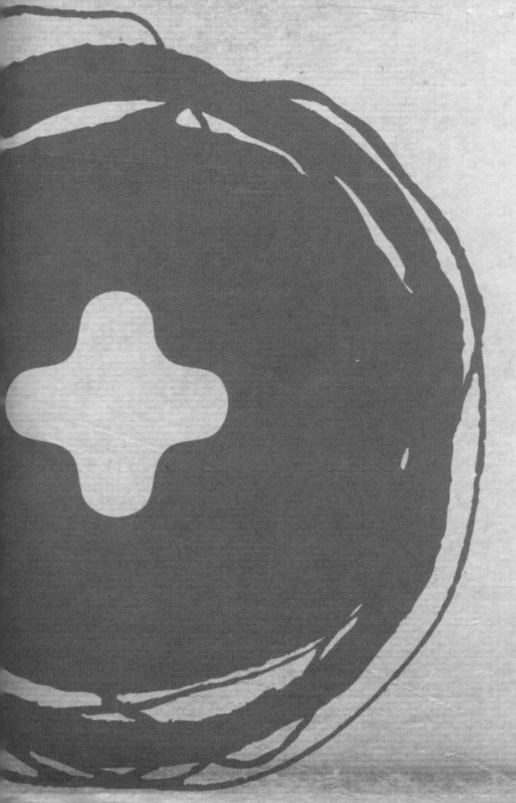

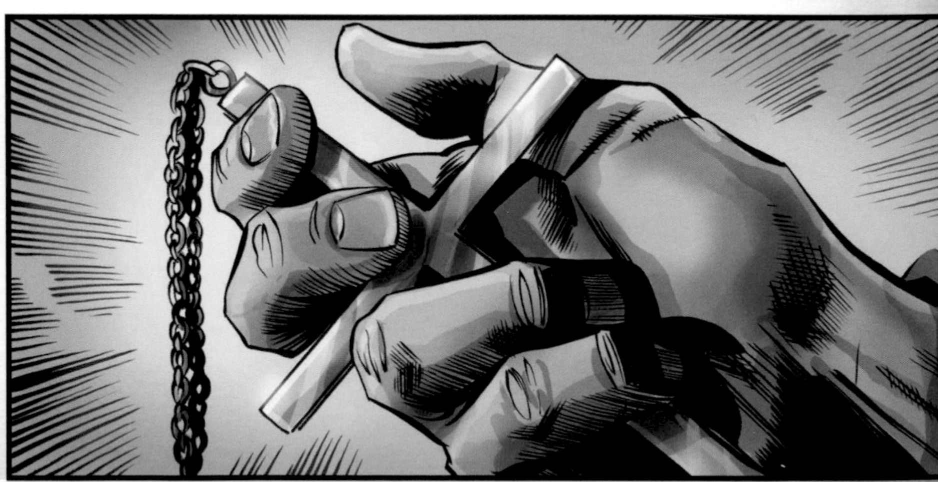

SMALL GROUP

SHARE, READ, TALK, PRAY, BLESS

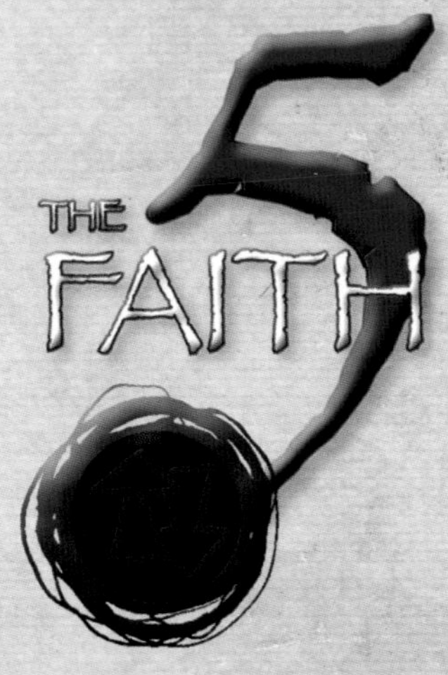

1. **SHARE** your highs and lows of the week one-on-one with another person. Listen carefully and record your friend's thoughts in the space below. Then return to small group and share your friend's highs and lows.

   MY HIGHS + LOWS THIS WEEK WERE:

   ....

   MY FRIEND'S HIGHS + LOWS THIS WEEK WERE:

   ....

2. **READ** and highlight the theme verse in your Bibles. Circle key words and learn the verse in song if time permits.

3. **TALK** about how today's verse relates to your highs and lows. Review the art for today, the Quiz Bowl questions, the terms, and the cartoons. Then write a sentence on each of the following:

   ONE NEW THING I LEARNED TODAY:

   ....

   ONE THING I ALREADY KNEW THAT IS WORTH REPEATING:

   ....

   ONE THING I WOULD LIKE TO KNOW MORE ABOUT:

   ....

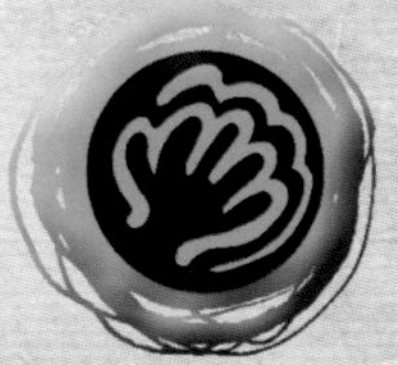

4. **PRAY** for one another, praising and thanking God for your highs, and asking God to be with you in your lows. Include your friend's highs and lows in your prayers.

   A PRAISING PRAYER: ....

   A THANKING PRAYER: ....

   AN ASKING PRAYER: ....

5. **BLESS** one another using the blessing of the week. (right) Mark each person with the sign of the cross as you bless them.

THIS WEEK'S BLESSING

(NAME), CHILD OF GOD, MAY YOU ALWAYS HAVE COURAGE TO DO THE RIGHT THING.

WEEK 1

THE FAITH 5 JOURNAL

Read the full devotions using FINKlink
LL03 @ www.faithink.com

DAY 1

TODAY'S BIBLE VERSE:

Haggai 2:4-5

Take courage, all you people of the land, says the Lord; work, for I am with you, says the Lord of hosts, according to the promise that I made you when you came out of Egypt. My spirit abides among you; do not fear.

my HIGH today was:

my LOW today was:

my PRAYER today is:

DAY 2

TODAY'S BIBLE VERSE:

Psalm 143:11

For your name's sake, O Lord, preserve my life. In your righteousness bring me out of trouble.

my HIGH today was:

my LOW today was:

my PRAYER today is:

DAY 3

TODAY'S BIBLE VERSE:

Habakkuk 2:4b

The righteous live by their faith.

my HIGH today was:

my LOW today was:

my PRAYER today is:

my HIGH today was:

my LOW today was:

my PRAYER today is:

DAY 4

TODAY'S BIBLE VERSE:

Isaiah 33:2

O Lord, be gracious to us; we wait for you. Be our arm every morning, our salvation in the time of trouble.

my HIGH today was:

my LOW today was:

my PRAYER today is:

DAY 5

TODAY'S BIBLE VERSE:

Proverbs 3:25-26

Do not be afraid of sudden panic, or of the storm that strikes the wicked; for the Lord will be your confidence and will keep your foot from being caught.

my HIGH today was:

my LOW today was:

my PRAYER today is:

DAY 6

TODAY'S BIBLE VERSE:

Job 30:22

You lift me up on the wind, you make me ride on it, and you toss me about in the roar of the storm.

my HIGHEST HIGH this week was:

my LOWEST LOW this week was:

my PRAYER for next week is:

DAY 7

THIS WEEK'S BLESSING

(NAME), CHILD OF GOD, MAY YOU ALWAYS HAVE COURAGE TO DO THE RIGHT THING.

Vorzeytten pfiff ich hin vnd her
Aus solcher Pfeiffen dicht vnd mer
Vil Fabel Trewm vnd Fantasey
Ist yetzundt auß vnd gar entzwey
Das ist mir leyd auch schwer vnd bang
Doch hoff ich es wer auch nit lang
Die weyl die welt so furwitz ist
Sündlich dückisch vol arger list.

WEEK 2

THE FAITH5 JOURNAL

Read the full devotions using FINKlink LL03 @ www.faithink.com

DAY 1

TODAY'S BIBLE VERSE:

JOEL 2:28

I will pour out my spirit on all flesh; your sons and your daughters shall prophesy, your old men shall dream dreams, and your young men shall see visions.

MY HIGH TODAY WAS:

MY LOW TODAY WAS:

MY PRAYER TODAY IS:

DAY 2

TODAY'S BIBLE VERSE:

PSALM 32:7

You are a hiding place for me; you preserve me from trouble; you surround me with glad cries of deliverance.

MY HIGH TODAY WAS:

MY LOW TODAY WAS:

MY PRAYER TODAY IS:

DAY 3

TODAY'S BIBLE VERSE:

DANIEL 6:16B

May your God, whom you faithfully serve, deliver you!

MY HIGH TODAY WAS:

MY LOW TODAY WAS:

MY PRAYER TODAY IS:

2. READ and highlight the verse of the day in your Bibles.

3. TALK about how today's verse relates to your highs & lows.

4. PRAY for your highs & lows, for your family and for the world.

5. BLESS one another using this week's blessing (on the previous page).

DAY 4

my HIGH today was:

my LOW today was:

my PRAYER today is:

today's Bible verse:

Psalm 50:15

Call on me in the day of trouble; I will deliver you, and you shall glorify me.

DAY 5

my HIGH today was:

my LOW today was:

my PRAYER today is:

today's Bible verse:

Nahum 1:7

The Lord is good, a stronghold in a day of trouble; he protects those who take refuge in him, even in a rushing flood.

DAY 6

my HIGH today was:

my LOW today was:

my PRAYER today is:

today's Bible verse:

Psalm 138:7

Though I walk in the midst of trouble, you preserve me against the wrath of my enemies; you stretch out your hand, and your right hand delivers me.

THEME IN REVIEW

Do the right thing.

Spike Lee

DAY 7

MY FAVORITE VERSE FROM THE THEME WAS:

THERE'S THIS RADICAL PASTOR WHO SAYS ANY CHRISTIAN CAN PERFORM ANY FUNCTION OF THE MINISTRY AT ANY TIME. BAPTISM HOLY COMMUNION. PREACHING. ABSOLUTION. ANYTHING!
WHAT DANGEROUS IDIOT SAID THAT?
MARTIN LUTHER

LOOKING BACK ON THESE TWO WEEKS, MY HIGHEST HIGH WAS:

MY LOWEST LOW THESE PAST WEEKS WAS:

ONE WAY GOD ANSWERED MY PRAYERS WAS:

ONE WAY GOD MIGHT USE ME AS A SACRED AGENT TO ANSWER THESE PRAYERS:

Family Covenant

We have shared *Highs & Lows* this week, read and highlighted the verses assigned in our Bible, talked about our lives, prayed for one another's highs and lows, and blessed one another.

Parent's Signature *Teen's Signature* *Date*

THE FINKMANIA QUIZBOWL

QUESTION 1:

Martin Luther's main problem with the church of his day was:

(A) Confirmation class,
(B) Pot luck dinners,
(C) The sale of indulgences for the forgiveness of sins and other practices he considered wrong from a biblical standard,
(D) Long sermons

QUESTION 2:

When Luther nailed his 95 Theses to the door on Oct. 31, 1517, his goal was:

(A) To get scholars and faculty to debate the unbiblical practices,
(B) To start the Protestant Reformation,
(C) To split the church between Catholic and Protestant,
(D) To get a cute nun named Katie to notice him

QUESTION 3:

Luther expected his Theses to be debated by scholars, but instead:

(A) Students copied them and put them on blogs,
(B) Students copied, translated and spread them all over Europe,
(C) The president of Wittenberg U told him to resign,
(D) Only a couple of janitors and the papal paper boy read them

QUESTION 4:

When Rome heard an obnoxious German monk was calling the pope's indulgences a sham:

(A) The pope repented and invited Luther to Sicily for spring break,
(B) The pope sent a cardinal and professor to tell Luther to shape up,
(C) The pope kicked Luther out of the church,
(D) Both B & C

QUESTION 5:

The pope's letter called Dr. Luther:

(A) A scabby sheep,
(B) A dirty duck,
(C) A wild bore in the vineyard of the Lord,
(D) Both A & C, and Luther returned the compliment by later calling the pope the Anti-Christ

QUESTION 6:

When Luther received the Papal Bull (letter kicking him out of the church), he immediately:

(A) Wrote a letter of apology to Rome,
(B) Had it framed,
(C) Threw it into the campus bonfire,
(D) Sold it on Ebay

QUESTION 7:

Luther's friend and protector in Wittenberg was:

(A) Frederick the Stout,
(B) Frederick the Wise,
(C) Frederick of CSI,
(D) Frederick of Hollywood

QUESTION 8:

In a pamphlet titled "On the Babylonian Captivity of the Church," Luther charged religious leaders with:

(A) Enslaving God's people,
(B) Annoying God's people,
(C) Empowering God's people,
(D) Boring sermons

QUESTION 9:

In a pamphlet titled "Address to the German Nobility" Luther claimed:

(A) All nobles are equal,
(B) All nobles should raise up peasant armies to fight against Rome,
(C) All people are equal before God and deserve the same dignity,
(D) All Germans were equal, but some were more equal than others

FINKMANIA FINAL QUESTION:

Haggai 2:4 - 5, the verse of the week, tells us:

(A) God has our back,
(B) The Lord likes to host dinner parties,
(C) God keeps promises,
(D) Both A & C

Play this online game using **FINKlink**
LL03 @ www.faithink.com

THE WEAKEST FINK

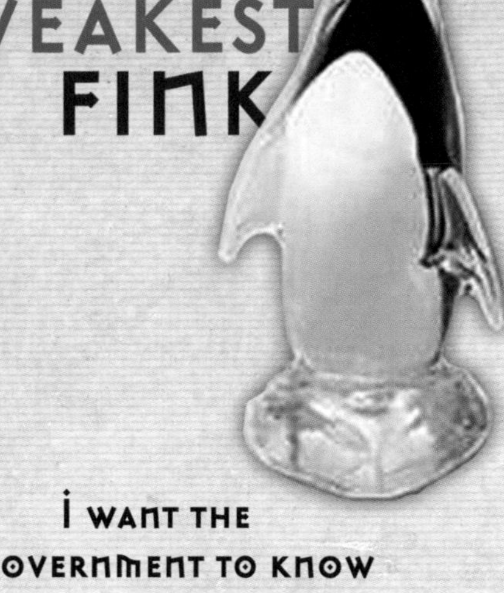

I WANT THE GOVERNMENT TO KNOW I'M NOT AFRAID OF THEM. ESPECIALLY IF I'M DOING WHAT GOD WANTS ME TO DO.

BISHOP DESMOND TUTU

TERMS

WRITE A DEFINITION BELOW.

DIET

FREDERICK THE WISE

PAPAL BULL

POLITICAL CARTOON

PROTESTANT REFORMATION

FAITH INKUBATORS

Heretic's Trial

"For by grace you have been saved through faith,
and this is not your own doing; it is a gift of God."

— Ephesians 2:8

Martin Luther was now on the empire's "Ten Most Wanted" list. There was a price on his head. A high price.

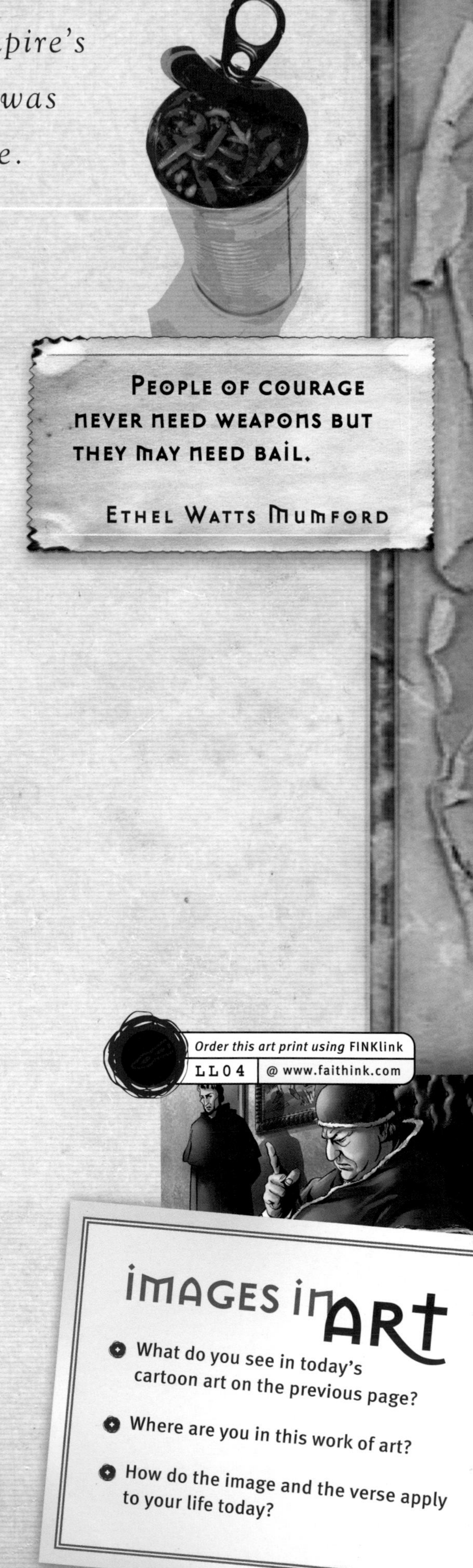

PEOPLE OF COURAGE NEVER NEED WEAPONS BUT THEY MAY NEED BAIL.
ETHEL WATTS MUMFORD
Order this art print using FINKlink
LL04
@ www.faithink.com
IMAGES IN ART
What do you see in today's cartoon art on the previous page?
Where are you in this work of art?
How do the image and the verse apply to your life today?

Charles V was twenty-five. The pope had just crowned him king of the Holy Roman Empire and was now pressuring him to silence the wayward monk once and for all. He called for a final trial on April 16, 1521, in the city of Worms. Duke Frederick saw to it that Luther was promised safe passage to and from the Diet of Worms. (No joke. That's the name.) Crowds lined the streets as the protesting professor's procession began its 300-mile trip to Worms under an imperial banner. Some cheered. Some jeered. Luther rode along in a two-wheeled cart, playing his guitar (lute), and singing hymns. Merchants, teachers, and peasants joined the caravan. Ulrich von Hutton, a scholar, knight, and friend, offered to join Luther with 100 armed knights. He was ready to start the war of independence against Rome right then and there. Luther told Hutton the gospel didn't need an army. It had God's word! In Erfurt, where Luther first joined the monastery, 2000 cheering students and faculty lined the parade route and greeted him like a hero. They threw a banquet to wish him well.

The Diet of Worms

Luther stood before the emperor, cardinals of the church, princes and government officials. Piles of his writings were stacked on a table before him and he was ordered to confess his errors. The monk whose parents once wanted him to be a lawyer moved to stall the proceedings. He requested a day to prepare a defense. It was granted. The second morning Luther asked for clarification. Which of the writings on the table was he supposed to reject? Some of the materials spoke about faith and life. Even his enemies agreed those writings were good. Some pamphlets targeted the sale of indulgences, the sinful lives of the pope's Vatican staff, and the unbiblical practices which the church was supporting. The famous prosecutor, Dr. Eck, asked, "Who do you think you are to put yourself above so many famous church leaders over the ages and claim to know more than they do?" He pressed Luther to recant. (back down) Luther's answer:

"Unless I am convicted by scripture and plain reason, I do not accept the authority of popes and councils, for they have contradicted each other. My conscience is captive to the word of God. I cannot, and I will not recant anything, for to go against conscience is neither right nor safe. God help me. Amen."

First accounts of this scene also have him saying the now famous words:

"Here I stand, I cannot and I will not recant."

1521

Luther travels to his trial, playing his lute and singing hymns

Diet of Worms

Luther refuses to back down

Kidnapped!

Luther's friend and protector, Duke Frederick, whisks him off to the spooky old castle at Wartburg

Junker George

Luther lays low and does a lot of rabbit hunting—just a knight out with the boys

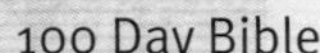

100 Day Bible

While at Wartburg, Luther translates the entire New Testament into German in 100 days. It will become the standard text book for German schools for the next 300 years.

The Birth of the Modern World

This was the pivotal point in 1500 years of Christianity. Some say the medieval era ended at this moment, and the modern era began. On this day, one simple monk armed with nothing but reason, conscience, and faith in the word of God stood before the powers of the vanishing Holy Roman Empire and said, "No! No church, pope, king, or state has power over an individual's conscience!"

Kidnapped

Luther was condemned. The young emperor kept his promise of safe passage and allowed the monk eight days to get home. After that, anyone who found Luther would be doing the state a favor by capturing or killing him. Further, anyone who harbored, helped, or sympathized with the heretic could also be condemned, banned from buying and selling property, and forbidden from taking communion. (Which, of course, meant hell!) Returning home on the night of April 16, 1521, Martin was asleep in his wagon as it creaked through the dark forest. Suddenly, a group of masked riders charged out of the woods. Luther was kidnapped and dragged away to the spooky old Wartburg Castle. To all the world, he simply disappeared. Rumors spread. Maybe he was captured. Maybe he was dead. Decades later it was revealed: his captor was none other than Duke Frederick.

The Wartburg Hideout

Martin spent the next ten months in hiding. He grew a beard, dressed like a knight, and took on the name "Junker (Knight) George." Days were spent hunting, writing, and waiting for word from the outside world. Nights were particularly eerie. Locked up in the creepy old castle, listening to bats whirl above his head and winds howl, the fugitive monk often sensed the presence of evil. One night, he felt Satan was right in the room with him, condemning him for being a sinner. Tradition has it Martin picked up an inkwell and threw it at Satan, smashing it against the wall. "I have been baptized!" he shouted. He belonged to God. Satan couldn't have him. "Yes, I'm a sinner, but I have been baptized! I belong to God! Get out!"

Translating the Bible

The months in hiding weren't entirely wasted. Luther used the time to write students, teachers, pastors and government officials to encourage them. This fanned the flames of reformation. He snuck out and returned to Wittenberg from time to time to preach, discuss the growing peasant unrest, and argue with other reform-minded leaders about the next steps. In his spare time, he cranked out a translation of the entire New Testament in 100 days. Placing God's word in the hands of ordinary people was a dangerous act. It would be key to removing power from Rome and recreating the church as a priesthood of all believers. The English reformer, William Tyndale, visited Luther and later translated the New Testament into English. For that offense Tyndale was burned at the stake!

Next Time: Luther - A Legacy

Five Keys to Luther's Theology

During this period of his life, Dr. Luther began to see a number of additional problems with the church—many practices and traditions with no biblical basis. To Luther, if a practice wasn't commanded in the Bible, it couldn't be demanded by the church. Below are five keys to Luther's basic theology.

Key 1: Justification by Grace Through Faith

Luther spent much of his young life trying to earn God's love and favor. He found his freedom and joy in the fact that Jesus had already done it all for him! We are justified - made "right in God's sight" - by the grace of God through faith in what Jesus has done for us, and even that faith is a gift of God!

Do Not Bend

Key 2: Grace, Faith & Word Alone

Luther began to draw on three central themes that would become his motto: God's grace alone (*sola gratia*), God's word alone (*sola scriptura*), and faith alone (*sola fide*). With indulgences, the church was selling what couldn't be sold. Grace was God's—a free gift, bought by the blood of Christ. The church had no right to sell it to anyone. The church also enforced many rules, laws, and traditions that had no scriptural base. Luther would rely on God's word alone—not the pope, the church, or any other voice to tell him what to do. It was not extra merits purchased from dead saints that saved. It was not even one's own good works. It was only by grace through faith in Jesus that anyone could hope to come to God. Remember Habakkuk 2:4b, Romans 1:17 and Ephesians 2:8? The Reformation motto became *Sola Gratia, Sola Scriptura, Sola Fide.*

Key 3: Saints & Sinners

Every believer in Jesus is *simul justus et peccator* (chant this five times)—at the same time both saint and sinner. We are all sinners, but trusting in Christ's sacrifice in our place and washed in his blood, we are saints in God's sight.

Key 4: Two Sacraments

Luther could find only two true sacraments commanded with physical elements attached—baptism and communion. He believed and taught that the other Catholic rites (confirmation, ordination, marriage, last rites, and even penance) were all valuable additions to the Christian life, but not essential for salvation.

Key 5: The Universal Church

The church claimed a person was damned apart from its blessings and sacraments. If you were kicked out of the Roman Church, there was no salvation for you. Luther saw the church as much larger than a particular earthly organization. The true church was a spiritual community of souls united in faith—all believers in Christ—whether connected with Rome or not. Christians don't need a priest or Pope as go-betweens between them and God. We can all go to God through Jesus!

> Here I stand.
> I cannot and I will not recant (back down).
>
> Martin Luther

So What Does This Mean?

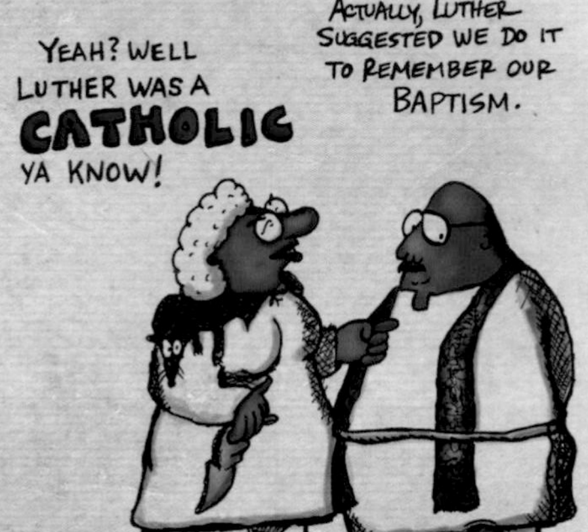

WHY DO YOU ALWAYS DO THAT CATHOLIC "CROSS YOUR HEART THING" IN CHURCH?
YEAH? WELL LUTHER WAS A CATHOLIC YA KNOW!
ACTUALLY, LUTHER SUGGESTED WE DO IT TO REMEMBER OUR BAPTISM.

REVOLUTIONARIES DO NOT MAKE REVOLUTIONS. REVOLUTIONARIES ARE THOSE WHO KNOW WHEN POWER IS LYING IN THE STREET AND PICK IT UP.

HANNAH ARENDT

Bible Time

Read and highlight Ephesians 2:8-9, writing "Grace!" in the margin.

Prayer

Dear God, I don't deserve anything, yet you give me everything. I don't deserve your love, yet you love me anyway. Plant the seeds of faith in me; so that, by your grace I may grow closer and closer to you. In Jesus' name. Amen.

Catechism Encounter

Find the two sacraments in Luther's Small Catechism. What are they? What do they have in common?

Questions to Ponder

1. What is a conscience? What do your conscience and the Holy Spirit have to do with one another?

2. What do each of these mean to you?

   God's Grace Alone (Sola Gratia)

   God's Word Alone (Sola Scriptura)

   Faith Alone (Sola Fide)

3. What is a saint? What is a sinner? How can Lutherans say Christians are both a saint and a sinner at the same time (simul justus et peccator)?

SMALL GROUP

SHARE, READ, TALK, PRAY, BLESS

1. **SHARE** your highs and lows of the week one-on-one with another person. Listen carefully and record your friend's thoughts in the space below. Then return to small group and share your friend's highs and lows.

   MY HIGHS + LOWS THIS WEEK WERE:

   ....

   MY FRIEND'S HIGHS + LOWS THIS WEEK WERE:

   ....

2. **READ** and highlight the theme verse in your Bibles. Circle key words and learn the verse in song if time permits.

3. **TALK** about how today's verse relates to your highs and lows. Review the art for today, the Quiz Bowl questions, the terms, and the cartoons. Then write a sentence on each of the following:

   ONE NEW THING I LEARNED TODAY:

   ....

   ONE THING I ALREADY KNEW THAT IS WORTH REPEATING:

   ....

   ONE THING I WOULD LIKE TO KNOW MORE ABOUT:

   ....

4. **PRAY** for one another, praising and thanking God for your highs, and asking God to be with you in your lows. Include your friend's highs and lows in your prayers.

   A PRAISING PRAYER: ....

   A THANKING PRAYER: ....

   AN ASKING PRAYER: ....

5. **BLESS** one another using the blessing of the week. (right) Mark each person with the sign of the cross as you bless them.

THIS WEEK'S BLESSING

(NAME), CHILD OF GOD, MAY GRACE, FAITH, AND GOD'S WORD BE ALL YOU NEED.

WEEK 1

FAITH JOURNAL

Read the full devotions using FINKlink
LL04 @ www.faithink.com

DAY 1

TODAY'S BIBLE VERSE:

Ephesians 2:8-9

For by grace you have been saved through faith, and this is not your own doing; it is the gift of God—not the result of works, so that no one may boast.

MY HIGH TODAY WAS:

MY LOW TODAY WAS:

MY PRAYER TODAY IS:

DAY 2

TODAY'S BIBLE VERSE:

Romans 8:38-39

I am convinced that neither death, nor life, nor angels, nor rulers, nor things present, nor things to come, nor powers, nor height, nor depth, nor anything else in all creation, will be able to separate us from the love of God...

MY HIGH TODAY WAS:

MY LOW TODAY WAS:

MY PRAYER TODAY IS:

DAY 3

TODAY'S BIBLE VERSE:

Galatians 5:1

For freedom Christ has set us free. Stand firm, therefore, and do not submit again to a yoke of slavery.

MY HIGH TODAY WAS:

MY LOW TODAY WAS:

MY PRAYER TODAY IS:

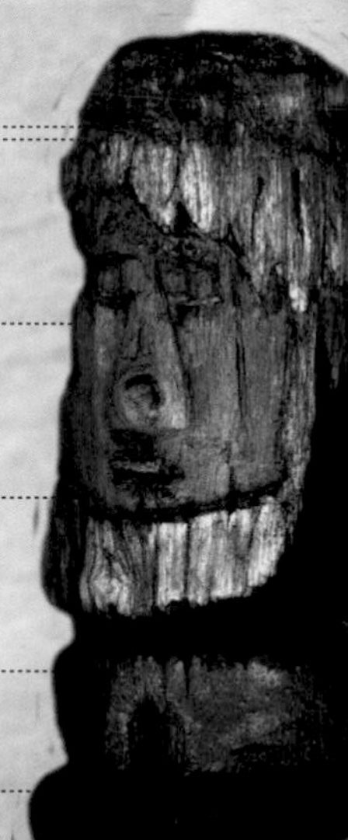

my HIGH today was:

my LOW today was:

my PRAYER today is:

DAY 4

TODAY'S BIBLE VERSE:

JAMES 2:26B

Faith without works is dead.

my HIGH today was:

my LOW today was:

my PRAYER today is:

DAY 5

TODAY'S BIBLE VERSE:

I PETER 4:12-13

Beloved, do not be surprised at the fiery ordeal that is taking place among you to test you... rejoice insofar as you are sharing Christ's sufferings...

my HIGH today was:

my LOW today was:

my PRAYER today is:

DAY 6

TODAY'S BIBLE VERSE:

REVELATION 2:10B

Be faithful until death, and I will give you the crown of life.

Standing in (on) your faith!

my HIGHEST HIGH this week was:

my LOWEST LOW this week was:

my PRAYER for next week is:

DAY 7

THIS WEEK'S BLESSING

(NAME), CHILD OF GOD, MAY GRACE, FAITH, AND GOD'S WORD BE ALL YOU NEED.

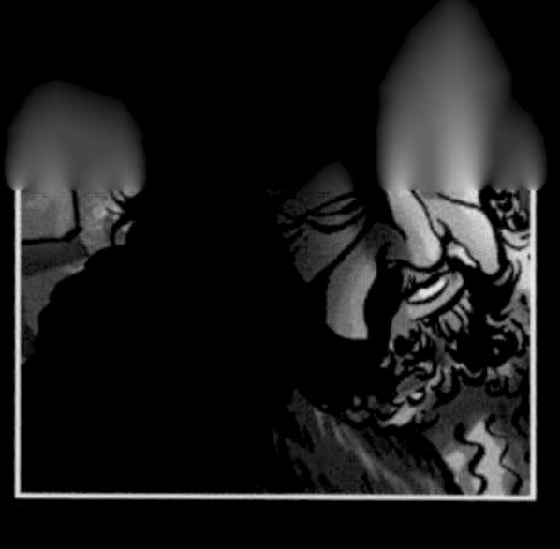

Read the full devotions using FINKlink

LL04 @ www.faithink.com

FAITH JOURNAL

WEEK 2

DAY 1

TODAY'S BIBLE VERSE:

Romans 8:31

If God is for us, who is against us?

MY HIGH TODAY WAS:

MY LOW TODAY WAS:

MY PRAYER TODAY IS:

DAY 2

TODAY'S BIBLE VERSE:

LUKE 9:23-24

If any want to become my followers, let them deny themselves and take up their cross daily and follow me. For those who want to save their life will lose it, and those who lose their life for my sake will save it.

MY HIGH TODAY WAS:

MY LOW TODAY WAS:

MY PRAYER TODAY IS:

DAY 3

TODAY'S BIBLE VERSE:

LUKE 21:13

This will give you an opportunity to testify.

MY HIGH TODAY WAS:

MY LOW TODAY WAS:

MY PRAYER TODAY IS:

3. TALK about how today's verse relates to your highs & lows.

4. PRAY for your highs & lows, for your family and for the world.

5. BLESS one another using this week's blessing (on the previous page).

my HIGH today was:

my LOW today was:

my PRAYER today is:

DAY 4

today's bible verse:

john 8:31a

Then Jesus said to the Jews who had believed in him, "If you continue in my word, you are truly my disciples."

my HIGH today was:

my LOW today was:

my PRAYER today is:

DAY 5

today's bible verse:

john 8:31b

"And you will know the truth, and the truth will make you free."

my HIGH today was:

my LOW today was:

my PRAYER today is:

DAY 6

today's bible verse:

john 15:13

No one has greater love than this, to lay down one's life for one's friends.

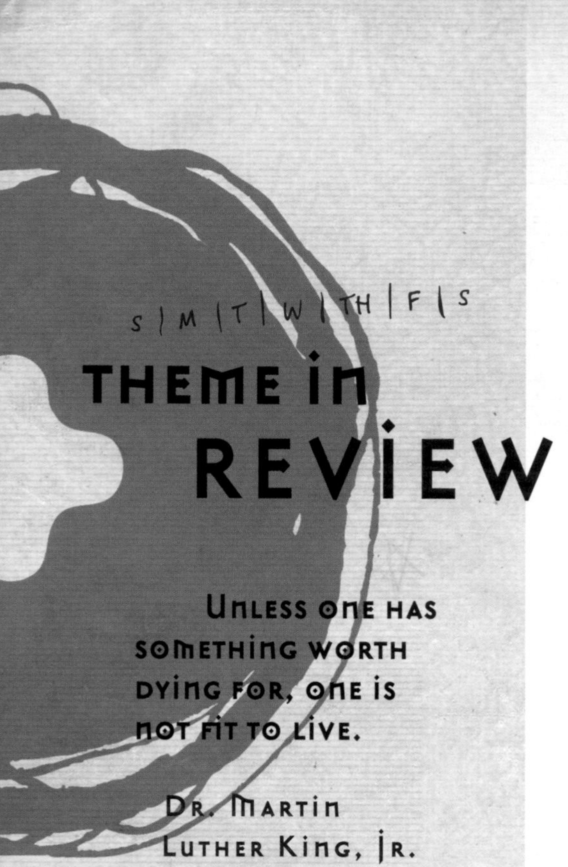

S | M | T | W | TH | F | S

THEME IN REVIEW

> Unless one has something worth dying for, one is not fit to live.
>
> Dr. Martin Luther King, Jr.

DAY 7

My favorite VERSE from the theme was:

....

....

....

....

....

Looking back on these two weeks, my highest HIGH was:

....

My lowest LOW these past weeks was:

....

One way God answered my PRAYERS was:

....

One way God might use me as a SACRED AGENT to answer these prayers:

....

....

Family Covenant

We have shared *Highs & Lows* this week, read and highlighted the verses assigned in our Bibles, talked about our lives, prayed for one another's highs and lows, and blessed one another.

Parent's Signature	*Teen's Signature*	*Date*

THE FINKMANIA QUIZBOWL

QUESTION 1:

When Luther would not back down, the pope:

(A) Issued a letter kicking him out of the church and calling all Christians to hunt him down,

(B) Issued a letter calling him a "scabby sheep infecting the fold,"

(C) Issued a letter calling him a "loose boar in God's vineyard,"

(D) All of the above

QUESTION 2:

Rather than allow Luther to go to Rome for a trial, Duke Frederick:

(A) Convinced the emperor, Charles V, to try "German matters on German soil,"

(B) Convinced the pope to forget the whole thing,

(C) Convinced a Lutheran insurance company to make a movie about Luther,

(D) Wrote his memoirs for Oprah's Book Club

QUESTION 3:

The "Diet of Worms" was:

(A) The trial where Luther denied his writings,

(B) The trial where Luther refused to deny (recant) his writings,

(C) A protein supplement paste used to make hot dishes in German middle school cafeterias,

(D) The trial where Luther had to eat nightcrawlers

QUESTION 4:

At the Diet of Worms, when Luther was ordered to recant his writings, he:

(A) Stalled by asking to separate writings that had no relevance in the case from those that did,

(B) Shouted "My soul is captive to the word of God!"

(C) Shouted "Here I stand!"

(D) All of the above, and Luther fully expected to be burned at the stake

QUESTION 5:

Instead of being burned at the stake, Luther was:

(A) Burned at the state,

(B) Served a burnt steak,

(C) Flogged, blogged and released,

(D) Condemned as a heretic and given eight days of safe passage to get home before the state declared open hunting season on him

QUESTION 6:

On his way home from the Diet of Worms, Luther was:

(A) Arrested and executed,

(B) Bumped from first class to coach,

(C) Kidnapped by his friend Frederick the Wise and hidden in Wartburg castle,

(D) Kidnapped by space aliens

QUESTION 7:

While laying low and hiding from the pope's assassination squad at Wartburg in 1521, Luther:

(A) Dressed up like a knight,

(B) Changed his name to Junker (Knight) George,

(C) Did a lot of rabbit hunting,

(D) All of the above, plus translated the New Testament into German so common people could read it for themselves

QUESTION 8:

Luther's German New Testament translation:

(A) Only took him 100 days to complete,

(B) Became the main text book to teach reading in German schools for the next 300 years,

(C) Became the best-selling book in Germany for the next 300 years,

(D) All of the above, and spawned an English Bible

QUESTION 9:

Some say the medieval era ended and the modern age began when:

(A) Luther stood up for his conscience against all the powers of Church and State,

(B) Luther was born,

(C) Apple introduced the iPod,

(D) Luther invented the Internet

FINKMANIA FINAL QUESTION:

Ephesians 2:8 says:

(A) "For by grace you have been saved through faith,"

(B) "For by faith you have been saved through grace,"

(C) "The one who is righteous shall live by faith,"

(D) "Go to the ant, you lazybones, consider its ways and be wise"

Play this online game using FINKlink

LL04 @ www.faithink.com

THE WEAKEST FINK

PEACE IF POSSIBLE, BUT TRUTH AT ANY RATE.

MARTIN LUTHER

TERMS

WRITE A DEFINITION BELOW.

DIET OF WORMS

....

HERE I STAND!

....

RECANT

....

SOLA GRATIA, SCRIPTURA, FIDE

....

WARTBURG CASTLE

....

FAITH INKUBATORS

The grass withers, the flower fades; but the word of our God will stand forever.

— Isaiah 40:8

Sometimes a leader has to disappear to get things done. With Luther in hiding and presumed dead, other bold Christians picked up the torch and continued the reform.

Under the leadership of reformers like Andreas von Carlstadt, the church began to change. On Christmas 1521, 2000 people in Wittenberg were offered both wine and bread at communion for the first time. (Wine had been reserved for priests.) Clergy stopped wearing robes. Monotonous chants were replaced with new hymns like Luther's "A Mighty Fortress" (inspired by his stay at the spooky old Wartburg castle). Legend has it some songs were set to beer hall tunes so everyone could sing along. Other songs were played on stringed instruments called lutes—the guitars of the day. Over time, people were allowed to become active participants in worship rather than mere spectators. The Mass (communion) remained central, but preaching took on a more important teaching role. People started calling pastors from their own towns rather than accepting priests from Rome.

Sola Gratia, Sola Scriptura, Sola Fide. (Grace alone, God's Word alone, Faith Alone.)

The Lutheran Motto

The Peasant Uprising

By January, the Wittenburg town council outlawed images and statues in the church. After that, things got ugly. Mobs destroyed stained glass windows, holy relics, and other symbols of Rome's power. Monks and nuns left monasteries. Peasants rose up against their masters. Finally, Luther came out of hiding to stop the slaughter. In despair for a spiritual reform that turned into a peasants' revolt, Luther wrote a pamphlet urging princes to put down the rebellion and restore order. By the time it was over, 70 cloisters and 70 castles were burned to the ground. Some estimate 10,000 peasants and soldiers were dead. Very sad.

Kicking the Habit

In 1523, twelve nuns were smuggled out of their convent in herring barrels and arrived in Wittenberg seeking protection. Luther decided to marry them off to friends and students for their safety. There was nothing in the Bible that said priests couldn't marry! In fact, the first command in Genesis is "be fruitful and multiply." (Genesis 1:28) Since the Bible, not the church, was the final authority for all matters of faith and life, priests, monks, and nuns were free to marry if they chose. The last nun, Katherine von Bora, decided she didn't want to marry anyone but Martin. On June 13, 1525, in part to defy the church, in part to enjoy the gifts of marriage, Martin and Katie were married. She was 26; he was 42. Duke Frederick gave them a wonderful wedding present—the whole Black Cloister monastery building—for their home. Together they shared 20 years, 6 children, 11 foster children, and 24 boarding students. The large family enjoyed talk, music and regular debates around their dinner table. One of their daughters, Elizabeth, died as a baby. Martin's favorite, sweet Magdalena, died in his arms at twelve. It broke his heart, but before she died, she told him: "You are my earthly father, but God is my heavenly Father."

Images in Art

- What do you see in today's cartoon art on the previous page?
- Where are you in this work of art?
- How do the image and the verse apply to your life today?

1521

Worship reforms, all take communion, hymns like "A Mighty Fortress" engage the masses in the Masses

1522

Peasant Revolt forces Luther out of hiding—castles attacked, churches smashed, 10,000 die

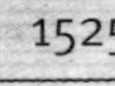

1523

Twelve nuns escape to Wittenberg seeking asylum

1525

Luther marries Katrina von Bora—raises family and eyebrows

1527

Luther writes small pamphlet for parents to teach their kids—first confirmation classes begin at home

Protestors called "Lutheran" by some, but Martin favors "Evangelical"

The Small Catechism

In 1527, while touring the countryside, Luther was shocked to find children weren't being taught even the basics of Christianity. Worse, most parents he met were ignorant and superstitious. He returned home and converted a pile of old sermons into a simple, easy-to-understand teaching tool. This Small Catechism was printed on pamphlets and wall-charts for families to use at home. According to Luther, children were the spiritual responsibility of their parents—not the church. He called parents "bishops" of their homes and said faith education was their daily responsibility—just like feeding, clothing and protecting a child.

That "Lutheran" Word

Some called the protest movement Lutheran—although Luther never wanted a church named after him. "Why should you name a church after me, filthy maggot that I am! Call it the Evangelical Church, instead," he is reported to have said. This word comes from the Greek: *Eu* = good; *angelion* = message. An evangelical is any messenger spreading the good news of Jesus. According to Luther, this joyful task is every Christian's job. It is not reserved for priests or those paid to do it.

The Augsburg Confession

For the next few years, Charles V was too busy fighting Islamic armies in eastern Europe to bother with Luther. Left alone, the reform grew and spread. In 1530, the empire struck back. The young emperor returned and Luther was forced back into hiding. To defend the movement, Luther's friend Philip Melanchthon wrote a document explaining exactly who these Evangelicals were and what they believed. Protesting princes presented their argument in 1530 to Charles in Augsburg, Germany. The famous Dr. Eck returned as prosecutor for the pope. Charles slept through some of the hearing, then declared Eck the winner. Before it was over, however, he did something very helpful. He asked the pope to look into the corruption charges responsible for this protest. After Augsburg, the princes siding with Luther's reform immediately created a mutual defense pact. Twenty-five years of civil war, killing, and burning followed pitting Catholics against the prostestors. The term Protestant was coined as a dirty word. It meant heathen heretic! To Protestants, it became a term of honor. They believed they were protesting abuses of the church and leading people back to the truth of the Bible.

Luther's Death

Due to harsh conditions, bad nutrition, and unsanitary medical treatments, the average life span in the 16th century was only 28 years. Luther was now 62. He often lamented the fact he hadn't died a martyr. His movement might have accomplished something! On February 17, 1546, while settling a dispute between two leaders in Eisleben, the town of his birth, Luther took sick. His pastor asked him if he was willing to die in the name of Jesus. The good Dr. Luther's last word recorded was a firm, "Yes!"

1530

German princes present their case to Charles V at Augsburg—he agrees to look into their grievances against the church

February 17, 1546

Luther dies with a firm "Yes!"

Eight Keys to Luther's Legacy

In his lifetime, the young lad who could have been a lawyer transformed from obedient monk to protesting professor to leader of an uncontrollable movement. After his death, seeds he planted grew, spread, and impacted society in many ways. Today 350 million Protestants and hundreds of millions of others owe a debt of thanks to the German monk who wouldn't back down. Below are some of the gifts and problems Luther left as a legacy to the world.

Legacy 1. Justification by Grace through Faith: St. Paul taught a person was saved by grace through faith. This central New Testament truth, lost by the church, was restored by Luther. Good works do not earn a person's salvation. Works sprout and grow from the life of a sinner saved by Christ. Luther taught a Christian was completely free from the requirements of the law. At the same time, however, a Christian was a complete slave, subject to all in love. (That's called a paradox.)

Legacy 2. Priesthood of All Believers: Luther saw every Christian emerging from the baptismal waters as a priest. Every Christian had the right and responsibility to go directly to God through Christ. You did not need a priest to access God. Sacraments weren't owned by the church. They were gifts of God, available to all with or without a priest's blessing. He did away with Rome's control over churches and set up a system where congregations could call their own pastors and leaders. Pastors became more like shepherds, preachers, and educators and less like gatekeepers of God's grace.

Legacy 3. Word and Worship for the People: Luther translated the Bible and worship services into the language of the people. He elevated the role of preaching, brought popular music into worship and allowed all to take wine at communion. Worship was for all. Priests didn't own it!

Legacy 4. Education Reform: Luther stressed the importance of reading, education, and critical thinking for everyone—even girls. Many at the time believed girls didn't have souls! Why teach them to read? Reading would fill their minds with distractions and keep them from housework! Luther taught this was nonsense. Everyone needed to learn to read and think for himself or herself.

Legacy 5. Marriage and Family: Luther's experience with a loving family changed and influenced his writing in a major way. He lifted parenting to the highest of callings, brought faith teaching directly into the home with his Small Catechism, and called parents bishops of their own households. He taught that parents—not the church—were accountable to God for children's spiritual welfare.

Legacy 6. Human Rights: Luther's bold stance in claiming all people are equally noble before God opened the door to everything from free enterprise, to free speech, to the intellectual freedoms millions enjoy today. Luther taught the importance of an individual's conscience and rights over the powers of government. The concept of human rights wouldn't be where it is today without Luther.

Legacy 7. The Dark Side: Luther's legacy had a dark side. His teachings on equality were taken out of the religious sphere and into the political arena. Hijacked by those who wanted a class war, they spawned a peasant's uprising that left 10,000 dead. Because of this, Germany's peasants wouldn't achieve any real power or rights for another 300 years. His movement also led to 30 years of bloody conflict between Catholics and Protestants in Germany and around the world. Some of this hatred—like that in Northern Ireland—is still smoldering five hundred years later. Luther's statements against all who denied Christ—whether pope or Moslem or Jew—were used and misused over the centuries to justify everything from the holocaust to hangings to Aryan hate groups in the world today. Nazi's quoted Luther to justify the murder of millions of Jews. This was not God's will!

Legacy 8. God's Word as Final Authority: Of all his work and influence, lifting the Bible up as our final authority in faith and life is perhaps Luther's greatest legacy. He translated and placed God's word into the hands of the common people, challenging all Christians to read it and think for themselves. You've got God's word. You've got a good mind. Use it. That's your legacy!

So What Does This Mean?

It WON'T BE THE INK THAT HE THREW, BUT THE INK THAT HE WROTE THAT WILL MAKE THE DIFFERENCE

Bible Time

Read and highlight Isaiah 40:8, writing "What lasts?" in the margins.

Catechism Encounter

When Luther became a monk, he made a vow of obedience to the church. What does Luther's explanation to the First Commandment say about our allegiance to church, state, governments and all other human institutions?

Reformation Prayer

Write a short prayer asking God to give you courage to make the world a better place. Now, squeeze your eyes tightly shut and picture protesting evil or working for change. Pray for the Spirit's power to begin using you to affect the change, first in your own heart, then in your home, then out into the community and world. Praise God for the witness of Martin Luther and others throughout history who have spoken out for God. Thank Jesus for the great works of faith he can and will accomplish in your life. Ask the Spirit to open your heart to the truth of God's word and keep you strong today. End in Jesus' name.

Together we confess: By grace alone, in faith in Christ's saving work and not because of any merit on our part, we are accepted by God and receive the Holy Spirit, who renews our hearts while equipping and calling us to good works.

– Joint Lutheran and Catholic Declaration on the Doctrine of Justification, Augsburg, October 31, 1999

Questions to Ponder

1. Business management author Peter Drucker once said: "There are essentially four kinds of risks: The risk you can afford to take; The risk you can't afford to take; The risk you can afford not to take; The risk you can't afford not to take." Based on Drucker's quotation, which kind of risk do you think Luther took by protesting against the abuses of the church 500 years ago? Why?

2. What kind of risk do you take by not protesting evil today? Why?

3. What do you risk when you stand up for God and truth? What do you risk when you remain silent?

SMALL GROUP

SHARE, READ, TALK, PRAY, BLESS

1. SHARE your highs and lows of the week one-on-one with another person. Listen carefully and record your friend's thoughts in the space below. Then return to small group and share your friend's highs and lows.

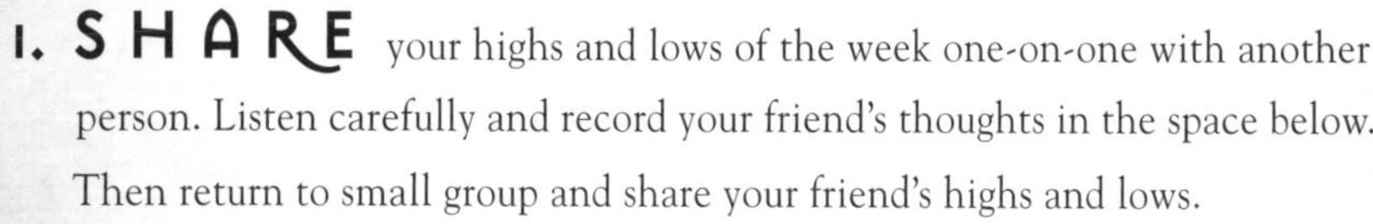

MY HIGHS + LOWS THIS WEEK WERE:

....

MY FRIEND'S HIGHS + LOWS THIS WEEK WERE:

....

2. READ and highlight the theme verse in your Bibles. Circle key words and learn the verse in song if time permits.

3. TALK about how today's verse relates to your highs and lows. Review the art for today, the Quiz Bowl questions, the terms, and the cartoons. Then write a sentence on each of the following:

ONE NEW THING I LEARNED TODAY:

....

ONE THING I ALREADY KNEW THAT IS WORTH REPEATING:

....

ONE THING I WOULD LIKE TO KNOW MORE ABOUT:

....

4. PRAY for one another, praising and thanking God for your highs, and asking God to be with you in your lows. Include your friend's highs and lows in your prayers.

A PRAISING PRAYER: ....

A THANKING PRAYER: ....

AN ASKING PRAYER: ....

5. BLESS one another using the blessing of the week. (right) Mark each person with the sign of the cross as you bless them.

THIS WEEK'S BLESSING

(NAME), CHILD OF GOD, MAY GOD'S WORD LIVE FOREVER IN YOUR HEART.

WEEK 1

THE FAITH JOURNAL

Read the full devotions using FINKlink
LL05 | @ www.faithink.com

DAY 1

TODAY'S BIBLE VERSE:

Isaiah 40:8

The grass withers, the flower fades; but the word of our God will stand forever.

MY HIGH TODAY WAS:

MY LOW TODAY WAS:

MY PRAYER TODAY IS:

DAY 2

TODAY'S BIBLE VERSE:

Deuteronomy 4:29

You will seek the Lord your God, and you will find him if you search after him with all your heart and soul.

MY HIGH TODAY WAS:

MY LOW TODAY WAS:

MY PRAYER TODAY IS:

DAY 3

TODAY'S BIBLE VERSE:

1 Samuel 3:10

Now the Lord came and stood there, calling as before, "Samuel! Samuel!" And Samuel said, "Speak, for your servant is listening."

MY HIGH TODAY WAS:

MY LOW TODAY WAS:

MY PRAYER TODAY IS:

my HIGH today was:

my LOW today was:

my PRAYER today is:

DAY 4

today's bible verse:

I Chronicles 16:10

Glory in his holy name; let the hearts of those who seek the Lord rejoice.

my HIGH today was:

my LOW today was:

my PRAYER today is:

DAY 5

today's bible verse:

Psalms 18:28

It is you who light my lamp; the Lord, my God, lights up my darkness.

my HIGH today was:

my LOW today was:

my PRAYER today is:

DAY 6

today's bible verse:

Psalm 27:4

One thing I asked of the Lord, that will I seek after: to live in the house of the Lord all the days of my life, to behold the beauty of the Lord, and to inquire in his temple.

my HIGHEST HIGH this week was:

my LOWEST LOW this week was:

my PRAYER for next week is:

DAY 7

this week's blessing

(NAME), child of God, may God's Word live forever in your heart.

Read the full devotions using FINKlink LL05 @ www.faithink.com

FAITH JOURNAL

WEEK 2

DAY 1

TODAY'S BIBLE VERSE:

Psalm 51:6

You desire truth in the inward being; therefore teach me wisdom in my secret heart.

MY HIGH TODAY WAS:

MY LOW TODAY WAS:

MY PRAYER TODAY IS:

DAY 2

TODAY'S BIBLE VERSE:

Psalm 119:160

The sum of your word is truth; and every one of your righteous ordinances endures forever.

MY HIGH TODAY WAS:

MY LOW TODAY WAS:

MY PRAYER TODAY IS:

DAY 3

TODAY'S BIBLE VERSE:

Isaiah 42:6

I am the Lord, I have called you in righteousness, I have taken you by the hand and kept you; I have given you as a covenant to the people, a light to the nations.

MY HIGH TODAY WAS:

MY LOW TODAY WAS:

MY PRAYER TODAY IS:

1. SHARE highs & lows of the day.

2. READ and highlight the verse of the day in your bibles.

3. TALK about how today's verse relates to your highs & lows.

4. PRAY for your highs & lows, for your family and for the world.

5. BLESS one another using this week's blessing (on the previous page).

my HIGH today was:

my LOW today was:

my PRAYER today is:

DAY 4

today's bible verse:

Jeremiah 23:28

Let the prophet who has a dream tell the dream, but let the one who has my word speak my word faithfully.

my HIGH today was:

my LOW today was:

my PRAYER today is:

DAY 5

today's bible verse:

Daniel 4:34

I blessed the Most High, and praised and honored the one who lives forever. For his sovereignty is an everlasting sovereignty, and his kingdom endures from generation to generation.

my HIGH today was:

my LOW today was:

my PRAYER today is:

DAY 6

today's bible verse:

Revelation 2:10b

Be faithful until death, and I will give you the crown of life.

PROTEST

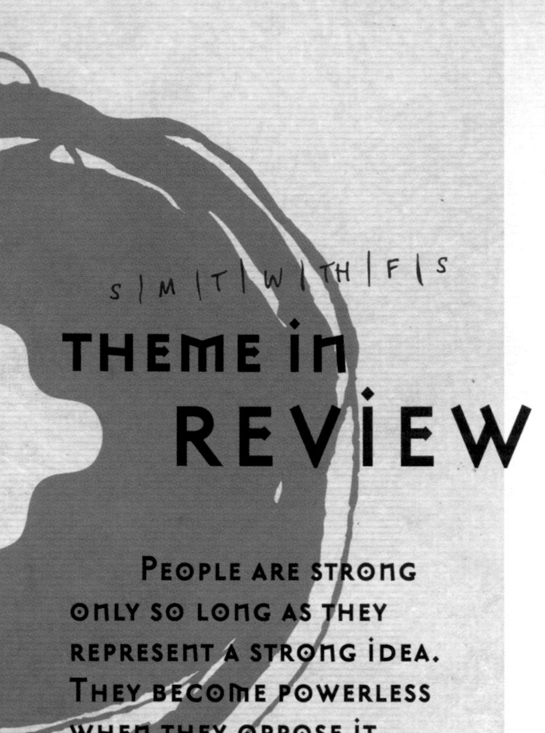

S | M | T | W | TH | F | S

THEME IN REVIEW

PEOPLE ARE STRONG ONLY SO LONG AS THEY REPRESENT A STRONG IDEA. THEY BECOME POWERLESS WHEN THEY OPPOSE IT.

SIGMUND FREUD

DAY 7

MY FAVORITE VERSE FROM THE THEME WAS:

LOOKING BACK ON THESE TWO WEEKS, MY HIGHEST HIGH WAS:

MY LOWEST LOW THESE PAST WEEKS WAS:

ONE WAY GOD ANSWERED MY PRAYERS WAS:

ONE WAY GOD MIGHT USE ME AS A SACRED AGENT TO ANSWER THESE PRAYERS:

FAMILY COVENANT

We have shared *Highs & Lows* this week, read and highlighted the verses assigned in our Bibles, talked about our lives, prayed for one another's highs and lows, and blessed one another.

Parent's Signature *Teen's Signature* *Date*

THE FINKMANIA QUIZ BOWL

Question 1:

Lutherans are closer theologically to:

(A) Catholics,
(B) Mormons,
(C) Agnostics,
(D) Republicans

Question 2:

When Luther heard they were trying to name a church after him, he:

(A) Celebrated with brats and beer,
(B) Quickly registered the name www.luther.com,
(C) Said, "Why do you name a church after me, filthy maggot that I am? Call it the Evangelical church,"
(D) Changed his name to Martin Baptist

Question 3:

A "Protestant" is:

(A) A heretic who opposes the one true church,
(B) A protester who opposed Catholic practices they considered unbiblical,
(C) A term for 342 million of the 2.1 billion Christians in the world who don't consider themselves Catholic, Orthodox or Independent,
(D) B and C, hopefully not A

Question 4:

Martin Luther wrote the Small Catechism for:

(A) Parents to teach their children in the home,
(B) Professors to teach their students at the seminary,
(C) Popes to teach their cardinals in Rome,
(D) Pastors to torture adolescent confirmation students

Question 5:

The Augsburg Confession was a statement given to:

(A) Lutherans by the Roman Catholics in 1999, saying Luther was right all along,
(B) Emperor Charles V in 1530 explaining the protesting princes' theology,
(C) Queen Latifah in 2006 explaining the prancing princes' dance moves
(D) Confirmation students to test their smarts

Question 6:

Martin Luther's greatest achievements included:

(A) Standing up against corruption and for an individual's conscience,
(B) Starting a movement which led to the rise of independent nation states in Europe,
(C) Translating the Bible and stressing God's word, grace, and faith
(D) All of the above

Question 7:

Which of the following is NOT a direct by-product of Luther's Reformation?:

(A) People receiving bread and wine at communion,
(B) Church music sung to popular tunes,
(C) Bibles translated into every major language in the world,
(D) Communion wafers that stack like poker chips and taste like Styrofoam

Question 8:

In his darker moments, Luther said a lot of nasty things about:

(A) The Pope,
(B) Moslems,
(C) Jews,
(D) All of the above, and anybody else who didn't agree with him that faith in Jesus was the only way to God

Question 9:

A Lutheran might be described as:

(A) A Catholic who asks too many questions,
(B) A protestor who listens to God's word before anything or anyone else,
(C) A Christian who believes in grace, God's word, and faith alone
(D) C, B, and sometimes A, depending on who you are talking to

FINKmania Final Question:

Isaiah 40:8 says, "The grass withers, the flower fades; but the word of our God..."

(A) "Is a two-edged sword,"
(B) "Is near you,"
(C) "Will stand forever,"
(D) "Will remain under the pew in a book that few will open"

Play this online game using FINKlink
LL05 | @ www.faithink.com

THE WEAKEST FINK

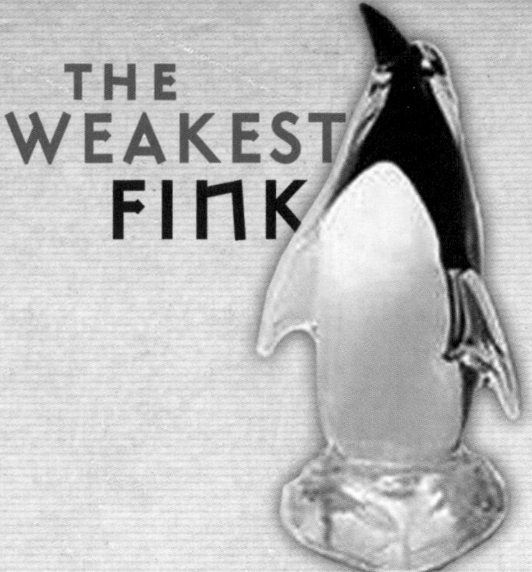

AS THE HEAD OF THE FAMILY SHOULD TEACH IN A SIMPLE WAY TO THE HOUSEHOLD...

INTRODUCTION TO MARTIN LUTHER'S SMALL CATECHISM

TERMS

WRITE A DEFINITION BELOW.

EVANGELICAL

....

....

KATHERINE VON BORA

....

....

LUTHERAN

....

....

PROTESTANT

....

....

SMALL CATECHISM

....

....

FAITH INKUBATORS

"I TREASURE YOUR WORD IN MY HEART,

SO THAT I MAY NOT SIN AGAINST YOU."

— PSALM 119:11

The mountainside is wrapped in smoke. The earth quakes as fearful nomads stand outside their tents looking up. The air is heavy and hot, like the smoke of a kiln.

One man steps from the crowd to head up the mountain. You follow him. His name is Moses. You enter into a thick darkness together, trembling. Then, in a still, small voice, you sense the presence of the Almighty. It is as if God is speaking to your soul. You whisper with Moses, "Everything that the Lord has spoken we will do." In a moment you are transported in time and space to a campfire outside a ravaged city. The great houses have been ransacked. A broken group of refugees huddles around a charcoal fire, fearful of the night. Three dark-eyed men step into the orange glow. People turn toward them as if imploring God for advice. How can we ever know the presence of God again? Isaiah rises and speaks, "Wash yourselves; make yourselves clean; remove the evil of your doings from before my eyes; cease to do evil, learn to do good; seek justice, rescue the oppressed, defend the orphan, plead for the widow."

Now the prophet Micah rises and speaks, "What does the Lord require of you but to do justice, and to love kindness, and to walk humbly with your God?"

A wild-eyed Amos stirs the coals and whispers, "Let justice roll down like waters, and righteousness like an ever-flowing stream." You answer with the huddling crowd, "Everything that the Lord has spoken we will do."

In another moment you are drawn through time and space to the side of Jesus. A man walks up to test the master, "Teacher, which commandment in the law is the greatest?" Jesus flashes a knowing smile and says, "You shall love the Lord your God with all your heart, with all your soul, and with all your mind. This is the greatest and first commandment. And a second is like it, 'You shall love your neighbor as yourself.'" You nod and grin back, whispering, "Everything that the Lord has spoken we will do."

The Ten Commandments

The Children of Israel were wandering in a foreign land. There were all kinds of dangers in this land. Powerful enemies waited to crush them. Strange cults and religious groups required child sacrifice and used temple prostitutes to coax their gods to do their bidding. How would God's people stay safe and strong and pure in the face of such temptations? God gave the Ten Commandments as a gift of love saying, "Do this and you will live." If you want to survive and know God's good and gracious will for your life as you wander through this foreign land called the new millennium, God's gift of the Ten Commandments still applies. It is a gift for your life.

THE BEST WAY TO SHOW THAT A STICK IS CROOKED IS NOT TO ARGUE ABOUT IT, BUT TO LAY A STRAIGHT STICK ALONGSIDE IT.

D.L. MOODY

Order this art print using FINKlink
LL06 @ www.faithink.com

IMAGES IN ART

- What do you see in today's painting by Dr. He Qi?
- Where are you in this work of art?
- How do the image and the verse apply to your life today?

So What Does This Mean?

NO MUKLESTERN, I DON'T THINK GOD WOULD TRADE SIX KEEPINGS OF THE 4TH COMMANDMENT EVEN UP FOR ONE BREAKING OF THE 6TH.

I don't need to compromise my principles, because they don't have the slightest bearing on what happens to me anyway.

Calvin and Hobbes

Bible Time

The Ten Commandments were given to Israel soon after their escape from Egypt (Exodus 20). This law wasn't the end of God speaking to the people. God continued to speak through the prophets to explain the "whys" of these commandments. Finally, at the exact right time, God came in Jesus to bring the Word to us in flesh. Read and highlight the following verses summarizing God's will for us. Write "God's Will" in the margins near each verse:

Exodus 19:8

Exodus 20:3

Isaiah 1:16-17

Micah 6:8

Amos 5:24

Matthew 22:36-40

Prayer

Holy God, help me to understand what it means to treasure you in my heart. Along with this understanding, help me find ways to live for you. Amen.

Catechism Encounter

Scan Luther's explanation of the First Commandment in your Small Catechism and circle three words that jump out at you. Write those words here:

Questions to Ponder

1. Which three commandments do you think are broken most often in the world? In your school? In your home?

2. What can you do to keep from breaking these three commandments?

3. How might loving God and loving your neighbor be connected?

SMALL GROUP

SHARE, READ, TALK, PRAY, BLESS

1. **SHARE** your highs and lows of the week one-on-one with another person. Listen carefully and record your friend's thoughts in the space below. Then return to small group and share your friend's highs and lows.

   MY HIGHS + LOWS THIS WEEK WERE:

   ....

   MY FRIEND'S HIGHS + LOWS THIS WEEK WERE:

   ....

2. **READ** and highlight the theme verse in your Bibles. Circle key words, and learn the verse in song if time permits.

3. **TALK** about how today's verse relates to your highs and lows. Review the art for today, the Quiz Bowl questions, the terms, and the cartoons. Then write a sentence on each of the following:

   ONE NEW THING I LEARNED TODAY:

   ....

   ONE THING I ALREADY KNEW THAT IS WORTH REPEATING:

   ....

   ONE THING I WOULD LIKE TO KNOW MORE ABOUT:

   ....

4. **PRAY** for one another, praising and thanking God for your highs, and asking God to be with you in your lows. Include your friend's highs and lows in your prayers.

   A PRAISING PRAYER: ....

   A THANKING PRAYER: ....

   AN ASKING PRAYER: ....

5. **BLESS** one another using the blessing of the week. (right) Mark each person with the sign of the cross as you bless them.

THIS WEEK'S BLESSING

(NAME), CHILD OF GOD, MAY YOU BE RIGHT AND PURE AND TRUE IN ALL YOU SAY AND DO.

Read the full devotions using FINKlink
LL06 @ www.faithink.com

FAITH

JOURNAL

WEEK 1

DAY 1

TODAY'S BIBLE VERSE:

Psalm 119:11

I treasure your word in my heart, so that I may not sin against you.

MY HIGH TODAY WAS:

MY LOW TODAY WAS:

MY PRAYER TODAY IS:

DAY 2

TODAY'S BIBLE VERSE:

Exodus 20:2-3

I am the Lord your God, who brought you out of the land of Egypt, out of the house of slavery; you shall have no other gods before me.

MY HIGH TODAY WAS:

MY LOW TODAY WAS:

MY PRAYER TODAY IS:

DAY 3

TODAY'S BIBLE VERSE:

Exodus 20:4

You shall not make for yourself an idol, whether in the form on anything that is in heaven above, or that is on the earth beneath...

MY HIGH TODAY WAS:

MY LOW TODAY WAS:

MY PRAYER TODAY IS:

my HIGH today was:

my LOW today was:

my PRAYER today is:

DAY 4

today's bible verse:

Exodus 20:7

You shall not make wrongful use of the name of the Lord your God, for the Lord will not acquit anyone who misuses his name.

my HIGH today was:

my LOW today was:

my PRAYER today is:

DAY 5

today's bible verse:

Exodus 20:8

Remember the sabbath day, and keep it holy.

my HIGH today was:

my LOW today was:

my PRAYER today is:

DAY 6

today's bible verse:

Exodus 20:12

Honor your father and your mother, so that your days may be long in the land that the Lord your God is giving you.

my HIGHEST HIGH this week was:

my LOWEST LOW this week was:

my PRAYER for next week is:

RE= Again
SPECT= SEE
OR LOOK

DAY 7

this week's blessing

(NAME), CHILD OF GOD, MAY YOU BE RIGHT AND PURE AND TRUE IN ALL YOU SAY AND DO.

WEEK 2

THE FAITH 5 JOURNAL

Read the full devotions using FINKlink LL06 @ www.faithink.com

DAY 1

TODAY'S BIBLE VERSE:

Exodus 20:13

You shall not murder.

MY HIGH TODAY WAS:

MY LOW TODAY WAS:

MY PRAYER TODAY IS:

DAY 2

TODAY'S BIBLE VERSE:

Exodus 20:14

You shall not commit adultery.

MY HIGH TODAY WAS:

MY LOW TODAY WAS:

MY PRAYER TODAY IS:

DAY 3

TODAY'S BIBLE VERSE:

Exodus 20:15

You shall not steal.

MY HIGH TODAY WAS:

MY LOW TODAY WAS:

MY PRAYER TODAY IS:

1. SHARE highs & lows of the day.

2. READ and highlight the verse of the day in your bibles.

3. TALK about how today's verse relates to your highs & lows.

4. PRAY for your highs & lows, for your family and for the world.

5. BLESS one another using this week's blessing (on the previous page).

DAY 4

today's bible verse:

Exodus 20:16

You shall not bear false witness against your neighbor.

my HIGH today was:

my LOW today was:

my PRAYER today is:

DAY 5

today's bible verse:

Exodus 20:17a

You shall not covet your neighbor's house.

my HIGH today was:

my LOW today was:

my PRAYER today is:

DAY 6

today's bible verse:

Exodus 20:17b

You shall not covet your neighbor's wife, or male or female slave, or ox, or donkey, or anything that belongs to your neighbor.

my HIGH today was:

my LOW today was:

my PRAYER today is:

S | M | T | W | TH | F | S

THEME IN REVIEW

I KNOW A FELLOW WHO'S AS BROKE AS THE TEN COMMANDMENTS.

JOHN MARQUAND

DAY 7

MY FAVORITE VERSE FROM THE THEME WAS:

LOOKING BACK ON THESE TWO WEEKS, MY HIGHEST HIGH WAS:

MY LOWEST LOW THESE PAST WEEKS WAS:

ONE WAY GOD ANSWERED MY PRAYERS WAS:

ONE WAY GOD MIGHT USE ME AS A SACRED AGENT TO ANSWER THESE PRAYERS:

FAMILY COVENANT

We have shared *Highs & Lows* this week, read and highlighted the verses assigned in our Bible, talked about our lives, prayed for one another's highs and lows, and blessed one another.

Parent's Signature   *Teen's Signature*   *Date*

THE FINKMANIA QUIZBOWL

Question 1:

The First Commandment is:

(A) "Don't get caught,"
(B) "Do unto others as you would have them do unto you,"
(C) "I am the Lord your God... you shall have no other gods before me,"
(D) "You shall not take the name of the Lord your God in vain"

Question 2:

The Second Commandment is:

(A) About cursing, swearing, lying and deceiving,
(B) About taking God's name in vain,
(C) About prayer, praise, and thanksgiving,
(D) All of the above

Question 3:

The Third Commandment is:

(A) "Remember the sabbath day,"
(B) "Remember the sabbath day, and keep it holy,"
(C) "Remember the sabbath day, and keep it frequently,"
(D) "Remember the sabbath day, and keep it occasionally"

Question 4:

The Fourth Commandment is:

(A) The only Commandment that comes with a promise attached,
(B) "Honor your father and mother when they aren't embarrassing you,"
(C) "Honor your father and mother so that your days may be long in the land the Lord your God is giving you,"
(D) A & C

Question 5:

The Fifth Commandment is:

(A) "You shall not murder,"
(B) "You shall not steal,"
(C) "You shall not kill on the fifth,"
(D) "You shall not steal on the fifth"

Question 6:

The Sixth Commandment is:

(A) About honoring marriage,
(B) About keeping sex pure,
(C) Directly related to the First, Fifth, Seventh, Eighth and Tenth Commandments because breaking it causes you to break them all at the same time,
(D) All of the above and then some

Question 7:

The Seventh Commandment is:

(A) "You shall not steal,"
(B) "You shall not steal,"
(C) "You shall not steal,"
(D) All of the above

Question 8:

The Eighth Commandment tells us:

(A) We aren't to betray, gossip, lie about, or slander our neighbor,
(B) We are to defend, speak well of, and explain our neighbor's actions in the kindest ways,
(C) "You shall not bear false witness against your neighbor,"
(D) All of the above and then some

Question 9:

The Ninth and Tenth Commandments are about:

(A) Coveting and scheming to get things and relationships that don't belong to you,
(B) Working to get things you want through honest means,
(C) A & B,
(D) Proper dental hygiene

FINKmania Final Question:

Jesus said all the commandments can be summed up by one four letter word:

(A) Love,
(B) Obey,
(C) Work,
(D) Pray

Play this online game using FINKlink
LL06 @ www.faithink.com

THE WEAKEST FINK

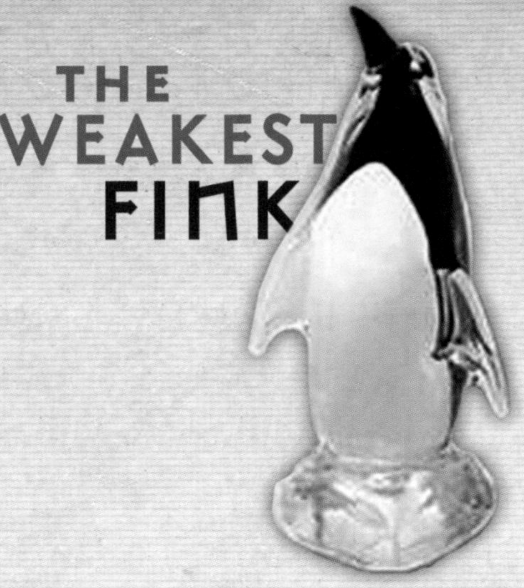

GOD DIDN'T CALL THEM "THE TEN SUGGESTIONS."

MIDORI KOTO

TERMS

WRITE A DEFINITION BELOW.

Love

Moses

Prophet

Sin

Ten Commandments

FAITH INKUBATORS

LORD'S PRAYER OVERVIEW

"Pray then in this way: Our Father in heaven, hallowed be your name. Your kingdom come. Your will be done, on earth as it is in heaven. Give us this day our daily bread. And forgive us our debts, as we also have forgiven our debtors. And do not bring us to the time of trial, but rescue us from the evil one."

—Matthew 6:9-13

Listen to this verse using FINKlink
LL07 @ www.faithink.com

f you Google the word "prayer," an entire digital world opens up to you with nearly 120 million results.

Google the phrase "teach us to pray" and you will have instant access to over thirteen million resources. These sites will do everything from teaching you to pray, to selling trinkets and coffee cups with prayers on them, to connecting you with a global web of praying people. If you narrow the search further by putting quotation marks around the phrase, you still have almost 167,000 results.

> **THE FEWER THE WORDS, THE BETTER THE PRAYER.**
>
> **MARTIN LUTHER**

THE LORD'S PRAYER

If someone asked, "What is prayer?" how would you respond? Would you say it involves talking to God? Would you say it has to do with listening to God? Imagine having a friend who only talked and never listened. Imagine having a friend who only spoke to you when they wanted you to give them something. That friendship would get old fast. True communication includes both talking and listening, both giving and taking. True prayer is a two-sided conversation. It includes everything a good relationship would include: talking and listening, asking and giving, laughing and crying, and sometimes saying, "I'm sorry" and "I love you." Prayer is all of these things—and more.

It has been two thousand years since Christ's disciples asked their Lord and friend for a lesson on how to pray. "Lord, teach us to pray," they said. Jesus responded with the words that have become the best-known prayer in history. This special prayer called "The Lord's Prayer" is found in two places in the Bible. In Matthew 6:9-15, the prayer is part of a larger teaching called "The Sermon on the Mount." In Luke 11:2-4, the prayer comes in response to the disciples asking Jesus to teach them. There must have been something about the way Christ communicated with God that motivated his friends to ask for a prayer lesson. Perhaps it was the humility, respect, and sincerity Jesus displayed. To Jesus, prayer was not a heaping of fancy words, a ritual, or a rote and rehearsed monologue. To Jesus, prayer was a natural communication with his Father. He once even called God "Abba"—or "Daddy"—in prayer. What is prayer to you?

PRAYER

Loving and listening God, thank you for giving me a way to communicate with you. Help me not only to speak, but also to listen. Help me not only to ask, but to give in prayer. Help me to make my whole life a prayer—an on-going conversation with you. In Jesus' name. Amen.

Order this art print using FINKlink LL07 @ www.faithink.com

IMAGES IN ART

- What do you see in today's painting by Dr. He Qi?
- Where are you in this work of art?
- How do the image and the verse apply to your life today?

So What Does This Mean?

The LORD'S PRAYER is sometimes known by its first two Latin words as the Pater Noster (Our Father). It includes an introduction ("Our Father in heaven..."), seven petitions (requests we make of God), and a traditional closing "Doxology" that wasn't part of the original prayer in the Bible ("For thine is the kingdom..."). Apart from minor changes and some capital letters, this prayer is essentially the same throughout the world for all Christians in all countries.

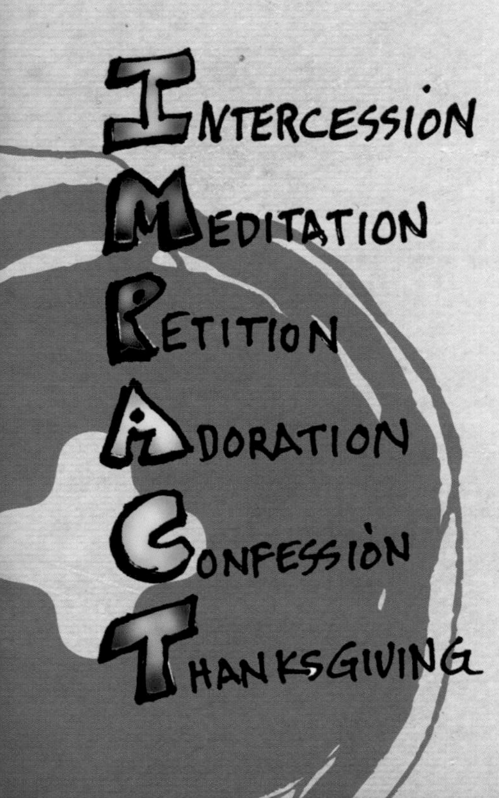

OUR TEACHER IS REALLY WEIRD! WE ASKED HER TO TEACH US HOW TO PRAY AND SHE TOLD US TO TAKE OFF OUR SHOES, LOOK UP AT THE STARS AND JUST LISTEN!

Bible Time

Read and highlight the Lord's Prayer in Matthew 6:9-13 and in Luke 11:2-4. Write "Lord's Prayer" in the margins. Now put the two versions side by side. What differences do you see?

Read and highlight Jeremiah 29:11-13. How does this verse relate to prayer?

Catechism Encounter

Scan the Lord's Prayer section of your Small Catechism for words that describe God. Circle five words that jump out at you. Write those words here:

Questions to Ponder

1. Who are three people you talk to most often when you really need to talk? Why do you trust these people with your inner thoughts?

2. How does trusting them make it easier for you to open up?

3. What are four qualities you think an ideal parent would have? How does God exhibit those qualities?

SMALL GROUP

SHARE, READ, TALK, PRAY, BLESS

1. **SHARE** your highs and lows of the week one-on-one with another person. Listen carefully and record your friend's thoughts in the space below. Then return to small group and share your friend's highs and lows.

   MY HIGHS + LOWS THIS WEEK WERE:

   ....

   MY FRIEND'S HIGHS + LOWS THIS WEEK WERE:

   ....

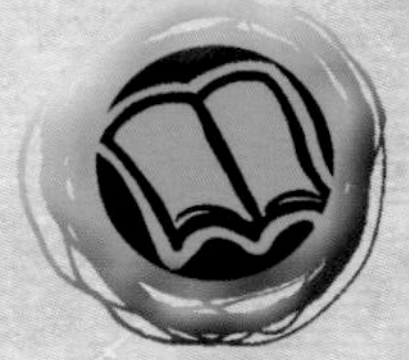

2. **READ** and highlight the theme verse in your Bibles. Circle key words, and learn the verse in song if time permits.

3. **TALK** about how today's verse relates to your highs and lows. Review the art for today, the Quiz Bowl questions, the terms, and the cartoons. Then write a sentence on each of the following:

   ONE NEW THING I LEARNED TODAY:

   ....

   ONE THING I ALREADY KNEW THAT IS WORTH REPEATING:

   ....

   ONE THING I WOULD LIKE TO KNOW MORE ABOUT:

   ....

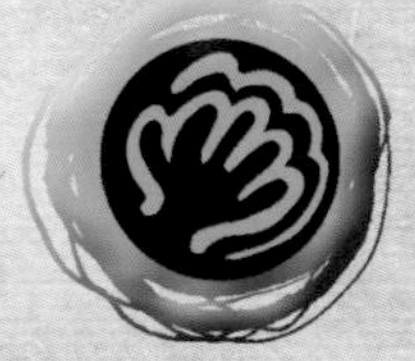

4. **PRAY** for one another, praising and thanking God for your highs, and asking God to be with you in your lows. Include your friend's highs and lows in your prayers.

   A PRAISING PRAYER: ....

   A THANKING PRAYER: ....

   AN ASKING PRAYER: ....

5. **BLESS** one another using the blessing of the week. (right) Mark each person with the sign of the cross as you bless them.

THIS WEEK'S BLESSING

(NAME), CHILD OF GOD, MAY YOU KNOW THE JOY OF BOTH TALKING AND LISTENING TO GOD IN PRAYER.

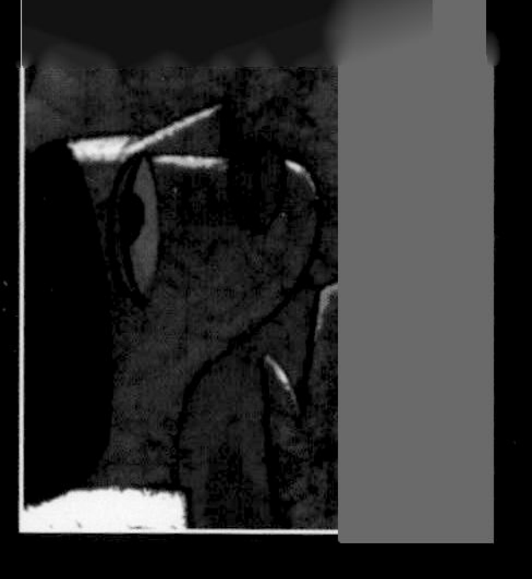

THE FAITH 5

Read the full devotions using FINKlink LL07 @ www.faithink.com

WEEK 1

journal

DAY 1

today's bible verse:

Matthew 6:9a

Our Father in heaven...

my HIGH today was:

my LOW today was:

my PRAYER today is:

DAY 2

today's bible verse:

Matthew 6:9b

Hallowed be your name.

my HIGH today was:

my LOW today was:

my PRAYER today is:

DAY 3

today's bible verse:

Matthew 6:10a

Your kingdom come.

my HIGH today was:

my LOW today was:

my PRAYER today is:

my HIGH today was:

my LOW today was:

my PRAYER today is:

DAY 4

today's bible verse:

Matthew 6:10b

Your will be done, on earth as it is in heaven.

my HIGH today was:

my LOW today was:

my PRAYER today is:

DAY 5

today's bible verse:

Matthew 6:11

Give us this day our daily bread.

my HIGH today was:

my LOW today was:

my PRAYER today is:

DAY 6

today's bible verse:

Matthew 6:12

And forgive us our debts, as we also have forgiven our debtors.

my HIGHEST HIGH this week was:

my LOWEST LOW this week was:

my PRAYER for next week is:

DAY 7

this week's blessing

(NAME), CHILD OF GOD, MAY YOU KNOW THE JOY OF BOTH TALKING AND LISTENING TO GOD IN PRAYER.

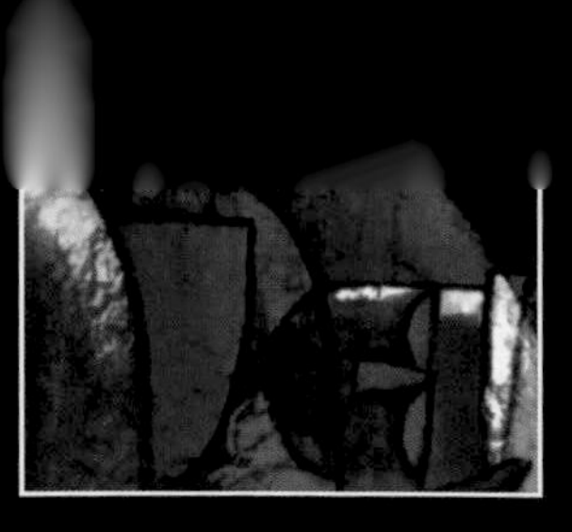

WEEK 2

FAITH JOURNAL

Read the full devotions using FINKlink LL07 @ www.faithink.com

DAY 1

TODAY'S BIBLE VERSE:

Matthew 6:13a

And do not bring us to the time of trial.

MY HIGH TODAY WAS:

MY LOW TODAY WAS:

MY PRAYER TODAY IS:

DAY 2

TODAY'S BIBLE VERSE:

Matthew 6:13b

But rescue us from the evil one.

MY HIGH TODAY WAS:

MY LOW TODAY WAS:

MY PRAYER TODAY IS:

DAY 3

TODAY'S BIBLE VERSE:

The Doxology

For the kingdom, the power, and the glory are yours, now and forever.

MY HIGH TODAY WAS:

MY LOW TODAY WAS:

MY PRAYER TODAY IS:

1. SHARE highs & lows of the day.
2. READ and highlight the verse of the day in your bibles.
3. TALK about how today's verse relates to your highs & lows.
4. PRAY for your highs & lows, for your family and for the world.
5. BLESS one another using this week's blessing (on the previous page).

DAY 4

today's bible verse:

Luke 11:9

So I say to you, "Ask, and it will be given you; search, and you will find; knock, and the door will be opened for you."

my HIGH today was:

my LOW today was:

my PRAYER today is:

Ask! SEEK! KNOCK!

DAY 5

today's bible verse:

Luke 11:13

If you then, who are evil, know how to give good gifts to your children, how much more will the heavenly Father give the Holy Spirit to those who ask him!

my HIGH today was:

my LOW today was:

my PRAYER today is:

DAY 6

today's bible verse:

Revelation 22:20

Amen. Come, Lord Jesus!

my HIGH today was:

my LOW today was:

my PRAYER today is:

S | M | T | W | TH | F | S

THEME IN REVIEW

WORK AS IF YOU WERE TO LIVE 100 YEARS. PRAY AS IF YOU WERE TO DIE TOMORROW.

BENJAMIN FRANKLIN

DAY 7

MY FAVORITE VERSE FROM THE THEME WAS:

....

....

....

....

....

....

....

POST CARD

DEAR GOD,
ARE YOU REALLY THERE
OR AM I ALL ALONE
HERE?
-CONCERNED

LOOKING BACK ON THESE TWO WEEK, MY HIGHEST HIGH WAS:

....

MY LOWEST LOW THESE PAST WEEKS WAS:

....

ONE WAY GOD ANSWERED MY PRAYERS WAS:

....

ONE WAY GOD MIGHT USE ME AS A SACRED AGENT TO ANSWER THESE PRAYERS:

....

....

FAMILY COVENANT

We have shared *Highs & Lows* this week, read and highlighted the verses assigned in our Bible talked about our lives, prayed for one another's highs and lows, and blessed one another.

....	....	....
Parent's Signature	*Teen's Signature*	*Date*

THE FINKMANIA QUIZBOWL

QUESTION 1:

The Lord's Prayer was given by:

(A) God to Moses,
(B) Jesus to the disciples,
(C) Jesus to Moses,
(D) Lord Sauron to Frodo Baggins

QUESTION 2:

The Lord's Prayer was given to the disciples when they asked Jesus:

(A) "Teach us to pray,"
(B) "Teach us to dance,"
(C) "Teach us something to pray every Sunday in church,"
(D) "Teach us how to get stuff from God"

QUESTION 3:

In the Lord's Prayer, Jesus addressed God as:

(A) Our Father,
(B) Our Mother,
(C) Your Holiness,
(D) Big Brother

QUESTION 4:

When it comes to the Lord's Prayer, a "petition" is:

(A) A prayer of praise,
(B) A request made of God,
(C) A paper you sign and send to God with at least 1000 signatures if you want your prayers answered,
(D) None of the above

QUESTION 5:

The First Petition of the Lord's Prayer is:

(A) Hallowed be your name,
(B) Hollowed be your name,
(C) Harold be your name,
(D) Give me lots of stuff

QUESTION 6:

"Your kingdom come, your will be done on earth as it is in heaven" is called:

(A) The Second Petition,
(B) The Second and Third Petitions,
(C) The Great Commission,
(D) Totally unrealistic

QUESTION 7:

The Fourth Petition of the Lord's Prayer is:

(A) "Give us this day our daily bread,"
(B) "Give me this day my daily bread,"
(C) "Give me this day everything I want,"
(D) "Give me more than my sister"

QUESTION 8:

The Fifth Petition is, "Forgive us our debts, as we...:"

(A) "...rack them up,"
(B) "...prove we are truly deserving,"
(C) "...also have forgiven our debtors,"
(D) "...try to get away with it"

QUESTION 9:

Two ways to pray the Sixth Petition of the Lord's Prayer are:

(A) "And do not bring us to the time of trial" and "Lead us not into temptation,"
(B) "Lead us not into temptation" and "Deliver us from evil,"
(C) Both A & B,
(D) Neither A nor B

FINKMANIA FINAL QUESTION:

The "Doxology" or final line in the traditional Lord's Prayer:

(A) Is "For the kingdom, the power, and the glory are yours now and forever,"
(B) Doesn't exist in most Bibles,
(C) Was added as a fitting ending to the prayer long after it was written,
(D) All of the above

Play this online game using FINKlink
LL07 @ www.faithink.com

THE WEAKEST FINK

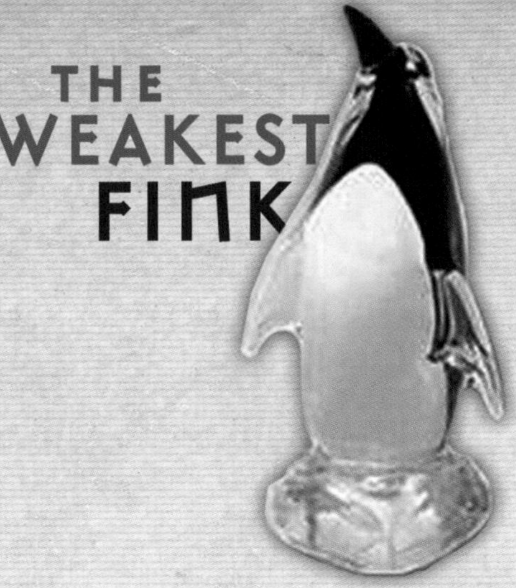

THE TRAGEDY OF OUR DAY IS NOT UNANSWERED PRAYER, BUT UNOFFERED PRAYER.

UNKNOWN

TERMS

WRITE A DEFINITION BELOW.

DISCIPLE

DOXOLOGY

LORD'S PRAYER

PETITION

PRAYER

FAITH INKUBATORS

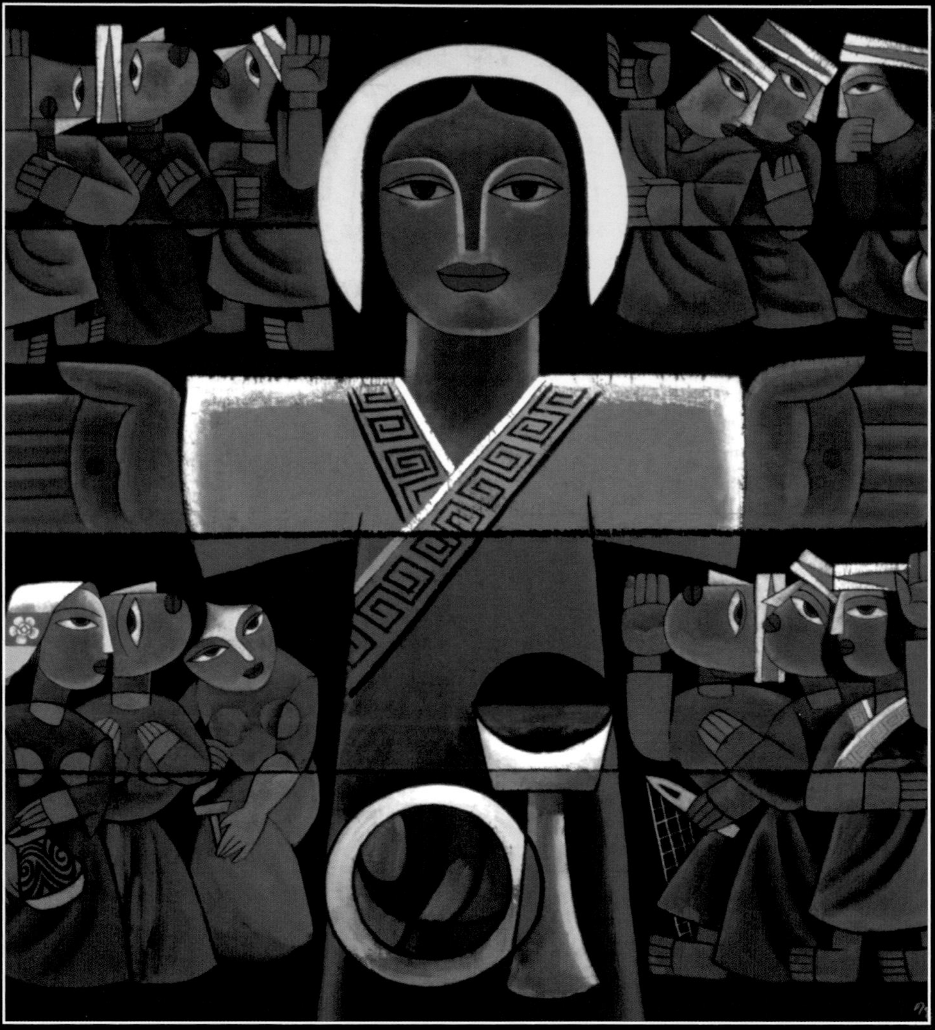

"The Risen Lord" Copyright © Dr. He Qi www.heqigallery.com

"The grace of the Lord Jesus Christ, the love of God, and the communion of the Holy Spirit be with all of you."

— II Corinthians 13:13

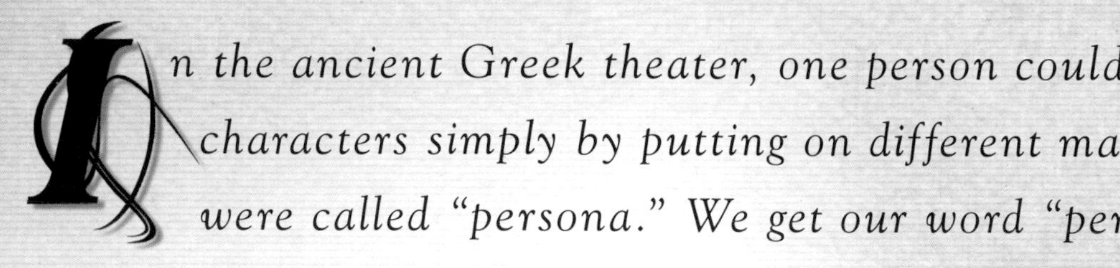

In the ancient Greek theater, one person could play many characters simply by putting on different masks. The masks were called "persona." We get our word "person" from it.

Sometimes the entire play was done by a single player, standing on stage in front of a table of masks. Everyone knew there was only one actor, but this actor came to the audience in different "persons."

After Jesus was raised from the dead and ascended into heaven, the early Christian church needed language to describe who Jesus was in relationship to God. Shortly after that, when the Holy Spirit came to empower the disciples on Pentecost, things became even more confusing. Who was God? Who was Jesus? Who or what was this Holy Spirit? Jesus said, "If you have seen me, you have seen the Father" and "I and the Father are one." He also called the Holy Spirit a "Comforter." Was this a being separate from God and Jesus?

From their Jewish roots, early Christians knew there was only one God. But how would they describe Jesus and the Holy Spirit? To explain the mystery of this "tri-unity" (trinity), they chose the language of the theater masks. The very earliest trinitarian creed simply said, "We believe in one God in three personas." There was only one actor, but this actor came in three special and distinct roles.

One God

There is only one God, but this God has three personas. It is a mystery and none of our words can fully describe it, but we may understand a little more about our amazing God by listening to Christ's final words to his disciples: "Go therefore and make disciples of all nations, baptizing them in the name of the Father and of the Son and of the Holy Spirit." If Jesus used these three names for God and instructed his Apostles to baptize and teach in the name of this trinity, then we, his followers today, will do just that.

The Apostles' Creed

A creed is a statement of faith. The word comes from the Latin *credo* meaning "I believe!" It is important to know that the original Apostles of Jesus did not write the Apostles' Creed. The first time parts of this statement appeared in written form was in 215 A.D., to summarize the teachings of the Apostles. The full creed as we have it today didn't show up until 542 A.D. The creed has three parts called "articles." The First Article teaches what Christians believe about God. The Second Article covers the life, death and resurrection of Jesus. The Third Article includes the Holy Spirit, our relationship to God and each other as the church and the promise of resurrection.

I BELIEVE IN GOD,
THE FATHER ALMIGHTY,
CREATOR OF HEAVEN AND EARTH.

I BELIEVE IN JESUS CHRIST, HIS ONLY SON, OUR LORD. HE WAS CONCEIVED BY THE POWER OF THE HOLY SPIRIT AND BORN OF THE VIRGIN MARY. HE SUFFERED UNDER PONTIUS PILATE, WAS CRUCIFIED, DIED, AND WAS BURIED.
HE DESCENDED INTO HELL.
ON THE THIRD DAY HE ROSE AGAIN. HE ASCENDED INTO HEAVEN AND IS SEATED AT THE RIGHT HAND OF THE FATHER. HE WILL COME AGAIN TO JUDGE THE LIVING AND THE DEAD.

I BELIEVE IN THE HOLY SPIRIT, THE HOLY CATHOLIC (CHRISTIAN) CHURCH, THE COMMUNION OF SAINTS, THE FORGIVENESS OF SINS, THE RESURRECTION OF THE BODY, AND THE LIFE EVERLASTING. AMEN.

Order this art print using FINKlink
LL08 @ www.faithink.com

IMAGES IN ART

- What do you see in today's painting by Dr. He Qi?
- Where are you in this work of art?
- How do the image and the verse apply to your life today?

So What Does This Mean?

NO FREIDA, I DON'T THINK THE TRINITY WOULD APPRECIATE BEING REFERRED TO AS "THE OLD MAN, THE BABY AND THE BIRD!"

One God, One Creed... 3 Parts

First Article
God the Almighty Creator

Second Article
Jesus, God's only Son

Third Article
The Holy Spirit, Church, Saints, Forgiveness, Resurrection and Eternal Life

Although the original Apostles of Jesus didn't write the Apostles' Creed and it didn't show up in its complete form until the end of the 5th Century, the Early Church used it and we continue to use it because it sums up the basics of the Apostles' teachings.

Bible Time

Read and highlight the verse of the week, II Corinthians 13:13, in your Bibles. Do the same with the following verses, writing key words in margins to help you remember what the verses are about:

Genesis 1:1-5	Write "God the Creator" in the margin
Psalm 19:1-4	Write "God the Creator" in the margin
John 1:1-18	Write "Christ, the living Word" in the margin
Colossians 1:15-20	Write "Christ, the visible presence of the invisible God"
John 14:25-27	Write "Holy Spirit as Counselor" in the margin
Acts 2:1-5	Write "Holy Spirit and Power" in the margin

Prayer

God of majesty and wonder, you are awesome and powerful, yet you want to know me. You have mystery wrapped about you, yet you want me to know you. Continue to show yourself to me. I am here. I am listening. Amen.

Catechism Encounter

Open your Small Catechism and scan the three articles of the Apostles' Creed. Circle three key words in each article that show the work of God, Jesus, and the Holy Spirit. Use these key words and the Bible Time verses above to help answer the questions below.

Questions to Ponder

1. List three things you know about God:

2. List three things you know about Jesus:

3. List three things you know about the work of the Holy Spirit:

SMALL GROUP

SHARE, READ, TALK, PRAY, BLESS

1. SHARE your highs and lows of the week one-on-one with another person. Listen carefully and record your friend's thoughts in the space below. Then return to small group and share your friend's highs and lows.

MY HIGHS + LOWS THIS WEEK WERE:

....

MY FRIEND'S HIGHS + LOWS THIS WEEK WERE:

....

2. READ and highlight the theme verse in your Bibles. Circle key words and learn the verse in song if time permits.

3. TALK about how today's verse relates to your highs and lows. Review the art for today, the Quiz Bowl questions, the terms, and the cartoons. Then write a sentence on each of the following:

ONE NEW THING I LEARNED TODAY:

....

ONE THING I ALREADY KNEW THAT IS WORTH REPEATING:

....

ONE THING I WOULD LIKE TO KNOW MORE ABOUT:

....

4. PRAY for one another, praising and thanking God for your highs, and asking God to be with you in your lows. Include your friend's highs and lows in your prayers.

A PRAISING PRAYER: ....

A THANKING PRAYER: ....

AN ASKING PRAYER: ....

5. BLESS one another using the blessing of the week. (right) Mark each person with the sign of the cross as you bless them.

THIS WEEK'S BLESSING

MAY THE GRACE OF OUR LORD JESUS CHRIST, THE LOVE OF GOD AND THE COMMUNION OF THE HOLY SPIRIT BE WITH YOU. (RESPONSE: AND ALSO WITH YOU.)

THE FAITH 5 JOURNAL

WEEK 1

Read the full devotions using FINKlink LL08 @ www.faithink.com

DAY 1

TODAY'S BIBLE VERSE:

2 Corinthians 13:13

The grace of the Lord Jesus Christ, the love of God, and the communion of the Holy Spirit be with all of you.

MY HIGH TODAY WAS:

MY LOW TODAY WAS:

MY PRAYER TODAY IS:

DAY 2

TODAY'S BIBLE VERSE:

1 Corinthians 8:6

Yet for us there is one God, the Father, from whom are all things and for whom we exist, and one Lord, Jesus Christ, through whom are all things and through whom we exist.

MY HIGH TODAY WAS:

MY LOW TODAY WAS:

MY PRAYER TODAY IS:

DAY 3

TODAY'S BIBLE VERSE:

Isaiah 40:28

Have you not known? Have you not heard? The Lord is the everlasting God, the Creator of the ends of the earth. He does not faint or grow weary; his understanding is unsearchable.

MY HIGH TODAY WAS:

MY LOW TODAY WAS:

MY PRAYER TODAY IS:

my HIGH today was:

my LOW today was:

my PRAYER today is:

DAY 4

today's bible verse:

Colossians 1:15

He is the image of the invisible God, the firstborn of all creation.

my HIGH today was:

my LOW today was:

my PRAYER today is:

DAY 5

today's bible verse:

Luke 1:31-32

And now, you will conceive in your womb and bear a son, and you will name him Jesus. He will be great, and will be called the Son of the Most High, and the Lord God will give to him the throne of his ancestor David.

my HIGH this week was:

my LOW this week was:

my PRAYER today is:

DAY 6

today's bible verse:

John 19:30

When Jesus had received the wine, he said, "It is finished." Then he bowed his head and gave up his spirit.

my HIGHEST HIGH today was:

my LOWEST LOW today was:

my PRAYER for next week is:

DAY 7

this week's blessing

May the grace of our Lord Jesus Christ, the love of God and the communion of the Holy Spirit be with you. (Response: And also with you.)

WEEK 2

THE FAITH 5
Read the full devotions using FINKlink
LL08 @ www.faithink.com
JOURNAL

DAY 1

TODAY'S BIBLE VERSE:

Acts 1:10-11

Men of Galilee, why do you stand looking up toward heaven? This Jesus, who has been taken up from you into heaven, will come in the same way as you saw him go into heaven.

MY HIGH TODAY WAS:

MY LOW TODAY WAS:

MY PRAYER TODAY IS:

DAY 2

TODAY'S BIBLE VERSE:

John 14:16

And I will ask the Father, and he will give you another Advocate, to be with you forever.

TRINITY = TRI-UNITY

MY HIGH TODAY WAS:

MY LOW TODAY WAS:

MY PRAYER TODAY IS:

DAY 3

TODAY'S BIBLE VERSE:

1 Corinthians 1:2-3

Grace to you and peace from God our Father and the Lord Jesus Christ.

MY HIGH TODAY WAS:

MY LOW TODAY WAS:

MY PRAYER TODAY IS:

2. READ AND HIGHLIGHT THE VERSE OF THE DAY IN YOUR BIBLES.

3. TALK ABOUT HOW TODAY'S VERSE RELATES TO YOUR HIGHS & LOWS.

4. PRAY FOR YOUR HIGHS & LOWS, FOR YOUR FAMILY AND FOR THE WORLD.

5. BLESS ONE ANOTHER USING THIS WEEK'S BLESSING (ON THE PREVIOUS PAGE).

DAY 4

TODAY'S BIBLE VERSE:

Philippians 3:10-11

I want to know Christ and the power of his resurrection and the sharing of his sufferings by becoming like him in his death, if somehow I may attain the resurrection from the dead.

MY HIGH TODAY WAS:

MY LOW TODAY WAS:

MY PRAYER TODAY IS:

DAY 5

TODAY'S BIBLE VERSE:

Psalm 51:11

Do not cast me away from your presence, and do not take your holy spirit from me.

MY HIGH TODAY WAS:

MY LOW TODAY WAS:

MY PRAYER TODAY IS:

DAY 6

TODAY'S BIBLE VERSE:

Genesis 1:1-3

In the beginning when God created the heavens and the earth, the earth was a formless void and darkness covered the face of the deep... Then God said, "Let there be light!" And there was light.

MY HIGH TODAY WAS:

MY LOW TODAY WAS:

MY PRAYER TODAY IS:

S | M | T | W | TH | F | S

THEME IN REVIEW

CHRISTIAN TRUTH COULD NOT POSSIBLY BE PUT INTO A SHORTER AND CLEARER STATEMENT THAN THAT WHICH IS CONTAINED IN THE APOSTLES' CREED.

MARTIN LUTHER

DAY 7

MY FAVORITE VERSE FROM THE THEME WAS:

....

....

....

....

....

....

....

....

....

CREED
CREDIT
INCREDIBLE
CREDENTIALS

LOOKING BACK ON THESE TWO WEEK, MY HIGHEST HIGH WAS:

....

MY LOWEST LOW THESE PAST WEEKS WAS:

....

ONE WAY GOD ANSWERED MY PRAYERS WAS:

....

ONE WAY GOD MIGHT USE ME AS A SACRED AGENT TO ANSWER THESE PRAYERS:

....

....

FAMILY COVENANT

We have shared *Highs & Lows* this week, read and highlighted the verses assigned in our Bible talked about our lives, prayed for one another's highs and lows, and blessed one another.

....	....	....
Parent's Signature	*Teen's Signature*	*Date*

THE FINKMANIA QUIZ BOWL

Question 1:

The Apostles' Creed was:

(A) Given by God to Moses,
(B) Dictated by Jesus to the Apostles,
(C) Written by the Apostles on the fiftieth day after Christ ascended into heaven,
(D) Found in its first written form in the Interrogatory Creed of Hippolytus, ca. 215 A.D., but not in its current form until 542 A.D.

Question 2:

The Apostles' Creed was originally written as:

(A) A summary of Christian faith,
(B) A statement for baptismal candidates in Rome in a question-and-answer format to affirm their faith,
(C) Both A & B,
(D) A test for adolescents to fill in the blanks on catacomb walls

Question 3:

Apostles are:

(A) Small furry creatures that eat bugs and grub worms,
(B) John, Paul, Luke and Ringo,
(C) All followers of Jesus who are "sent out" into the world to share the good news of Jesus,
(D) All followers of Jesus who worship but don't tell anyone

Question 4:

The word "Apostle" means:

(A) Small furry creatures that eats bugs and grub worms,
(B) To "go postal,"
(C) To "go willingly,"
(D) To "send out or away from"

Question 5:

The word "Creed":

(A) Comes from the same root as the words credit, credible and credentials,
(B) Comes from a Latin word meaning "I believe,"
(C) Means a formal statement of religious beliefs and faith,
(D) All of the above and then some

Question 6:

The First Article (part) of the Apostles' Creed is:

(A) "One God in three persons,"
(B) The funniest part
(C) "I believe in God the Father almighty, creator of heaven and earth,"
(D) "I am the Lord your God, you shall have no other gods before me"

Question 7:

The Second Article (part) of the Apostles' Creed is:

(A) "You shall not take the name of the Lord your God in vain,"
(B) "Your kingdom come,"
(C) "I believe in Jesus Christ, his only Son, our Lord..."
(D) "Don't forget to floss"

Question 8:

The Third Article (part) of the Apostles' Creed is:

(A) "Remember the sabbath day, and keep it holy,"
(B) "Your will be done on earth as in heaven,"
(C) "I believe in the Holy Spirit..."
(D) C, plus the church, the communion of saints, the forgiveness of sins, the resurrection of the body and life everlasting

Question 9:

Christians recite the Apostles' Creed every Sunday in order to:

(A) Impress the pastor
(B) Remember who they are and what they believe,
(C) Stand together with 2.1 billion Christians around the world in a common witness to their faith in the triune God,
(D) Both B & C

FINKmania Final Question:

The final line in the Apostles' Creed is:

(A) "He will come again to judge the living and the dead,"
(B) "This is most certainly true!"
(C) "Tip your waitress,"
(D) "...and the life everlasting. Amen."

Play this online game using **FINKlink**
LL08 @ www.faithink.com

THE WEAKEST FINK

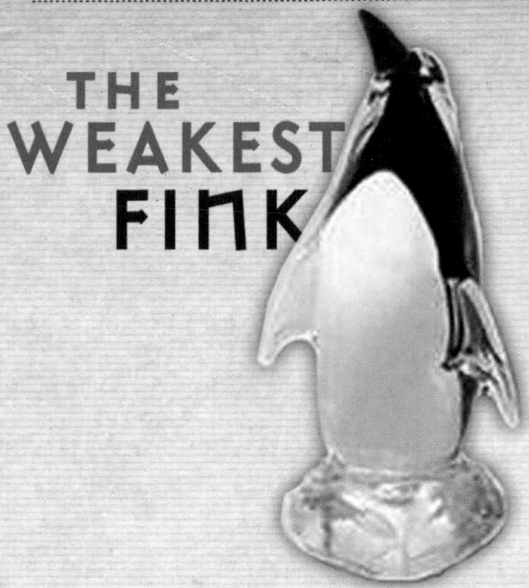

Snow is water, and ice is water, and water is water, these three are one.

Joseph Dare

TERMS

WRITE A DEFINITION BELOW.

Apostles' Creed

....

Article

....

Creed

....

Persona

....

Trinity

....

FAITH INKUBATORS

The Sacrament of Baptism

"But when the goodness and loving kindness of God our Savior appeared, he saved us, not because of any works of righteousness that we had done, but according to his mercy, through the water of rebirth and renewal by the Holy Spirit. This Spirit he poured out on us richly through Jesus Christ our Savior, so that, having been justified by his grace, we might become heirs according to the hope of eternal life." — Titus 3:4-7

Listen to this song using FINKlink
LL09 @ www.faithink.com

ike. McDonalds. Coca Cola. Target. Apple. Google. Amazon. Ebay.

These are eight of the most recognizable brands in the world. Just by hearing the word or seeing the logo, you know what they represent. Companies spend millions and millions on branding. They develop the brand, market the brand, position the brand, and protect it. Getting instant recognition means they can charge a premium price. Brands matter.

The concept of branding can be traced back to ancient nomads and herders. Because wandering animals could sometimes mix with other herds at scarce water holes, owners needed a way to protect their possessions and prove that a beast actually belonged to them. To accomplish this, they created unique symbols and marks on an iron brand, setting the tool into the fire until it was white-hot, then searing their mark of ownership into the hides of their animals. (Ouch!) The mark was a sign that the animal belonged to the brander. Even if the animal wandered and was separated for a time, the true owner could find and claim the member of the herd.

Some say baptism is a like branding. God places a mark on us and adopts us into the Christian family. We are sealed with the mark of Christ. We belong to God's herd.

Holy Baptism

When John the Baptist appeared in the wilderness telling everyone to prepare for Jesus, he baptized them with water as a symbolic act to show they had repented. He said one would come after him who would baptize with the Holy Spirit and fire! When Jesus was baptized, John announced, "Look! The Lamb of God who takes away the sin of the world!" From that day on, everything changed. When Jesus' disciples went out into the world "baptising in the name of the Father, Son, and Holy Spirit" as Jesus had instructed, they baptized whole families. Baptism in the early church was for young and old alike - all who wanted to be part of the Christian community and their children.

Today Lutherans see baptism as God's idea and God's act. A little baby doesn't know she's adopted until she's old enough to understand, but that doesn't make the baby any less a child of the adoptive parent. God names us and claims us. In these common, yet holy, waters, God creates a relationship with you. By that physical act of baptism, through the water and the Word, you have been branded and belong to God. You are a child of God, sealed with the Holy Spirit and marked—branded—with the cross of Christ forever!

God went out and womped us with the water and the Word;

we're branded and now we are part of the herd.

Monty Lysne

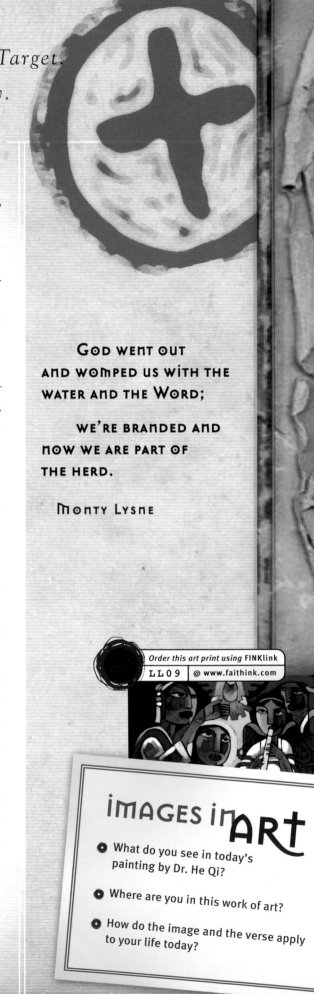

Order this art print using FINKlink
LL09 @ www.faithink.com

Images in Art

- What do you see in today's painting by Dr. He Qi?
- Where are you in this work of art?
- How do the image and the verse apply to your life today?

So What Does This Mean?

I HAD A SIMILIAR REACTION ON THE DAY I JOINED THIS CHURCH.

"SACRAMENTS" ARE:

1. Gifts of God's Grace
2. Commanded by Christ
3. Given with a Physical Element Attached

The Lutheran church honors and practices two special gifts from God that fit this definition: HOLY BAPTISM and HOLY communion.

Identification Card

NAME

ADDRESS

CITY STATE

TEL. NO.

in case of accident or serious illness please notify.

NAME

ADDRESS

Bible Time

Does baptism save us? Does sprinkling water on a baby's head and saying some words from the Bible make any real difference? Read and highlight Titus 3: 4-7. What exactly is happening in Holy Baptism? Write some thoughts here:

Prayer

God, our spirits are often dry. We are tired and thirsty for you. Be the water of our lives. We are tired of trying to do everything all alone. Brand us as your own. Help us walk in baptismal grace anew today. We pray in Jesus' name. Amen.

Catechism Encounter

Open your Small Catechism to Luther's explanation of the Sacrament of Holy Baptism. Circle five words that help you understand what Baptism is. Write those words here:

Questions to Ponder

1. What does a brand mean on an animal? What does God's brand in baptism mean on you?

2. Baptism is like being adopted into God's family. What rights and responsibilities do adopted children have? What rights and responsibilities does someone who is adopted by God have?

3. Is the water used for baptism magic, holy or different from regular water? Why or why not?

4. Role Play: You come upon a bad car accident. The victim is dying and asks to be baptized. What do you do?

A twelve-year-old girl was diagnosed with a rare blood disease. The only possible thing that could save her was a blood transfusion.

After exhaustive tests, it was discovered that her little brother's blood was the closest to her own type. The parents approached the young boy and asked if he would be willing to give his blood to save the life of his sister. He thought for a moment, then requested he be given the night to think about it. They agreed. The next morning, the boy was sitting on his parents' bed when they awoke. He told them he would do this for his sister—he would give his blood. Later that day, as both children lay side-by-side with his blood running into her veins, the young boy turned to his parents and asked a simple, startling question: "When do I start to die?"

His parents didn't know how to answer. It slowly dawned on them the child believed that—in participating in the blood transfusion—he would be giving up his own life to save his sister. He made this decision freely to save her life.

Two thousand years ago, Jesus made a decision. He chose to give up his life to save all of us. "This is my body, which is given for you." He made the ultimate sacrifice—the giving of life—so we could live. In the ancient world, it was thought and taught that a high price had to be paid and blood had to be shed to show sorrow for sin. For a nomadic people, sacrificing a precious, spotless animal was the sign of repentance to God. People believed the life of the animal was somehow held and housed in its blood. Blood sacrifices were seen as paying the price for sin. Blood held power. Blood gave life. The shedding of blood was an awesome and meaningful act of sorrow for sins.

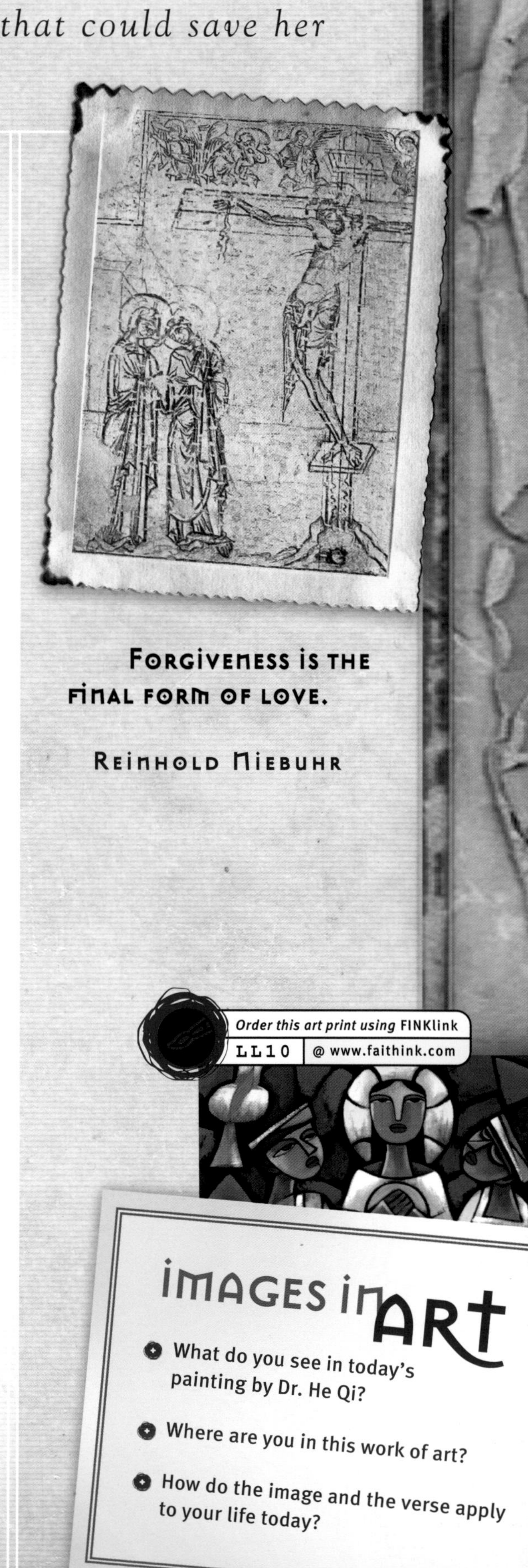
Order this art print using FINKlink
LL10
@ www.faithink.com

Forgiveness is the final form of love.

Reinhold Niebuhr

The Sacrament of Communion

Lutherans believe Jesus is really present in the gifts of this supper. They don't teach, as the Roman Catholic church does, that the bread and wine mysteriously become actual flesh and blood (transubstantiation). Neither do they teach that the bread and wine are mere symbols of Christ. Rather, they believe Christ comes in a real, special, unexplainable way to be real to us, to forgive us, and to begin the process of restoring us to communion with God and one another. Lutheran's call this mystery the "real presence." Where is Jesus in Holy Communion? Lutherans like to say Jesus is "in, with, and under" this meal. Bread isn't just bread. Wine isn't simply wine. It is a living bread. It is Christ's blood given for you! When we hear Christ's promise, examine our hearts, pray for Christ's forgiving presence, and eat and drink the bread and wine, Jesus comes to us in a very real way. In this meal we are fed, forgiven, restored, and strengthened for the journey ahead.

Images in Art

- What do you see in today's painting by Dr. He Qi?
- Where are you in this work of art?
- How do the image and the verse apply to your life today?

So What Does This Mean?

The Lord Jesus on the night when he was betrayed took bread, and when he had given thanks, he broke it, and said, "This is my body which is for you. Do this in remembrance of me."

In the same way also he took the cup, after supper, saying, "This cup is the New Covenant in my blood. Do this, as often as you drink it, in remembrance of me."

Words of Institution
I Corinthians 11:23-24

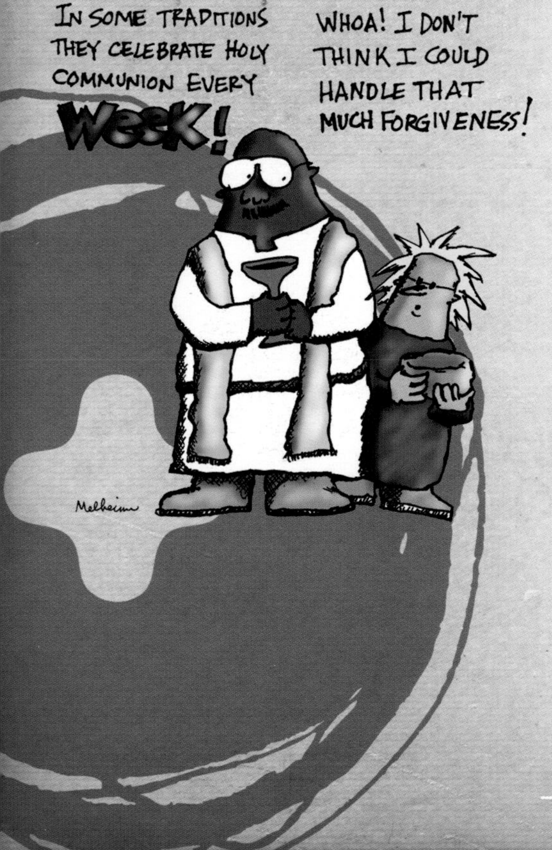

IN SOME TRADITIONS THEY CELEBRATE HOLY COMMUNION EVERY WEEK!
WHOA! I DON'T THINK I COULD HANDLE THAT MUCH FORGIVENESS!
Melheim

Bible Time

Read and highlight the words of institution in Matthew, Mark, Luke and I Corinthians, writing "Words of Institution" in the margins:

Matthew 26:26-28

Mark 14:22-24

Luke 22:19-20

I Corinthians 11:23-26.

Prayer

Holy Jesus, thank you for the unexpected and undeserved gift of your living real presence in Holy Communion. Thank you that this gift is "given for me" and that you are always near. Amen.

Catechism Encounter

Scan Luther's explanation of Holy Communion in the Small Catechism. What does Luther say are the gifts and benefits of the Sacrament?

Questions to Ponder

1. What do you remember about the first time you took communion?

2. Can you have communion all alone by yourself? Why or why not?

3. What are some good ways to prepare your mind and heart before going up to take Holy Communion?

Small Group

share, read, talk, pray, bless

1. **SHARE** your highs and lows of the week one-on-one with another person. Listen carefully and record your friend's thoughts in the space below. Then return to small group and share your friend's highs and lows.

   MY HIGHS + LOWS THIS WEEK WERE:

   ....

   MY FRIEND'S HIGHS + LOWS THIS WEEK WERE:

   ....

2. **READ** and highlight the theme verse in your Bibles. Circle key words and learn the verse in song if time permits.

3. **TALK** about how today's verse relates to your highs and lows. Review the art for today, the Quiz Bowl questions, the terms, and the cartoons. Then write a sentence on each of the following:

   ONE NEW THING I LEARNED TODAY:

   ....

   ONE THING I ALREADY KNEW THAT IS WORTH REPEATING:

   ....

   ONE THING I WOULD LIKE TO KNOW MORE ABOUT:

   ....

4. **PRAY** for one another, praising and thanking God for your highs, and asking God to be with you in your lows. Include your friend's highs and lows in your prayers.

   A PRAISING PRAYER: ....

   A THANKING PRAYER: ....

   AN ASKING PRAYER: ....

5. **BLESS** one another using the blessing of the week. (right) Mark each person with the sign of the cross as you bless them.

THIS WEEK'S BLESSING

(NAME), CHILD OF GOD, MAY THE BEAUTY OF JESUS BE SEEN IN YOU THIS DAY. AMEN.

WEEK 1

THE
FAITH
5
JOURNAL
Read the full devotions using FINKlink
LL10
@ www.faithink.com

DAY 1

TODAY'S BIBLE VERSE:

1 Corinthians 11:26

For as often as you eat this bread and drink the cup, you proclaim the Lord's death until he comes.

MY HIGH TODAY WAS:

MY LOW TODAY WAS:

MY PRAYER TODAY IS:

DAY 2

TODAY'S BIBLE VERSE:

1 Corinthians 11:23

For I received from the Lord what I also handed on to you, that the Lord Jesus on the night when he was betrayed took a loaf of bread...

MY HIGH TODAY WAS:

MY LOW TODAY WAS:

MY PRAYER TODAY IS:

DAY 3

TODAY'S BIBLE VERSE:

1 Corinthians 11:24

And when he had given thanks, he broke it and said, "This is my body that is for you. Do this in remembrance of me.

MY HIGH TODAY WAS:

MY LOW TODAY WAS:

MY PRAYER TODAY IS:

my HIGH today was:

my LOW today was:

my PRAYER today is:

DAY 4

today's bible verse:

I Corinthians 11:25a

In the same way he took the cup also after supper, saying, "This cup is the new covenant in my blood."

my HIGH today was:

my LOW today was:

my PRAYER today is:

DAY 5

today's bible verse:

I Corinthians 11:25b

"Do this, as often as you drink it, in remembrance of me."

my HIGH today was:

my LOW today was:

my PRAYER today is:

DAY 6

today's bible verse:

I Corinthians 11:27

Whoever, therefore, eats the bread or drinks the cup of the Lord in an unworthy manner will be answerable for the body and blood of the Lord.

my HIGHEST HIGH this week was:

my LOWEST LOW this week was:

my PRAYER for next week is:

DAY 7

this week's blessing

(NAME), CHILD OF GOD, MAY THE BEAUTY OF JESUS BE SEEN IN YOU THIS DAY. AMEN.

WEEK 2

DAY 1

TODAY'S BIBLE VERSE:

I Corinthians 11:28

Examine yourselves, and only then eat of the bread and drink of the cup.

MY HIGH TODAY WAS:

MY LOW TODAY WAS:

MY PRAYER TODAY IS:

DAY 2

TODAY'S BIBLE VERSE:

I Chronicles 29:17

I know, my God, that you search the heart, and take pleasure in uprightness.

MY HIGH TODAY WAS:

MY LOW TODAY WAS:

MY PRAYER TODAY IS:

DAY 3

TODAY'S BIBLE VERSE:

Psalm 51:10

Create in me a clean heart, O God, and put a new and right spirit within me.

MY HIGH TODAY WAS:

MY LOW TODAY WAS:

MY PRAYER TODAY IS:

my HIGH today was:

my LOW today was:

my PRAYER today is:

DAY 4

today's bible verse:

Psalm 130:3-4

If you, O Lord, should mark iniquities, Lord, who could stand? But there is forgiveness with you, so that you may be revered.

my HIGH today was:

my LOW today was:

my PRAYER today is:

DAY 5

today's bible verse:

Psalm 139:23

Search me, O God, and know my heart; test me and know my thoughts.

my HIGH today was:

my LOW today was:

my PRAYER today is:

DAY 6

today's bible verse:

Lamentation 3:40

Let us test and examine our ways, and return to the Lord.

S | M | T | W | TH | F | S

THEME IN REVIEW

THERE IS ONLY ONE PLACE WE CAN PUT OUR GUILT TO FIND A TRUE SENSE OF FORGIVENESS: ON THE BACK OF THE CRUCIFIED CHRIST.

DAVID SEAMANDS

DAY 7

MY FAVORITE VERSE FROM THE THEME WAS:

....

....

....

....

....

....

....

....

....

LOOKING BACK ON THESE TWO WEEKS, MY HIGHEST HIGH WAS:

....

MY LOWEST LOW THESE PAST WEEKS WAS:

....

ONE WAY GOD ANSWERED MY PRAYERS WAS:

....

ONE WAY GOD MIGHT USE ME AS A SACRED AGENT TO ANSWER THESE PRAYERS:

....

....

FAMILY COVENANT

We have shared *Highs & Lows* this week, read and highlighted the verses assigned in our Bible talked about our lives, prayed for one another's highs and lows, and blessed one another.

....	....	....
Parent's Signature	*Teen's Signature*	*Date*

THE FINKMANIA QUIZBOWL

QUESTION 1:

Not forgiving someone is like a long-term illness because both:

(A) Can cause you injury and harm,
(B) Happen only to evil people,
(C) Need treatment for you to get better,
(D) A & C

QUESTION 2:

The meal of bread and wine makes a special communion with God because of:

(A) The quality of the ingredients,
(B) How they are prepared,
(C) The addition of the Word of God,
(D) Their power to change into real blood and flesh

QUESTION 3:

The benefits of Holy Communion include:

(A) Receiving forgiveness of sin, life, and salvation,
(B) Realizing how much God has forgiven us, so that we are more able to forgive others,
(C) Understanding we are part of a Christian community,
(D) All of the above and then some

QUESTION 4:

Who is rightly prepared to receive Holy Communion?:

(A) All who believe the words, "Given and shed for you for the forgiveness of sins,"
(B) All who believe the words, "Given and shed for you for the forgiveness of sins,"
(C) All who believe the words, "Given and shed for you for the forgiveness of sins,"
(D) All of the above

QUESTION 5:

A person should take Holy Communion:

(A) As often as they feel a need for forgiveness, are willing to confess, and want to be closer to Christ and others,
(B) Once a month whether they think they need it or not,
(C) Only when they have committed a terrible sin,
(D) Go ask my pastor

QUESTION 6:

Where might a person celebrate communion?:

(A) In a church building,
(B) On a hillside,
(C) In a jail cell
(D) All of the above, plus anywhere the God's word is present with the bread and wine

QUESTION 7:

Do the bread and wine actually turn into the flesh and blood of Jesus in Holy Communion?:

(A) Catholics say yes—it's called transubstantiation,
(B) Most Protestants say no and believe in a symbolic presence,
(C) Lutherans say no, but believe in a mystical "Real Presence",
(D) All of the above. What do you believe?

QUESTION 8:

The sacred act of taking the bread and wine in remembrance of Jesus is called:

(A) Holy Communion,
(B) The Eucharist (good grace),
(C) The Sacrament of the Altar,
(D) All of the above, plus the Lord's Supper, depending on your tradition

QUESTION 9:

Who is the "Lord" in the "Lord's Supper":

(A) Jesus,
(B) Jesus,
(C) Jesus,
(D) All of the above

FINKMANIA FINAL QUESTION:

In I Corinthians 11:26, St. Paul tells us:

(A) Every time you eat you should speak as well,
(B) If you eat too much you'll die,
(C) Every time you take communion, you are proclaiming Christ died for our sins,
(D) Absolutely nothing

Play this online game using **FINKlink**
LL10 @ www.faithink.com

THE WEAKEST FINK

IF WE REALLY WANT TO LOVE, WE MUST LEARN TO FORGIVE.

MOTHER TERESA

TERMS

WRITE A DEFINITION BELOW.

FORGIVENESS

HOLY COMMUNION

REAL PRESENCE

SACRAMENT

WORDS OF INSTITUTION

"The Risen Lord" Copyright © Dr. He Qi www.heqigallery.com

THE APOSTLES' CREED

1. GOD THE CREATOR
2. GOD THE PROVIDER
3. GOD THE PRESERVER
4. JESUS THE SAVIOR
5. JESUS THE REDEEMER
6. JESUS THE LORD
7. THE HOLY SPIRIT
8. THE CHURCH AND THE SAINTS
9. THE FORGIVENESS OF SINS
10. RESURRECTION AND ETERNAL LIFE

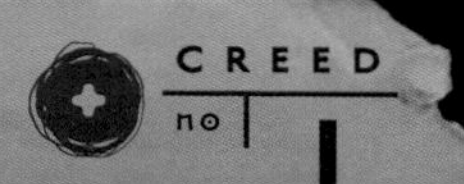

God the Creator

"Have you not known? Have you not heard? The LORD is the everlasting God, the Creator of the ends of the earth... Even youths will faint and be weary, and the young will fall exhausted; but those who wait for the Lord shall renew their strength, they shall mount up with wings like eagles, they shall run and not be weary, they shall walk and not faint." — Isaiah 40:28a, 30-31

Listen to this verse using **FINK**link
LL11 | @ www.faithink.com

orrington: "You are without a doubt the worst pirate I've ever heard of."
Captain Jack Sparrow: "But you have heard of me."

In the movie *Pirates of the Caribbean*, actor Jonny Depp plays a pirate who loves recognition. Captured and interrogated by a British officer, Sparrow lets it be known that he is happy to be recognized, even if for a bad reason. Most people like to be known for something good. They like others to recognize and remember them for their accomplishments.

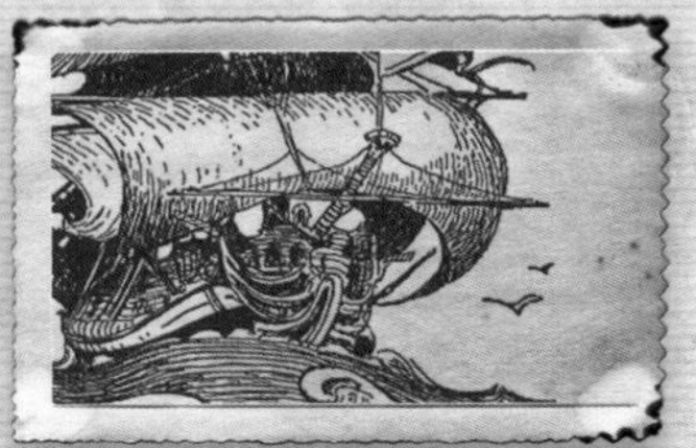

I DANCE TO THE TUNE OF AN INVISIBLE PIPER. HE STANDS BEHIND THE UNIVERSE. HE IS GOD.

ALBERT EINSTEIN

SMART AND SMARTER

As a school boy, Albert Einstein was considered a slow student. He had trouble following directions, paying attention, and listening. But Einstein was no dummy, even though his teachers thought so. He just didn't learn the same way other kids learned. Einstein was actually a genius. He grew up to be one of the most gifted physicists of the last century. His special theory of relativity ($E=MC^2$) changed our understanding of the fabric of the universe and modern science forever.

GOD THE CREATOR

Einstein was a scientist, but he was also a person of faith. He studied the stars and atoms and found God everywhere he looked. He wondered about the deepest questions puzzling science and discovered a beautiful order in all that wonder. He once said, "I want to know God's thoughts, the rest is detail." Another time he said, "I dance to the tune of an Invisible Piper. He stands behind the Universe. He is God."

There are people who will tell you the universe was created by chance. Others say God is simply the invention of superstitious minds trying to explain the unexplainable—certainly not a being in whom a scientist could believe. Yet, even an atheist will admit there exists an amazing order in the universe. From the smallest sub-atomic particles to the greatest super nova, everything in the universe holds together in an elegant, intricate, and infinitely fine-tuned balance. It is beautiful and perfect.

Can there be a work of art without an artist? A mathematically complex creation without a creator? An invention without an inventor?

What do you think?

Order this art print using FINKlink
LL11 | @ www.faithink.com

IMAGES IN ART

- What do you see in today's painting by Dr. He Qi?
- Where are you in this work of art?
- How do the image and the verse apply to your life today?

So What Does This Mean?

I DONT' KNOW ANYONE WHO BELIEVES IN GOD.
EINSTEIN BELIEVED IN GOD. HE WROTE: "I DANCE TO THE TUNE OF AN INVISIBLE PIPER. HE STANDS BEHIND THE UNIVERSE. HE IS GOD!"
YEAH? WHAT DID HE KNOW?

I believe in God the Father Almighty, creator of heaven and earth.

First Article
Apostles' Creed

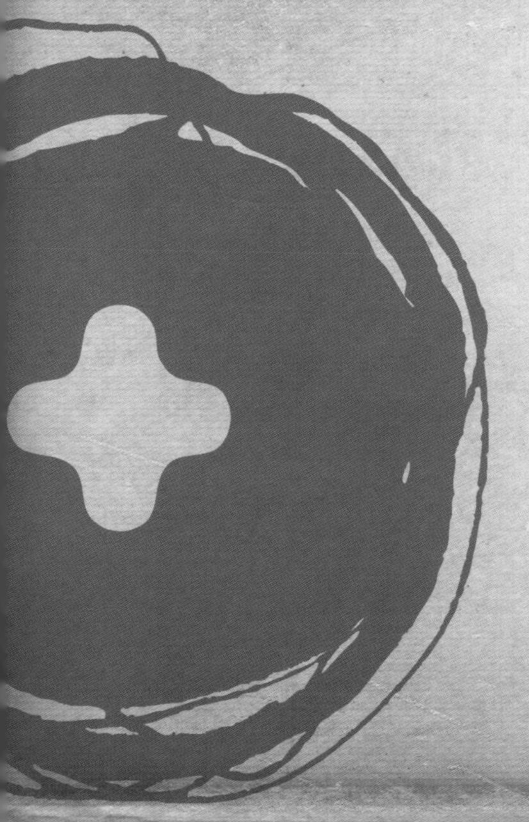

Bible Time

Read and highlight Isaiah 40:28a, 30-31. In this chapter God is saying, "Have you heard of me? Have you not known? Have you not heard? I made it all!" Why do you think God wants you to know this? Why is it important people recognize God as God?

The Bible says the Creator God didn't just make the world and walk away like some grand old computer designer who builds a self-replicating computer, drops it on a planet, then disappears. This inventor loves the invention! This creator is here to help. "I believe in God the Creator" means I believe God is with me all the time. God is watching over and taking care of everything in creation. That everything includes you! When you are tired and exhausted, God can give you strength and stamina. When you are heartbroken and hurting, God listens, loves and will come to your aid. This God wants to be known by you and help you!

Prayer

Creator God, sometimes I don't know what I believe, but I sense you are calling me to find you. Help me to believe. Help me to know you. Continue to create in me a space for you. In Jesus' name I pray. Amen.

Catechism Encounter

Open your Small Catechism to the First Article of the Apostles' Creed. Circle five words that describe God and write them here:

Questions to Ponder

1. Why do people want to be noticed? Do you think God wants to be noticed? Why or why not?

2. What can you notice about God by looking at creation? What do you think God wants you to know and notice about creation?

3. How would you answer a person who said, "You can't be much of a scientist and believe in God!"

SMALL GROUP

SHARE, READ, TALK, PRAY, BLESS

1. **SHARE** your highs and lows of the week one-on-one with another person. Listen carefully and record your friend's thoughts in the space below. Then return to small group and share your friend's highs and lows.

   MY HIGHS + LOWS THIS WEEK WERE:

   ....

   MY FRIEND'S HIGHS + LOWS THIS WEEK WERE:

   ....

2. **READ** and highlight the theme verse in your Bibles. Circle key words and learn the verse in song if time permits.

3. **TALK** about how today's verse relates to your highs and lows. Review the art for today, the Quiz Bowl questions, the terms, and the cartoons. Then write a sentence on each of the following:

   ONE NEW THING I LEARNED TODAY:

   ....

   ONE THING I ALREADY KNEW THAT IS WORTH REPEATING:

   ....

   ONE THING I WOULD LIKE TO KNOW MORE ABOUT:

   ....

4. **PRAY** for one another, praising and thanking God for your highs, and asking God to be with you in your lows. Include your friend's highs and lows in your prayers.

   A PRAISING PRAYER: ....

   A THANKING PRAYER: ....

   AN ASKING PRAYER: ....

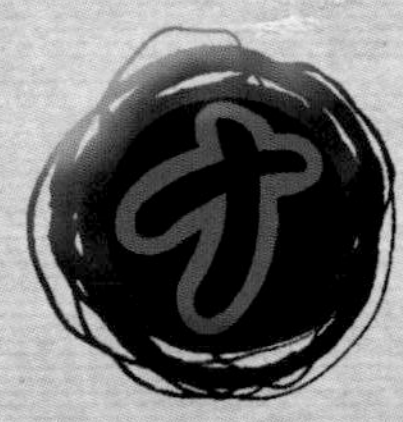

5. **BLESS** one another using the blessing of the week. (right) Mark each person with the sign of the cross as you bless them.

THIS WEEK'S BLESSING

(NAME), CHILD OF GOD, MAY ALMIGHTY GOD CREATE SOMETHING WONDERFUL AND NEW IN YOU THIS DAY.

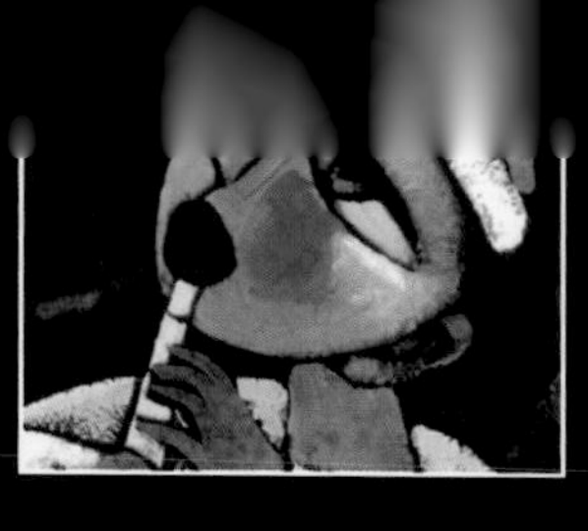

Read the full devotions using FINKlink
LL11 @ www.faithink.com

FAITH JOURNAL

WEEK 1

DAY 1

TODAY'S BIBLE VERSE:

Isaiah 40:21

Have you not known? Have you not heard? The Lord is the everlasting God, the creator of the ends of the earth.

MY HIGH TODAY WAS:

MY LOW TODAY WAS:

MY PRAYER TODAY IS:

DAY 2

TODAY'S BIBLE VERSE:

Psalm 19:1-2

The heavens are telling the glory of God; and the firmament proclaims his handiwork. Day to day pours forth speech, and night to night declares knowledge.

MY HIGH TODAY WAS:

MY LOW TODAY WAS:

MY PRAYER TODAY IS:

DAY 3

TODAY'S BIBLE VERSE:

Psalm 111:2

Great are the works of the Lord, studied by all who delight in them.

MY HIGH TODAY WAS:

MY LOW TODAY WAS:

MY PRAYER TODAY IS:

my HIGH today was:

my LOW today was:

my PRAYER today is:

DAY 4

today's bible verse:

Psalm 139:13

For it was you who formed my inward parts; you knit me together in my mother's womb. I praise you, for I am fearfully and wonderfully made.

my HIGH today was:

my LOW today was:

my PRAYER today is:

DAY 5

today's bible verse:

Isaiah 45:19

I did not speak in secret, in a land of darkness; I did not say to the offspring of Jacob, "Seek me in chaos." I the Lord speak the truth, I declare what is right.

my HIGH today was:

my LOW today was:

my PRAYER today is:

DAY 6

today's bible verse:

Joel 1:3

Tell your children of it, and let your children tell their children, and their children another generation.

my HIGHEST HIGH this week was:

my LOWEST LOW this week was:

my PRAYER for next week is:

DAY 7

this week's blessing

(NAME), CHILD OF GOD, MAY ALMIGHTY GOD CREATE SOMETHING WONDERFUL AND NEW IN YOU THIS DAY.

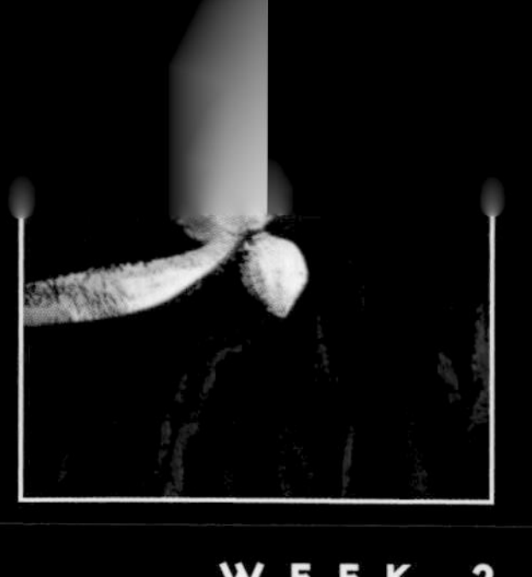

FAITH JOURNAL

WEEK 2

Read the full devotions using FINKlink
LL11 @ www.faithink.com

DAY 1

TODAY'S BIBLE VERSE:

Psalm 8:3-4

When I look at your heavens, the work of your fingers, the moon and the stars that you have established, what are human beings that you are mindful of them, mortals that you care for them.

MY HIGH TODAY WAS: ....

MY LOW TODAY WAS: ....

MY PRAYER TODAY IS: ....

....

DAY 2

TODAY'S BIBLE VERSE:

Genesis 1:1-2

In the beginning when God created the heavens and the earth, the earth was a formless void and darkness covered the face of the deep, while a wind from God swept over the face of the waters.

MY HIGH TODAY WAS: ....

MY LOW TODAY WAS: ....

MY PRAYER TODAY IS: ....

....

DAY 3

TODAY'S BIBLE VERSE:

Genesis 1:3

Then God said, "Let there be light"; and there was light.

MY HIGH TODAY WAS: ....

MY LOW TODAY WAS: ....

MY PRAYER TODAY IS: ....

....

1. SHARE highs & lows of the day.

2. READ and highlight the verse of the day in your bibles.

3. TALK about how today's verse relates to your highs & lows.

4. PRAY for your highs & lows, for your family and for the world.

5. BLESS one another using this week's blessing (on the previous page).

my HIGH today was:

my LOW today was:

my PRAYER today is:

DAY 4

today's bible verse:

Genesis 1:24

And God said, "Let the earth bring forth living creatures of every kind: cattle and creeping things and wild animals of the earth of every kind." And it was so.

my HIGH today was:

my LOW today was:

my PRAYER today is:

DAY 5

today's bible verse:

Genesis 1:27-28a

So God created humankind in his image, in the image of God he created them; male and female he created them. God blessed them and God said to them, "Be fruitful and multiply..."

my HIGH today was:

my LOW today was:

my PRAYER today is:

DAY 6

today's bible verse:

Genesis 1:31a

God saw everything that he had made, and indeed, it was very good.

S | M | T | W | TH | F | S

THEME IN REVIEW

GOD IS A SCIENTIST, NOT A MAGICIAN.

ALBERT EINSTEIN

DAY 7

MY FAVORITE VERSE FROM THE THEME WAS:

....

....

....

....

....

....

....

....

....

LOOKING BACK ON THESE TWO WEEKS, MY HIGHEST HIGH WAS:

....

MY LOWEST LOW THESE PAST WEEKS WAS:

....

ONE WAY GOD ANSWERED MY PRAYERS THIS WEEK WAS:

....

ONE WAY GOD MIGHT USE ME AS A SACRED AGENT TO ANSWER THESE PRAYERS:

....

....

FAMILY COVENANT

We have shared *Highs & Lows* this week, read and highlighted the verses assigned in our Bibles, talked about our lives, prayed for one another's highs and lows, and blessed one another.

....	....	....
Parent's Signature	*Teen's Signature*	*Date*

THE FINKMANIA QUIZBOWL

Question 1:

The First Article of the Apostles' Creed is:

(A) "I am the Lord your God. You shall have no other gods before me,"
(B) "Hallowed be your name,"
(C) "I believe in God the Father Almighty, creator of heaven and earth,"
(D) Right after the Second Article of the Apostles' Creed

Question 2:

Jesus called God:

(A) Abba ("Daddy" in Aramaic) and Father,
(B) The Ground of His Being,
(C) The Big Bang,
(D) The Big Coincidence

Question 3:

Which of the following did Albert Einstein NOT say?:

(A) "I want to know God's thoughts, the rest is detail,"
(B) "God is a scientist, not a magician,"
(C) "I dance to the tune of an Invisible Piper. He stands behind the Universe,"
(D) "Bad hair day? Call mine a bad hair life!"

Question 4:

Martin Luther explained the First Article by writing:

(A) "I believe God has created me and all that exists,"
(B) "God has given me life, and still preserves my body and soul with all of their powers,"
(C) "God provides me with food and clothing, home and family, daily work," and all I need,"
(D) All of the above

Question 5:

What else did Luther say about God?:

(A) God protects me in time of danger and guards me from evil,
(B) God does this out of fatherly and divine goodness and mercy,
(C) God does all this even though I don't deserve it,
(D) All of the above and "this is most certainly true!"

Question 6:

According to Luther, what is the proper response to all the wonderful gifts of God?:

(A) I surely ought to thank God,
(B) I surely ought to thank and praise God,
(C) I surely ought to thank, praise, serve and obey God,
(D) I ought to go to church once or twice a year and throw a couple bucks in the offering plate

Question 7:

You can't expect a fish to understand algebra any more than:

(A) You can expect a human being to understand the mysteries of God,
(B) You can expect an adult to understand the mysteries of a seventh grader,
(C) You can expect a seventh grader to understand algebra,
(D) None of the above

Question 8:

God has true authority over the universe because:

(A) God likes to boss us around,
(B) God "wrote the book" on all that exists,
(C) God is the author of creation and continues to sustain all that exists,
(D) Both B & C

Question 9:

The masterful design of the universe must have had:

(A) A sharp bunch of lawyers,
(B) A big crew of workers,
(C) A Master Designer according to Einstein
(D) Natural selection, random mutation and an infinite amount of time to come into being, according to Charles Darwin

Finkmania Final Question:

Because God has created me and all that exists, I should:

(A) Wreck creation,
(B) Take care of creation,
(C) Thank, praise, serve and obey God,
(D) B & C, and this is most certainly true!

Play this online game using FINKlink
LL11 @ www.faithink.com

THE WEAKEST FINK

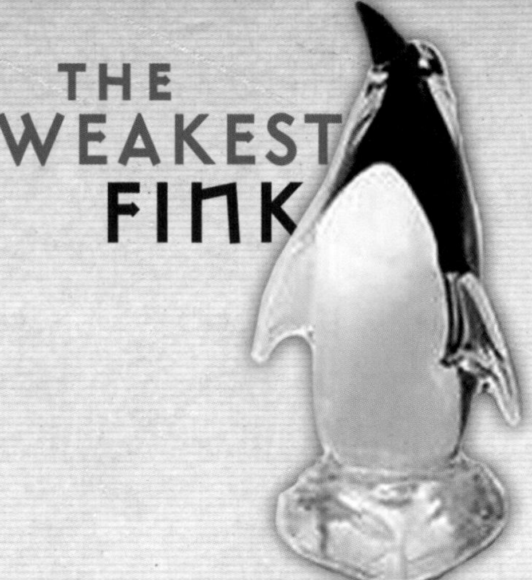

Calling Atheism a religion is like calling bald a hair color.

Don Hirschberg

TERMS

Write a definition below.

Belief

....

Creation

....

Creator

....

Faith

....

Science

....

FAITH INKUBATORS

God the Provider

"For in him all things in heaven and on earth were created, things visible and invisible, whether thrones or dominions or rulers or powers—all things have been created through him and for him. He himself is before all things, and in him all things hold together."

— Colossians 1:16–17

Imagine waking up one day to find your whole family missing. Vanished. Gone. Without a trace.

You look through every room in the house, but they have all disappeared. No parents. No siblings. Even your pets are gone. You run to the neighbor's house, but no one answers the door. Walking inside, you discover they've all vanished as well. Hungry, you return to your house to eat breakfast and think things over. The refrigerator, however, is empty. So are the cupboards. The kitchen is entirely void of food. Even the salt shaker is empty. You head to the store and slowly come to realize a deafening silence in the streets. No cars. No people. The grocery store parking lot is empty. The automatic doors open for you and you pull down a box of Pop-Tarts from the shelf. It feels light as you tear it open. Empty. You grab another box. Empty. You run down the dairy aisle for some milk, but all the cartons and bottles are empty. You rush about the store grabbing packages here and there, but every single one is filled with only air. What is happening here? How are you going to live? Where is your family? Where are your friends? All the fears you've ever had in your life rush in on you like an avalanche. You turn your eyes heavenward and raise hands to God.

What do you pray?

A GOD WISE ENOUGH TO CREATE ME AND THE WORLD I LIVE IN IS WISE ENOUGH TO WATCH OUT FOR ME.

PHILIP YANCY

God the Provider

Everything you have is a gift. Every moment, second, breath, and heartbeat is provided for you by God. When was the last time you said thanks to God for the hot water in your shower? For the music of a waterfall? For clean air to breathe? For that pesky little brother of yours?

Have you ever given a gift to someone who didn't say thanks? Have you ever felt like someone was taking advantage of your kindness? Maybe you had a friend who only wanted to hang around you for your money, your homework, or your status. Friends who only want to use you get old fast.

Do you ever wonder how God feels when people continue to take and take without saying thanks? God gives a new day, a new sunrise, oxygen to breathe, food on the table, a warm place to sleep, rains to replenish the earth and all good gifts that make and sustain life. These gifts are given to those who say thanks, and to those who don't. The sun shines both on those who acknowledge the giver of the gifts and on those who just keep on taking and taking and taking and taking and taking and taking and taking and taking and taking and taking and taking and taking without so much as a word of thanks.

Order this art print using FINKlink
LL12
@ www.faithink.com

IMAGES IN ART

- What do you see in today's painting by Dr. He Qi?
- Where are you in this work of art?
- How do the image and the verse apply to your life today?

So What Does This Mean?

SO GOD PROVIDES ME WITH FOOD, CLOTHING, HOME, FAMILY, DAILY WORK AND ALL I NEED. WHAT'S THE CATCH?
YOU ARE.

Dear Lord:

The gods have been good to me. For the first time in my life, everything is absolutely perfect just the way it is. So here's the deal: You freeze everything the way it is, and I won't ask for anything more. If that is OK, please give me absolutely no sign. OK, deal.

In gratitude, I present you this offering of cookies and milk. If you want me to eat them for you, give me no sign. Thy will be done.

Homer Simpson

Bible Time

The word "Providence" is an old term for our gracious providing God. The word comes from the Latin *providere* meaning "to prepare for." Read and highlight Colossians 1:16-17, writing "God holds it all together" in the margin. Think about how God holds the world together. Think about how God has held you together recently. What has God provided for you? Make a list of the top ten things God provided for you this week:

1.	2.
3.	4.
5.	6.
7.	8.
9.	10.

Prayer

Dear Giver of All Good Gifts, thank you for holding the universe together, and for holding me together this day. Thank you for all the blessings you provide for me: food, clothing, home, family, friends, a community of faith, your word, and all that I need from day to day. Help me to recognize you, and to receive these gifts with thanks. In Jesus' name. Amen.

Catechism Encounter

Read Luther's explanation of the First Article of the Apostles' Creed in your Small Catechism. Circle five things God provides. List them here:

Questions to Ponder

1. What is the difference between a want and a need? Does God always provide both?
2. Brainstorm a list of five essential things you need to survive.
3. How does God provide for each of these needs?
4. How can you show God you are thankful?

SMALL GROUP

SHARE, READ, TALK, PRAY, BLESS

1. **SHARE** your highs and lows of the week one-on-one with another person. Listen carefully and record your friend's thoughts in the space below. Then return to small group and share your friend's highs and lows.

   MY HIGHS + LOWS THIS WEEK WERE:

   ....

   MY FRIEND'S HIGHS + LOWS THIS WEEK WERE:

   ....

2. **READ** and highlight the theme verse in your Bibles. Circle key words and learn the verse in song if time permits.

3. **TALK** about how today's verse relates to your highs and lows. Review the art for today, the Quiz Bowl questions, the terms, and the cartoons. Then write a sentence on each of the following:

   ONE NEW THING I LEARNED TODAY:

   ....

   ONE THING I ALREADY KNEW THAT IS WORTH REPEATING:

   ....

   ONE THING I WOULD LIKE TO KNOW MORE ABOUT:

   ....

4. **PRAY** for one another, praising and thanking God for your highs, and asking God to be with you in your lows. Include your friend's highs and lows in your prayers.

   A PRAISING PRAYER: ....

   A THANKING PRAYER: ....

   AN ASKING PRAYER: ....

5. **BLESS** one another using the blessing of the week. (right) Mark each person with the sign of the cross as you bless them.

THE FAITH 5

THIS WEEK'S BLESSING

MAY THE GOOD AND GRACIOUS GIFTS OF GOD FILL YOUR LIFE AND SPILL OUT TO OTHERS TODAY.

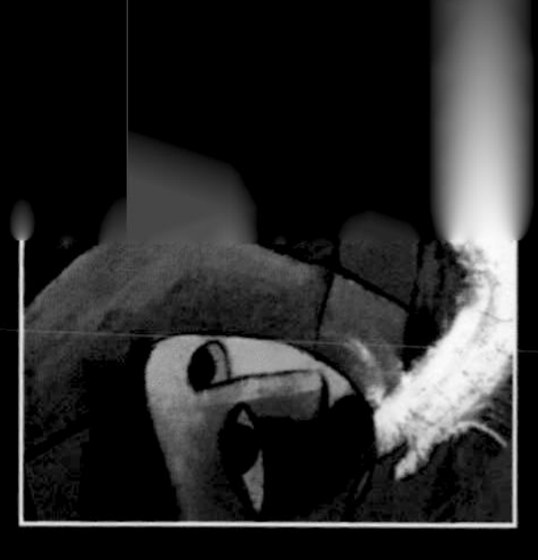

FAITH

Read the full devotions using FINKlink
LL12 @ www.faithink.com

WEEK 1 JOURNAL

DAY 1

TODAY'S BIBLE VERSE:

Colossians 1:16

For in him all things in heaven and on earth were created, things visible and invisible, whether thrones or dominions or rulers or powers—all things have been created through him and for him.

MY HIGH TODAY WAS:

MY LOW TODAY WAS:

MY PRAYER TODAY IS:

DAY 2

TODAY'S BIBLE VERSE:

Colossians 1:17

He himself is before all things, and in him all things hold together.

MY HIGH TODAY WAS:

MY LOW TODAY WAS:

MY PRAYER TODAY IS:

DAY 3

TODAY'S BIBLE VERSE:

Matthew 6:31-32

Therefore do not worry, saying "What will we eat?' or "What will we drink?' or "What will we wear?' For it is the Gentiles who strive for all these things; and indeed your heavenly Father knows that you need all these things.

MY HIGH TODAY WAS:

MY LOW TODAY WAS:

MY PRAYER TODAY IS:

my HIGH today was:

my LOW today was:

my PRAYER today is:

DAY 4

today's bible verse:

Matthew 6:33

But strive first for the kingdom of God and his righteousness, and all these things will be given to you as well.

my HIGH today was:

my LOW today was:

my PRAYER today is:

DAY 5

today's bible verse:

John 6:35

I am the bread of life. Whoever comes to me will never be hungry, and whoever believes in me will never be thirsty.

my HIGH today was:

my LOW today was:

my PRAYER today is:

DAY 6

today's bible verse:

2 Corinthians 12:9

My grace is sufficient for you, for power is made perfect in weakness.

my HIGHEST HIGH this week was:

my LOWEST LOW this week was:

my PRAYER for next week is:

DAY 7

this week's blessing

May the good and gracious gifts of God fill your life and spill out to others today.

Read the full devotions using FINKlink LL12 @ www.faithink.com

WEEK 2

FAITH JOURNAL

DAY 1

TODAY'S BIBLE VERSE:

Genesis 28:15

Know that I am with you and will keep you wherever you go, and will bring you back to this land; for I will not leave you until I have done what I have promised you.

MY HIGH TODAY WAS:

MY LOW TODAY WAS:

MY PRAYER TODAY IS:

DAY 2

TODAY'S BIBLE VERSE:

Deuteronomy 7:9

Know therefore that the Lord your God is God, the faithful God who maintains covenant loyalty with those who love him and keep his commandments, to a thousand generations.

MY HIGH TODAY WAS:

MY LOW TODAY WAS:

MY PRAYER TODAY IS:

DAY 3

TODAY'S BIBLE VERSE:

Psalm 1:1

Happy are those who do not follow the advice of the wicked, or take the path that sinners tread, or sit in the seat of scoffers.

MY HIGH TODAY WAS:

MY LOW TODAY WAS:

MY PRAYER TODAY IS:

1. SHARE HIGHS & LOWS OF THE DAY.

2. READ AND HIGHLIGHT THE VERSE OF THE DAY IN YOUR BIBLES.

3. TALK ABOUT HOW TODAY'S VERSE RELATES TO YOUR HIGHS & LOWS.

4. PRAY FOR YOUR HIGHS & LOWS, FOR YOUR FAMILY AND FOR THE WORLD.

5. BLESS ONE ANOTHER USING THIS WEEK'S BLESSING (ON THE PREVIOUS PAGE).

DAY 4

TODAY'S BIBLE VERSE:

Psalm 23:1

The Lord is my shepherd, I shall not want.

my HIGH today was:

my LOW today was:

my PRAYER today is:

DAY 5

TODAY'S BIBLE VERSE:

Psalm 23:2-31

He makes me lie down in green pastures; he leads me beside still waters; he restores my soul.

my HIGH today was:

my LOW today was:

my PRAYER today is:

DAY 6

TODAY'S BIBLE VERSE:

Proverbs 3:5-6

Trust in the Lord with all your heart, and do not rely on your own insight. In all your ways acknowledge him, and he will make straight your paths.

my HIGH today was:

my LOW today was:

my PRAYER today is:

S | M | T | W | TH | F | S

THEME IN REVIEW

GOD PROVIDES FOOD AND CLOTHING, HOME AND FAMILY, DAILY WORK AND ALL THAT I NEED FROM DAY TO DAY.

MARTIN LUTHER,
THE SMALL CATECHISM

DAY 7

MY FAVORITE VERSE FROM THE THEME WAS:

....

....

....

....

....

....

....

....

....

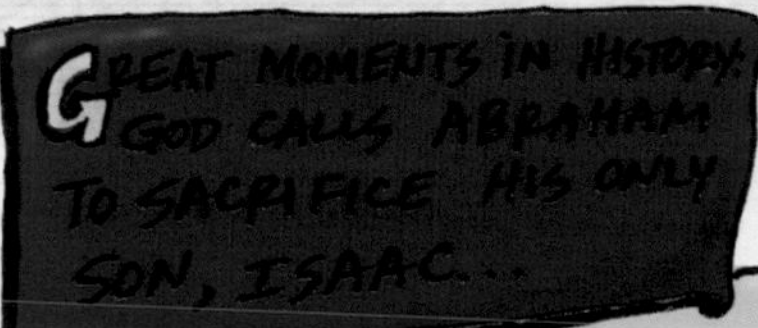

LOOKING BACK ON THESE TWO WEEKS, MY HIGHEST HIGH WAS:

....

MY LOWEST LOW THESE PAST WEEKS WAS:

....

ONE WAY GOD ANSWERED MY PRAYERS WAS:

....

ONE WAY GOD MIGHT USE ME AS A SACRED AGENT TO ANSWER THESE PRAYERS:

....

....

FAMILY COVENANT

We have shared *Highs & Lows* this week, read and highlighted the verses assigned in our Bible talked about our lives, prayed for one another's highs and lows, and blessed one another.

....	....	....
Parent's Signature	*Teen's Signature*	*Date*

The FinkMania QuizBowl

Question 1:

The First Article of the Apostles' Creed is:

(A) "I believe in God the Father Almighty, creator of heaven and earth,"

(B) "I believe in Jesus Christ, his only Son, our Lord,"

(C) "I believe in the Holy Spirit, the holy catholic (Christian) church,"

(D) "I am the Lord, your God. You shall have no other gods before me"

Question 2:

The word "provide":

(A) Comes from the Latin words meaning "to prepare for,"

(B) Comes from the same root word as "providence,"

(C) Means to supply ones' needs,

(D) All of the above and then some

Question 3:

What does God provide for us?:

(A) Not much,

(B) Food and clothing, home and family, daily work and all that we need from day to day,

(C) Protection,

(D) B & C

Question 4:

Why does God preserve and provide for us?:

(A) Just for the fun of it,

(B) Out of guilt for letting the world fall apart the way it has,

(C) Out of the kind of goodness and mercy a loving and parent has for precious children,

(D) Both A and B

Question 5:

What gives us life and sustains us?:

(A) Exercise,

(B) Exercise and bran muffins,

(C) Exercise, bran muffins and the little purple pill, *Nexium*,

(D) God

Question 6:

Something God gives to sustain us on a daily basis is called:

(A) School lunch,

(B) Daily Bread,

(C) iPod,

(D) Flintstones Multiple Vitamins

Question 7:

Giving up something special and giving it to God is called:

(A) A bad move,

(B) A sacrifice,

(C) A waste of money,

(D) A sanctuary

Question 8:

When God asked Abraham to sacrifice his only son, Isaac:

(A) It wasn't much of a sacrifice because Isaac was a teenager,

(B) It wasn't much of a sacrifice because Isaac wasn't really Abraham's son,

(C) It wasn't much of a sacrifice because Father Abraham had seven sons, sir,

(D) None of the above

Question 9:

At the last moment before Abraham's sacrifice of Isaac, God provided:

(A) Agent Jack Bauer and CTU to set him free,

(B) A stay of execution by the governor of Canaan,

(C) An angel to cut Isaac free,

(D) A ram caught in a nearby thicket in Isaac's place

FinkMania Final Question:

Colossians 1:16-17 tells us:

(A) God created everything,

(B) God holds everything together,

(C) Both A and B,

(D) God made everything visible, but the invisible stuff of the universe is made by chance

Play this online game using **FINKlink**

LL12 | **@ www.faithink.com**

The Weakest Fink

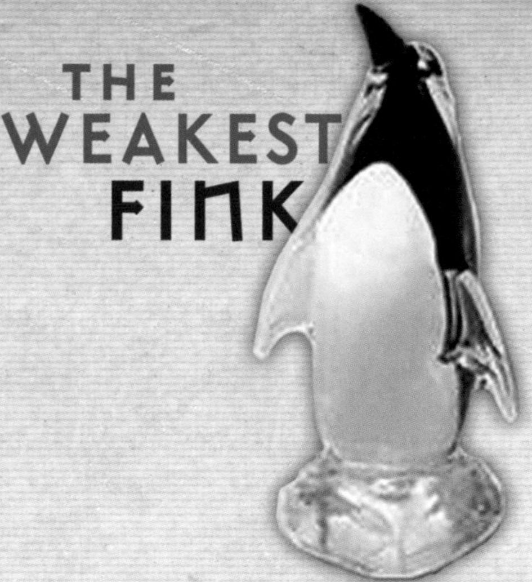

I know God will not give me anything I can't handle. I just wish that God didn't trust me so much.

Mother Teresa

Terms

Write a definition below.

Apostles' Creed

Needs

Provide

Providence

Wants

CREED no 3

God the Preserver

"The Lord is good, a stronghold in a day of trouble;

atrina crashes ashore with all the fury of an angry sea monster. A hundred-year-old levy in the city of New Orleans doesn't have a chance. Where is God in all of this?

Before the devastated Gulf Coast has a chance to recover, a huge offshore oil rig explodes. Millions of gallons of crude oil spew into the ocean. Thousands lose their jobs in the midst of the Great Recession. They watch the news night after night for months. Helpless. Hopeless. It is the greatest environmental disaster in American history. Where is God in all of this?

A tiny baby is born premature and unable to survive on her own. The little one barely weighs two pounds. An emergency nurse can hold her in the palm of her hand. Thirty years ago, this baby would have never made it. Today she will be nurtured, fed, monitored, and incubated until she's six pounds. Then she'll go home and lead a normal life. Where is God in all of this?

Some people blame God for all of the madness in the world. Some bless God for tiny miracles. Some say God has nothing to do with any of it—that God is an eternal watch maker who built the universe, wound it, and walked away. Others say God is merely an illusion created by ancient humans to explain the unexplainable. Still others see God as the very force behind the universe. If God would turn away for but a moment, they believe the universe would vanish into cosmic dust.

Sometimes I think we are alone. Sometimes I think we are not. In either case, the thought is staggering.

Buckminster Fuller

God the Preserver

As a boy, Martin Luther saw God as a stern, angry judge waiting for him to mess up so he could toss a bolt of lightning his way and make him pay. One day while studying the Bible in a tower, he saw something different. He looked at Jesus and saw God as a God of love. God was for him, not against him.

There was a day when the Children of Israel wouldn't even whisper the name of God out loud for fear of taking the holy name in vain. Then Jesus came along and called God "Abba." This was a term small children would use for their father. "Daddy" might be the best translation for us today. Jesus showed God as a loving daddy who cared about preserving and providing for his children. To Jesus, God was not some vague "may the force be with you" God. Jesus said, "If you have seen me, you have seen the Father."

What can we tell about God from Jesus? God loves. God heals. God listens. God forgives. God teaches. God cares. God saves. This God is not only the Creator, but also the provider and preserver. We can call in times of trouble, and this God will act. This God is bigger than your biggest problems. This God's love is more powerful than your deepest pain.

Ask. Seek. Knock.

Order this art print using FINKlink
LL13 @ www.faithink.com

Images in Art

- What do you see in today's painting by Dr. He Qi?
- Where are you in this work of art?
- How do the image and the verse apply to your life today?

So What Does This Mean?

A PRESERVER? HA! I DON'T THINK I'LL BE NEEDING A PRESERVER. THINGS ARE LOOKING PRETTY GOOD FROM WHERE I'M SITTING...

THE WELL OF PROVIDENCE IS DEEP. IT IS THE BUCKETS WE BRING TO IT THAT ARE SMALL.

MARY WEBB

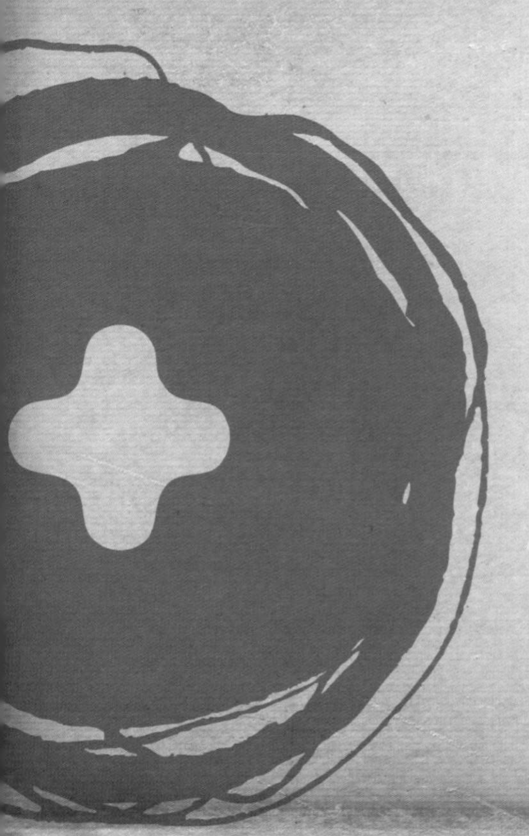

Bible Time

Read and highlight Nahum 1:7-8. When you feel afraid, anxious, worried, or overwhelmed, remember this verse and these three things about God:

1. God is good.

2. God is a stronghold in the time of trouble. (God will give you emotional, moral, or mental strength.)

3. God will protect you. (God will care for, champion, chaperone, defend, keep safe, look after, preserve, save, shelter, shield, stand guard, support, and watch over you!)

Write these three things in the margin of your Bible next to Nahum 1:7-8.

Prayer

Dear God, you are my preserver, provider, and protector. Help me when I am afraid and angry. Help me to believe that you are good, you are strong, and you will always provide for me. I pray in the powerful name of Jesus. Amen.

Catechism Encounter

Open Luther's Small Catechism to the explanation of the First Article of the Apostles' Creed. What does it say about God as protector and preserver?

Flip over to the explanation to the sixth and seventh petitions of the Lord's Prayer. What do these explanations tell you about God as protector?

Questions to Ponder

1. Talk about things that scare you. What do you normally do when you are afraid?

2. Name three people or groups who need protection today. How can God work through you to help offer protection?

3. A friend at school tells you: "There is no God. We're all alone here. And if there is a God, he, she or it certainly doesn't care for puny humans!" How do you answer?

SMALL GROUP

SHARE, READ, TALK, PRAY, BLESS

1. SHARE your highs and lows of the week one-on-one with another person. Listen carefully and record your friend's thoughts in the space below. Then return to small group and share your friend's highs and lows.

MY HIGHS + LOWS THIS WEEK WERE:

....

MY FRIEND'S HIGHS + LOWS THIS WEEK WERE:

....

2. READ and highlight the theme verse in your Bibles. Circle key words and learn the verse in song if time permits.

3. TALK about how today's verse relates to your highs and lows. Review the art for today, the Quiz Bowl questions, the terms, and the cartoons. Then write a sentence on each of the following:

ONE NEW THING I LEARNED TODAY:

....

ONE THING I ALREADY KNEW THAT IS WORTH REPEATING:

....

ONE THING I WOULD LIKE TO KNOW MORE ABOUT:

....

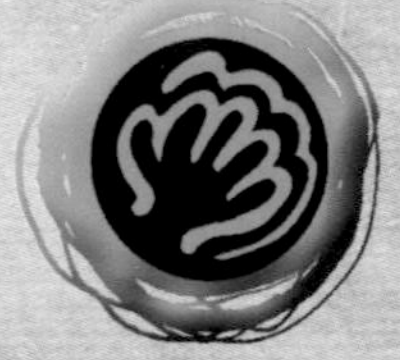

4. PRAY for one another, praising and thanking God for your highs, and asking God to be with you in your lows. Include your friend's highs and lows in your prayers.

A PRAISING PRAYER: ....

A THANKING PRAYER: ....

AN ASKING PRAYER: ....

5. BLESS one another using the blessing of the week. (right) Mark each person with the sign of the cross as you bless them.

THIS WEEK'S BLESSING

MAY GOD THE PRESERVER SHIELD YOU FROM HARM AND PROTECT YOU FROM EVERY EVIL THIS DAY.

Read the full devotions using FINKlink LL13 @ www.faithink.com

WEEK 1

FAITH JOURNAL

DAY 1

TODAY'S BIBLE VERSE:

Nahum 1:7, 8

The Lord is good, a stronghold in a day of trouble; he protects those who take refuge in him, even in a rushing flood.

MY HIGH TODAY WAS:

MY LOW TODAY WAS:

MY PRAYER TODAY IS:

DAY 2

TODAY'S BIBLE VERSE:

Mark 4:39

He woke up and rebuked the wind, and said to the sea, "Peace! Be still!" Then the wind ceased, and there was a dead calm.

MY HIGH TODAY WAS:

MY LOW TODAY WAS:

MY PRAYER TODAY IS:

DAY 3

TODAY'S BIBLE VERSE:

John 10:11

I am the good shepherd. The good shepherd lays down his life for the sheep.

MY HIGH TODAY WAS:

MY LOW TODAY WAS:

MY PRAYER TODAY IS:

my HIGH today was:

my LOW today was:

my PRAYER today is:

DAY 4

today's bible verse:

John 16:33

I have said this to you, so that in me you may have peace. In the world you face persecution. But take courage; I have conquered the world!

my HIGH today was:

my LOW today was:

my PRAYER today is:

DAY 5

today's bible verse:

Romans 8:38-39

I am convinced that neither death, nor life, nor angels, nor rulers, nor things present, nor things to come, nor powers, nor height, nor depth, nor anything else in all creation, will be able to separate us from the love of God in Christ Jesus our Lord.

my HIGH today was:

my LOW today was:

my PRAYER today is:

DAY 6

today's bible verse:

Ephesians 6:10-11

Finally, be strong in the Lord and in the strength of his power. Put on the whole armor of God, so that you may be able to stand against the wiles of the devil.

my HIGHEST HIGH this week was:

my LOWEST LOW this week was:

my PRAYER for next week is:

DAY 7

this week's blessing

MAY GOD THE PRESERVER
SHIELD YOU FROM HARM
AND PROTECT YOU FROM
EVERY EVIL THIS DAY.

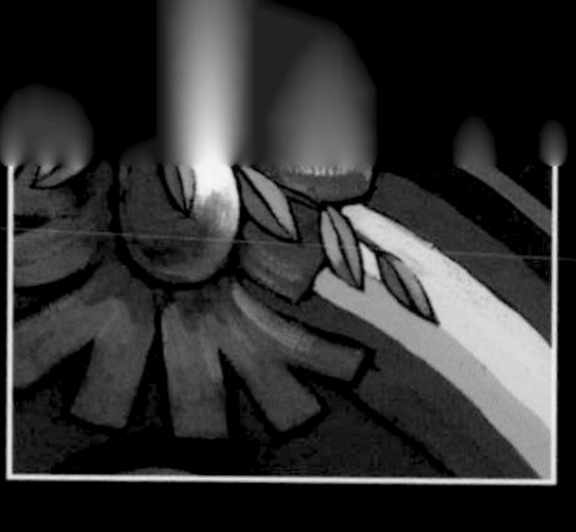

Read the full devotions using FINKlink LL13 @ www.faithink.com

WEEK 2

FAITH JOURNAL

DAY 1

TODAY'S BIBLE VERSE:

Psalm 27:1

The Lord is my light and my salvation; whom shall I fear? The Lord is the stronghold of my life; of whom shall I be afraid?

MY HIGH TODAY WAS:

MY LOW TODAY WAS:

MY PRAYER TODAY IS:

DAY 2

TODAY'S BIBLE VERSE:

Psalm 46:1-2

God is our refuge and our strength, a very present help in trouble. Therefore we will not fear, though the earth should change, though the mountains shake in the heart of the sea.

MY HIGH TODAY WAS:

MY LOW TODAY WAS:

MY PRAYER TODAY IS:

DAY 3

TODAY'S BIBLE VERSE:

Joshua 1:9

I hereby command you: Be strong and courageous; do not be frightened or dismayed, for the Lord your God is with you wherever you go.

MY HIGH TODAY WAS:

MY LOW TODAY WAS:

MY PRAYER TODAY IS:

HIGHS & LOWS OF THE DAY.

AND HIGHLIGHT THE VERSE OF THE DAY IN YOUR BIBLES.

ABOUT HOW TODAY'S VERSE RELATES TO YOUR HIGHS & LOWS.

PRAY FOR YOUR HIGHS & LOWS, FOR YOUR FAMILY AND FOR THE WORLD.

BLESS ONE ANOTHER USING THIS WEEK'S BLESSING (ON THE PREVIOUS PAGE).

DAY 4

TODAY'S BIBLE VERSE:

JOB 5:17

How happy is the one whom God reproves; therefore do not despise the discipline of the Almighty.

MY HIGH TODAY WAS:

MY LOW TODAY WAS:

MY PRAYER TODAY IS:

DAY 5

TODAY'S BIBLE VERSE:

PSALM 18:2

The Lord is my rock, my fortress, and my deliverer, my God, my rock in whom I take refuge, my shield, and the horn of my salvation, my stronghold.

MY HIGH TODAY WAS:

MY LOW TODAY WAS:

MY PRAYER TODAY IS:

DAY 6

TODAY'S BIBLE VERSE:

PSALM 121:7-8

The Lord will keep you from evil; he will keep your life. The Lord will keep your going out and your coming in from this time on and forevermore.

MY HIGH TODAY WAS:

MY LOW TODAY WAS:

MY PRAYER TODAY IS:

S | M | T | W | TH | F | S

THEME IN REVIEW

Nobody seriously believes the universe was made by God without being persuaded that He takes care of His works.

John Calvin

DAY 7

MY FAVORITE VERSE FROM THE THEME WAS:

GOD NOT ONLY CREATED IT ALL, GOD ALSO SUSTAINS AND PRESERVES YOUR BODY AND SOUL WITH ALL OF THEIR POWERS. WERE GOD TO WITHOLD YOUR BREATH OR TURN AWAY FOR EVEN A MOMENT, THE ENTIRE UNIVERSE WOULD DISINTEGRATE INTO DUST!

DUST? DUST? WHOA! INTO DUST...

WHAT ARE YOU DOING UNDER THE BUNK?

WHOA! THERE'S A WHOLE UNIVERSE UNDER HERE THAT GOD IGNORED!

NO, THAT WOULD BE MY OLD UNDERWEAR.

(SNIFF) I CAN SEE WHY GOD IGNORED THEM...

Melhorn

LOOKING BACK ON THESE TWO WEEKS, MY HIGHEST HIGH WAS:

MY LOWEST LOW THESE PAST WEEKS WAS:

ONE WAY GOD ANSWERED MY PRAYERS WAS:

ONE WAY GOD MIGHT USE ME AS A SACRED AGENT TO ANSWER THESE PRAYERS:

FAMILY COVENANT

We have shared *Highs & Lows* this week, read and highlighted the verses assigned in our Bible talked about our lives, prayed for one another's highs and lows, and blessed one another.

Parent's Signature   *Teen's Signature*   *Date*

THE FINKMANIA QUIZ BOWL

Question 1:

The First Article of the Apostles' Creed is:

(A) "You shall have no other gods before me,"
(B) "Hallowed be your name,"
(C) "I believe in God the Father Almighty, creator of heaven and earth,"
(D) Spelled "Apostle's" and not "Apostles'"

Question 2:

A "preserver":

(A) Always comes in during the ninth inning and strikes out the other side in fewer than 12 pitches,
(B) Comes in before a "post server,"
(C) Protects from injury and keeps you going,
(D) None of the above

Question 3:

Behaviors that ignore God's protection are:

(A) Stupid choices,
(B) Taking risks with sex, drugs and fast cars,
(C) Thinking we know more about what we need than God,
(D) All of the above and then some

Question 4:

Martin Luther explained the First Article of the Creed with the words...:

(A) "I believe that God has created me and all that exists,"
(B) "God has given me, and still preserves my body and soul with all of their powers,
(C) Both A & B
(D) "There is a God, and it ain't you!"

Question 5:

What does "God preserves my body and soul" mean?:

(A) God puts me in a pickle jar,
(B) God fills me full of Botox,
(C) God keeps me alive from day to day,
(D) God will protect me from myself when I engage in risky behavior or make stupid decisions

Question 6:

God helps preserve the human body by:

(A) Giving us an immune system,
(B) Giving us good doctors,
(C) Giving us common sense,
(D) All of the above

Question 7:

God's children are protected by:

(A) Body armor,
(B) An intricate alarm system,
(C) Guns and tanks,
(D) The good and gracious will and loving power of God

Question 8:

God protects us through:

(A) Baptism, God's Word, and faith,
(B) The still, small voice of the Holy Spirit, our conscience, and advice from our parents,
(C) A really big guy named Guido,
(D) Both A & B

Question 9:

Why do bad things happen to good people if God is our protector?:

(A) Good question,
(B) Go ask the pastor,
(C) If I knew, I would be outselling Dr. Phil right now,
(D) All of the above, and this is a fallen world

FINKmania Final Question:

Nahum 1:7, 8 tells us:

(A) The Lord is good,
(B) The Lord is good, a stronghold in the day of trouble,
(C) The Lord is good, a stronghold in the day of trouble; he protects those who take refuge in him, even in a raging flood,
(D) All of the above, and isn't it grand?

Play this online game using **FINKlink**
LL13 | **@ www.faithink.com**

THE WEAKEST FINK

If God loves me, why can't I get my locker open?

Ron Klug

TERMS

Write a definition below.

Creator

Preserver

Protect

Stronghold

Afraid

FAITH INKUBATORS

Jesus the Savior

"For God so loved the world that he gave his only Son,

so that everyone who believes in him may not perish

but may have eternal life."

—John 3:16

Listen to this song using FINKlink
LL14 @ www.faithink.com

You are moving back in time to a lonely, rocky hill outside the city walls. There is a stench of death about the place and flies are buzzing, buzzing, buzzing...

The sun is beating down as you join a crowd of people walking toward the top of the hill. There are three motionless images etched against the sky, hanging on crosses. You brush the flies from your face but you can't brush the foul smell from your nostrils. The two figures on either side are writhing in agony. You hear them curse and spit and cry. Blood is dripping from their matted hair. Their eyes are crazed. But the man in the middle—there's something different about him. You can feel it, though you can't bring your eyes to meet his. You can't bear to look directly at him, though you feel his eyes piercing your soul.

He's saying something to his mother and asking his friend John to take care of her. He's saying something to the criminal on his right telling the thief he will wake on the other side of death in Paradise. Suddenly you are ashamed. Even in death he is thinking of others. And all you could think about in these last hours was yourself. Again, you feel drawn to his eyes, but you dare not look.

Only hours ago you stood in the courtyard and swore you didn't know him. You pledged loyalty to the death last night and then ran away. And now, only now, slinking through the darkness like a dog, you join the crowd to watch the end. Like a spectator in some gruesome sport—not like a friend by a friend's side. He had been your strength, your teacher, your wisdom. He had been your hope, your future, your dreams. He had once said, "No greater love has anyone than to lay down his life for his friends."

And now he has done this. For you.

Jesus the Savior

The chasm was too wide—you could never cross it. The stain runs too deep—you could never remove it. You were condemned to die, with no possible way out. Then, in the love of God, the one who loved you into existence became a human being and sought you out. Even when you couldn't look at Jesus because of your guilt, Jesus turned his eyes upon you. And there, in those God-like eyes you see no judgment, no blame, no anger, no bitterness. In those eyes, all you see is love.

Love.

You are loved by the God of the universe.

What will you do with this love?

I believe in JESUS CHRIST, his only Son, our LORD. He was conceived by the power of the HOLY SPIRIT, born of the Virgin Mary, suffered under Pontius Pilate, was crucified, died and was buried. He descended into hell. On the third day he rose again from the dead. He ascended into heaven. He is seated at the right hand of GOD the FATHER ALMIGHTY. He will come again to judge the living and the dead.

Second Article,
The Apostles' Creed

Images in Art

- What do you see in today's painting by Dr. He Qi?
- Where are you in this work of art?
- How do the image and the verse apply to your life today?

So What Does This Mean?

EGADS! THE BODY IS GONE! DO YOU REALIZE THE TROUBLE WE'RE IN?

He carried the cross so the cross could carry you.

Archie Jordan & Dennis Morgan

Bible Time

Read and highlight the theme verse, John 3:16, in your Bible. Some call this verse "The Little Gospel" because it sums up the entire Bible in one sentence. Write "The Little Gospel" in the margin. Now look up Luke 9:18-20. Write "Who is Jesus?" in the margin. There is perhaps only one question more important than "Who is Jesus?" That question is "Who is Jesus to me?" Why is this question so important? What hangs in the balance?

Prayer

Lover of the world, thank you for loving me. Never let me forget how great is your love for me. Every time I see your cross, let me see your love. Every time I see your children in need, let me be your love. I pray in Jesus' name. Amen.

Catechism Encounter

Open your Small Catechism to the Second Article of the Apostles' Creed. Circle words that describe Jesus. Write five of them here:

Questions to Ponder

1. When was the last time you gave someone a gift? What did you give? How did they say thanks?

2. When was the last time someone sacrificed something for you? Why did they do it? How did you say thanks?

3. Why did Jesus have to die?

4. How would you respond to someone who said, "Jesus was just like every other religious leader who ever walked on the earth?"

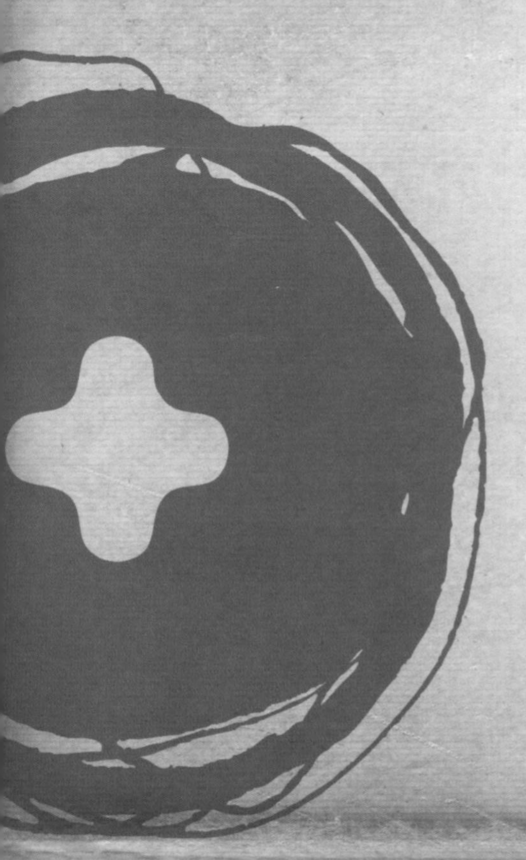

Small Group

share, read, talk, pray, bless

1. **SHARE** your highs and lows of the week one-on-one with another person. Listen carefully and record your friend's thoughts in the space below. Then return to small group and share your friend's highs and lows.

   MY HIGHS + LOWS THIS WEEK WERE:

   ....

   MY FRIEND'S HIGHS + LOWS THIS WEEK WERE:

   ....

2. **READ** and highlight the theme verse in your Bibles. Circle key words and learn the verse in song if time permits.

3. **TALK** about how today's verse relates to your highs and lows. Review the art for today, the Quiz Bowl questions, the terms, and the cartoons. Then write a sentence on each of the following:

   ONE NEW THING I LEARNED TODAY:

   ....

   ONE THING I ALREADY KNEW THAT IS WORTH REPEATING:

   ....

   ONE THING I WOULD LIKE TO KNOW MORE ABOUT:

   ....

4. **PRAY** for one another, praising and thanking God for your highs, and asking God to be with you in your lows. Include your friend's highs and lows in your prayers.

   A PRAISING PRAYER: ....

   A THANKING PRAYER: ....

   AN ASKING PRAYER: ....

5. **BLESS** one another using the blessing of the week. (right) Mark each person with the sign of the cross as you bless them.

THIS WEEK'S BLESSING

(NAME), MAY YOU LIVE FOR THE ONE WHO DIED IN LOVE FOR YOU. AMEN.

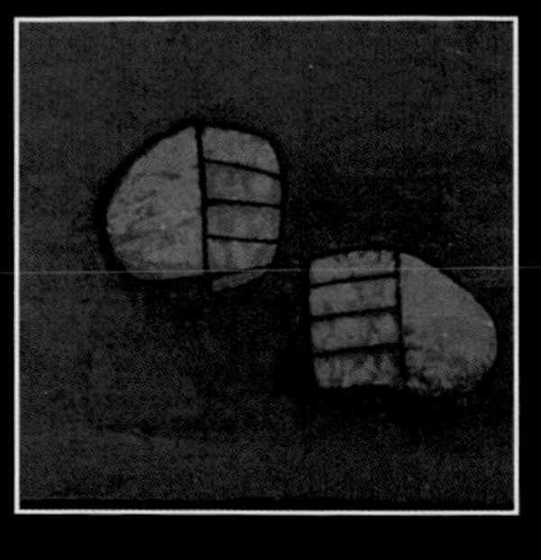

THE FAITH 5

Read the full devotions using FINKlink
LL14 @ www.faithink.com

WEEK 2

JOURNAL

DAY 1

TODAY'S BIBLE VERSE:

JOHN 3:16

For God so loved the world that he gave his only Son, so that everyone who believes in him may not perish but may have eternal life.

MY HIGH TODAY WAS:

MY LOW TODAY WAS:

MY PRAYER TODAY IS:

DAY 2

TODAY'S BIBLE VERSE:

JOHN 3:17

Indeed, God did not send the Son into the world to condemn the world, but in order that the world might be saved through him.

MY HIGH TODAY WAS:

MY LOW TODAY WAS:

MY PRAYER TODAY IS:

DAY 3

TODAY'S BIBLE VERSE:

PSALM 17:7

Wondrously show your steadfast love, O savior of those who seek refuge from their adversaries at your right hand.

MY HIGH TODAY WAS:

MY LOW TODAY WAS:

MY PRAYER TODAY IS:

my HIGH today was:

my LOW today was:

my PRAYER today is:

DAY 4

today's bible verse:

Romans 5:8

God proves his love for us in that while we still were sinners Christ died for us.

my HIGH today was:

my LOW today was:

my PRAYER today is:

DAY 5

today's bible verse:

1 Timothy 1:15

The saying is sure and worthy of full acceptance, that Christ Jesus came into the world to save sinners—of whom I am the foremost.

my HIGH today was:

my LOW today was:

my PRAYER today is:

DAY 6

today's bible verse:

Revelation 1:7

Look! He is coming with the clouds; every eye will see him, even those who pierced him; and on his account all the tribes of the earth will wail. So it is to be. Amen.

my HIGHEST HIGH this week was:

my LOWEST LOW this week was:

my PRAYER for next week is:

DAY 7

this week's blessing

(NAME), MAY YOU LIVE FOR THE ONE WHO DIED IN LOVE FOR YOU. AMEN

WEEK 2

THE FAITH5

JOURNAL

Read the full devotions using FINKlink
LL14 @ www.faithink.com

DAY 1

TODAY'S BIBLE VERSE:

MARK 16:7

Go, tell his disciples and Peter that he is going ahead of you to Galilee; there you will see him, just as he told you.

MY HIGH TODAY WAS:

MY LOW TODAY WAS:

MY PRAYER TODAY IS:

DAY 2

TODAY'S BIBLE VERSE:

JOHN 20:19

When it was evening on that day, the first day of the week, and the doors of the house where the disciples had met were locked for fear of the Jews, Jesus came to them and say, "Peace be with you!"

MY HIGH TODAY WAS:

MY LOW TODAY WAS:

MY PRAYER TODAY IS:

DAY 3

TODAY'S BIBLE VERSE:

JOHN 20:20, 28

Then the disciples rejoiced when they saw the Lord. Thomas answered him, "My Lord and my God!"

MY HIGH TODAY WAS:

MY LOW TODAY WAS:

MY PRAYER TODAY IS:

4. PRAY FOR YOUR HIGHS & LOWS, FOR YOUR FAMILY AND FOR THE WORLD.

5. BLESS ONE ANOTHER USING THIS WEEK'S BLESSING (ON THE PREVIOUS PAGE).

DAY 4

TODAY'S BIBLE VERSE:

HEBREWS 5:7

In the days of his flesh, Jesus offered up prayers and supplications, with loud cries and tears, to the one who was able to save him from death, and he was heard because of his reverent submission.

MY HIGH TODAY WAS:

MY LOW TODAY WAS:

MY PRAYER TODAY IS:

DAY 5

TODAY'S BIBLE VERSE:

HEBREWS 9:28

So Christ, having been offered once to bear the sins of many, will appear a second time, not to deal with sin, but to save those who are eagerly waiting for him.

MY HIGH TODAY WAS:

MY LOW TODAY WAS:

MY PRAYER TODAY IS:

DAY 6

TODAY'S BIBLE VERSE:

REVELATION 11:15

The seventh angel blew his trumpet, and there were loud voices in heaven, "The kingdom of the world has become the kingdom of our Lord and of his Messiah, and he will reign forever and ever."

MY HIGH TODAY WAS:

MY LOW TODAY WAS:

MY PRAYER TODAY IS:

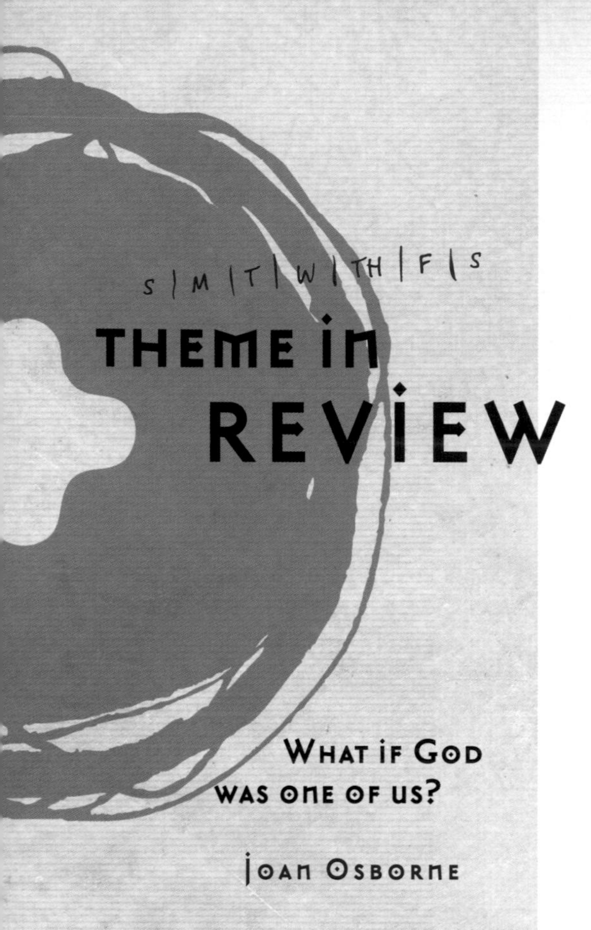

S | M | T | W | TH | F | S

THEME IN REVIEW

WHAT IF GOD WAS ONE OF US?

JOAN OSBORNE

LET'S NOT SAY A CARPENTER. HEAVENS NO! LET'S SAY A DIAMOND MOGUL OR A PRINCE OR A KING OR SOMETHING.

AND LET'S NOT SAY BETHLEHEM. LET'S SAY ATHENS OR ROME OR BAGHDAD.

THAT'S THE TICKET!

YEAH. TICKET! THE TICKET.

AND THIS SUFFERING SERVANT BIT. I MEAN PUL-EESE! LOSE IT! IT DOES ABSOLUTELY NOTHING IN THE POLLS!

DAY 7

MY FAVORITE VERSE FROM THE THEME WAS:

....

....

....

....

....

....

....

....

....

LOOKING BACK ON THESE TWO WEEKS, MY HIGHEST HIGH WAS:

....

MY LOWEST LOW THESE PAST WEEKS WAS:

....

ONE WAY GOD ANSWERED MY PRAYERS WAS:

....

ONE WAY GOD MIGHT USE ME AS A SACRED AGENT TO ANSWER THESE PRAYERS:

....

....

FAMILY COVENANT

We have shared *Highs & Lows* this week, read and highlighted the verses assigned in our Bibles, talked about our lives, prayed for one another's highs and lows, and blessed one another.

Parent's Signature	*Teen's Signature*	*Date*

THE FINKMANIA QUIZ BOWL

Question 1:

The Second Article of the Apostles' Creed is:

(A) "I believe in God the Father Almighty, creator of heaven and earth,"
(B) "I believe in Jesus Christ, his only Son, our Lord,"
(C) "I believe in the Holy Spirit,"
(D) "Thou shalt not use the words 'rap' and 'music' in the same breath, for the Lord will not hold him guiltless who does this"

Question 2:

Jesus of Nazareth was and is:

(A) True God, Son of the Father from eternity,
(B) True man, born of the Virgin Mary,
(C) Both A & B,
(D) Neither A nor B

Question 3:

Jesus was different from every other religious leader because:

(A) He said he was God,
(B) He was God, and proved it by dying and rising from the dead,
(C) He was better looking,
(D) He had a better speaking voice

Question 4:

Jesus is called the "Lamb of God" because:

(A) He was white and fluffy,
(B) He liked to graze at salad bars,
(C) He was sacrificed to pay for sin, like the sacrificial lambs of the Old Testament,
(D) None of the above

Question 5:

From what did Jesus free us?:

(A) Having to watch *Dancing With the Stars* reruns,
(B) Sin, death, and really, really bad hair days,
(C) Sin, death, and the power of the devil,
(D) Algebra

Question 6:

What price did Jesus pay to set you free from sin and death?:

(A) 30 pieces of silver,
(B) His holy and precious blood,
(C) His innocent suffering and death,
(D) Both B & C

Question 7:

For what did Jesus free us?:

(A) So that we could be his own,
(B) So that we could live under him in his kingdom,
(C) So that we could serve him in everlasting righteousness, innocence, and blessedness,
(D) According to Luther, all of the above

Question 8:

The word XRISTOS or "Christ" is the Greek translation of the Hebrew word:

(A) Message,
(B) Messiah,
(C) Masseuse,
(D) Mess with Me and You're Toast

Question 9:

The word "Messiah" is the Hebrew word for:

(A) The Anointed One of God,
(B) The Annotated one of God,
(C) The Greek word "Christ,"
(D) Both A & C

משיח= Χριστός

FINKmania Final Question:

John 3:16, the verse of the week, tells us:

(A) Out of a powerful love, God came as Jesus to die for the world,
(B) Anyone believing in Jesus will live forever,
(C) Jesus is our Savior,
(D) All of the above and then some

Play this online game using FINKlink LL14 @ www.faithink.com

THE WEAKEST FINK

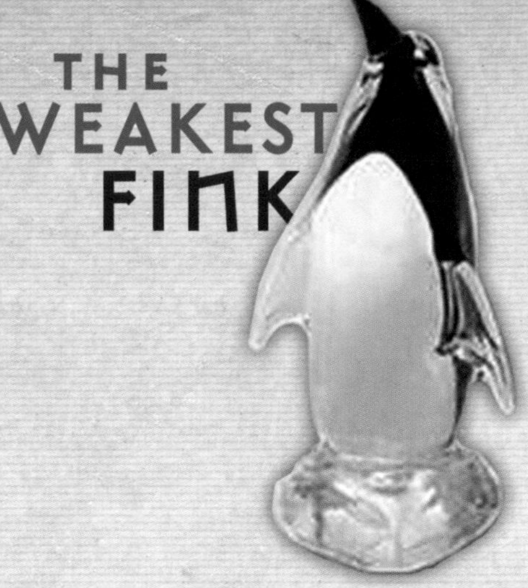

SANTA CLAUS NEVER DIED FOR ANYBODY.

CRAIG WILSON

TERMS

WRITE A DEFINITION BELOW.

CHRIST

....

....

GOD THE SON

....

....

JESUS

....

....

MESSIAH

....

....

SAVIOR

....

....

FAITH INKUBATORS

Jesus the Redeemer

"He has rescued us from the power of darkness

and transferred us into the kingdom of his beloved Son,

in whom we have redemption, the forgiveness of sins."

— Colossians 1:13-14

Listen to this verse using FINKlink

LL15 @ www.faithink.com

Imagine you are a prisoner of war. You sit on the dusty floor of a very small desert hut. The sun bakes the roof and walls until sweat pours off you. You are afraid.

Your mouth is dry. Your hands are swollen and sore from the ropes that bind you. Every day you are taken for interrogation with a rifle in your ribs and a blindfold tight around your eyes. Sometimes you are beaten. Sometimes during the night, soldiers come into your cell and drag your fellow prisoners out. Sometimes they don't come back.

You think of your family back home. You think of your friends. You think of swimming in a lake, of ice cream, of your last goodbye with someone you loved. You wonder if anyone knows you are alive. You wonder if anyone cares.

A distant sound pulls you back from your dream. What is that? A low whup, whup, whup. It's getting louder. Helicopters. Your body tenses at the sound. Your enemy doesn't have helicopters. This might be a rescue operation! Just as the thought crosses your mind, you hear gunships fire on the streets. You peer through a small crack in the wall to see what is happening. The helicopters land in the yard outside and soldiers jump out, scouring the compound for prisoners. Will they find you? Will they leave without you? The door cracks off its hinges as a soldier kicks it open and pulls you out. Too weak with exhaustion to walk, the soldier carries you to the helicopter.

And as you lift off, you look down on the shack that has been your prison and lift up a prayer to God. I know that my Redeemer lives...

What is to give light must endure burning.

Viktor Frankl

Jesus the Redeemer

Have you ever felt trapped? Alone? Lost? Have you ever waited, hoped or prayed for someone to rescue you from a seemingly hopeless situation?

The Bible says we are all lost. Trapped. Imprisoned by sin and destined for death. It also says Jesus came to "redeem" us. The American Heritage Dictionary defines "redeem" as "recover ownership of by paying a specified sum."

How much did Christ pay for you? It cost him his life. Jesus is called the Redeemer because he recovered ownership of you by paying the ultimate price so that you could be free. Christ died to buy you back—redeem you—from death. He went to hell for you so you wouldn't have to. He took the beating. He took the punishment. He took the pain. He took the nails. And he would do it again for you. Why? Only one reason.

Love.

Order this art print using FINKlink LL15 @ www.faithink.com

Images in Art

- What do you see in today's painting by Dr. He Qi?
- Where are you in this work of art?
- How do the image and the verse apply to your life today?

So What Does This Mean?

Do you have to be "deemed" before you can be re-deemed?

He left his Father's throne above, So free, so infinite His grace!

Emptied Himself of all but love, And bled for Adam's helpless race.

Charles Wesley

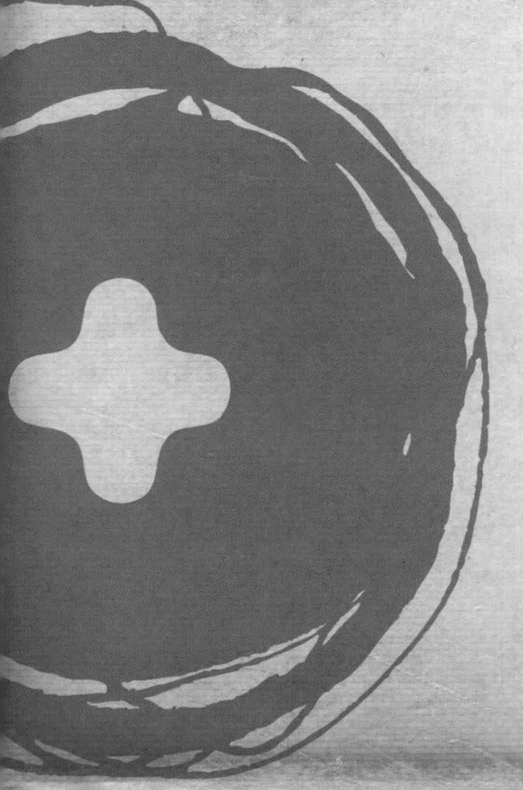

Bible Time

Jesus accomplished the greatest rescue mission of all time when he rescued you. Read and highlight the theme verse, Colossians 1:13-14, in your Bible. Circle the word "redemption" with a red pen. Why? Because it cost Christ more than money to rescue you. It cost him his life.

The Message Bible interprets the verse in this way, "God rescued us from dead-end alleys and dark dungeons. He's set us up in the kingdom of the Son he loves so much, the Son who got us out of the pit we were in, got rid of the sins we were doomed to keep repeating."

Jesus died for you. Now, here's the question: will you live for him?

Prayer

Redeeming God, don't let me ever forget how much it cost you to love me. I'm not used to being loved with "no strings attached." Help me not to be afraid to love you back. In Jesus' precious name I pray. Amen.

Catechism Encounter

Scan Luther's explanation of the Second Article of the Apostles' Creed. From what did Luther say Jesus redeemed you? Why did he redeem you?

Questions to Ponder

1. Who are your best friends? Would you ever take a punishment for them if they were in trouble? Why or why not?

2. Who is someone you would risk death to save? Why would you do such a thing?

3. Have you ever been rescued from a punishment you deserved? If so, how did you thank the rescuer?

4. How might you show your thanks to Jesus for rescuing you?

Small Group

share, read, talk, pray, bless

1. **SHARE** your highs and lows of the week one-on-one with another person. Listen carefully and record your friend's thoughts in the space below. Then return to small group and share your friend's highs and lows.

   my highs + lows this week were:

   ....

   my friend's highs + lows this week were:

   ....

2. **READ** and highlight the theme verse in your Bibles. Circle key words and learn the verse in song if time permits.

3. **TALK** about how today's verse relates to your highs and lows. Review the art for today, the Quiz Bowl questions, the terms, and the cartoons. Then write a sentence on each of the following:

   one new thing i learned today:

   ....

   one thing i already knew that is worth repeating:

   ....

   one thing i would like to know more about:

   ....

4. **PRAY** for one another, praising and thanking God for your highs, and asking God to be with you in your lows. Include your friend's highs and lows in your prayers.

   a praising prayer: ....

   a thanking prayer: ....

   an asking prayer: ....

5. **BLESS** one another using the blessing of the week. (right) Mark each person with the sign of the cross as you bless them.

this week's blessing

(NAME), child of God, may you always know how precious you are to the one who redeemed you from death.

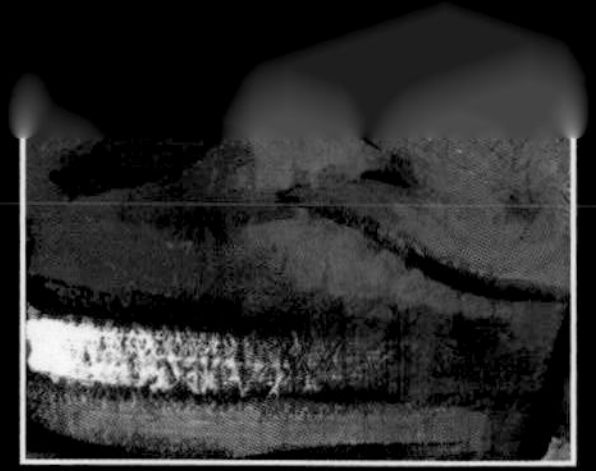

WEEK 1

FAITH jOURNAL

Read the full devotions using FINKlink

LL15 @ www.faithink.com

DAY 1

TODAY'S BIBLE VERSE:

Colossians 1:13-14

He has rescued us from the power of darkness and transferred us into the kingdom of his beloved Son, in whom we have redemption, the forgiveness of sins.

MY HIGH TODAY WAS:

MY LOW TODAY WAS:

MY PRAYER TODAY IS:

DAY 2

TODAY'S BIBLE VERSE:

Mark 2:17

When Jesus heard this, he said to them, "Those who are well have no need of a physician, but those who are sick; I have come to call not the righteous but sinners."

MY HIGH TODAY WAS:

MY LOW TODAY WAS:

MY PRAYER TODAY IS:

DAY 3

TODAY'S BIBLE VERSE:

Romans 3:23

All have sinned and fall short of the glory of God.

MY HIGH TODAY WAS:

MY LOW TODAY WAS:

MY PRAYER TODAY IS:

my HIGH today was:

my LOW today was:

my PRAYER today is:

DAY 4

today's bible verse:

Romans 5:10-11

For if while we were enemies, we were reconciled to God through the death of his Son, much more surely, having been reconciled, will we be saved by his life.

my HIGH today was:

my LOW today was:

my PRAYER today is:

DAY 5

today's bible verse:

2 Corinthians 5:17

So if anyone is in Christ, there is a new creation: everything old has passed away; see, everything has become new!

my HIGH today was:

my LOW today was:

my PRAYER today is:

DAY 6

today's bible verse:

Galatians 3:13

Christ redeemed us from the curse of the law by becoming a curse for us—for it is written, "Cursed is everyone who hangs on a tree."

my HIGHEST HIGH this week was:

my LOWEST LOW this week was:

my PRAYER for next week is:

DAY 7

this week's blessing

(NAME), CHILD OF GOD, MAY YOU ALWAYS KNOW HOW PRECIOUS YOU ARE TO THE ONE WHO REDEEMED YOU FROM DEATH.

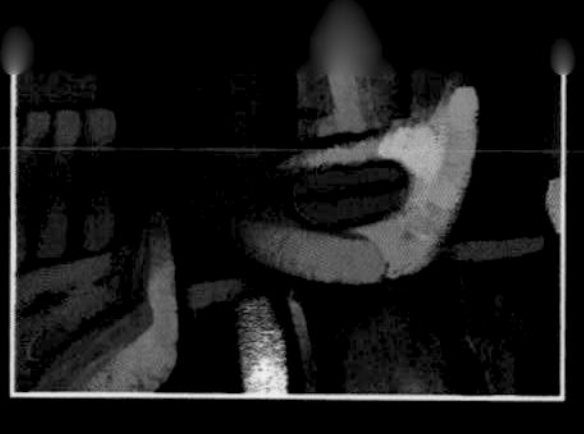

Read the full devotions using FINKlink LL15 @ www.faithink.com

WEEK 2

FAITH JOURNAL

DAY 1

TODAY'S BIBLE VERSE:

Psalm 130:7-8

O Israel, hope in the Lord! For with the Lord there is steadfast love, and with him is great power to redeem. It is he who will redeem Israel from all its iniquities.

MY HIGH TODAY WAS:

MY LOW TODAY WAS:

MY PRAYER TODAY IS:

DAY 2

TODAY'S BIBLE VERSE:

Exodus 15:13

In your steadfast love you led the people whom you redeemed; you guided them by your strength to your holy abode.

MY HIGH TODAY WAS:

MY LOW TODAY WAS:

MY PRAYER TODAY IS:

DAY 3

TODAY'S BIBLE VERSE:

Deuteronomy 30:2-3

Return to the Lord your God, and you and your children obey him with all your soul... then the Lord your God will restore your fortunes and have compassion on you.

MY HIGH TODAY WAS:

MY LOW TODAY WAS:

MY PRAYER TODAY IS:

my HIGH today was:

my LOW today was:

my PRAYER today is:

DAY 4

TODAY'S BIBLE VERSE:

Psalm 19:14

Let the words of my mouth and the meditation of my heart be acceptable to you, O Lord, my rock and my redeemer.

my HIGH today was:

my LOW today was:

my PRAYER today is:

DAY 5

TODAY'S BIBLE VERSE:

Psalm 51:10-12

Create in me a clean heart, O God, and put a new and right spirit within me. Do not cast me away from your presence, and do not take your holy spirit from me. Restore to me the joy of your salvation, and sustain in me a willing spirit.

my HIGH today was:

my LOW today was:

my PRAYER today is:

DAY 6

TODAY'S BIBLE VERSE:

Psalm 107:2

Let the redeemed of the Lord say so, those he redeemed from trouble...

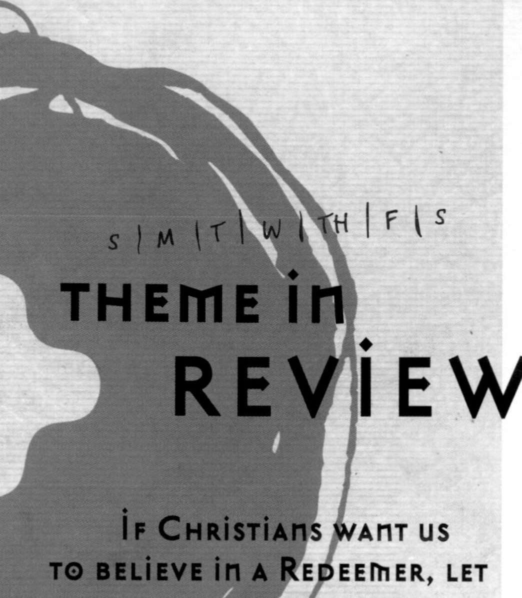

S | M | T | W | TH | F | S

THEME IN REVIEW

If Christians want us to believe in a Redeemer, let them act redeemed.

Voltaire

SO YOU'RE SAYING THAT JESUS CHRIST ALREADY PAID FOR MY SINS?

YUP...

I'M OFF THE HOOK? FORGIVEN? FREE AND CLEAR DEBT PAID? CASE CLOSED?

REDEEMED. REDEEMED. YUP. YUP. YUP.

WOW. IF JESUS CAN DO THAT, JESUS CAN DO ANYTHING!

YUP...

UH... REV... DO YOU THINK JESUS COULD DO SOMETHING ABOUT GETTING ME MY OWN CELL PHONE?

YOU'LL HAVE TO TALK TO HIM ABOUT THAT ONE ON YOUR OWN, FREIDA. I'M IN SALES, NOT MANAGEMENT.

Melheim

DAY 7

MY FAVORITE VERSE FROM THE THEME WAS:

....

....

....

....

....

....

....

....

....

LOOKING BACK ON THESE TWO WEEKS, MY HIGHEST HIGH WAS:

....

MY LOWEST LOW THESE PAST WEEKS WAS:

....

ONE WAY GOD ANSWERED MY PRAYERS WAS:

....

ONE WAY GOD MIGHT USE ME AS A SACRED AGENT TO ANSWER THESE PRAYERS:

....

....

Family Covenant

We have shared *Highs & Lows* this week, read and highlighted the verses assigned in our Bibles, talked about our lives, prayed for one another's highs and lows, and blessed one another.

Parent's Signature	*Teen's Signature*	*Date*

THE FINKMANIA QUIZBOWL

QUESTION 1:

The Second Article of the Apostles' Creed is:

(A) "I believe in God the Father Almighty, creator of heaven and earth,"

(B) "I believe in Jesus Christ, his only Son, our Lord...,"

(C) "I believe in the Holy Spirit,"

(D) None of the above

QUESTION 2:

The word "redeem" means:

(A) To "deem" again,

(B) To cut coupons,

(C) To buy back,

(D) To control

QUESTION 3:

Jesus is our Redeemer because:

(A) He bought us back with coupons,

(B) He bought us back with his holy and precious blood and 30 pieces of silver,

(C) He bought us back with his holy and precious blood and his innocent suffering and death,

(D) I haven't the foggiest

QUESTION 4:

I need Jesus to pay the cost for my sin because:

(A) I can't pay for it myself,

(B) The wages of sin is death,

(C) A sinful person cannot come into the presence of a Holy God without being covered by the blood of Christ,

(D) All of the above

QUESTION 5:

When I stand before God's judgment, I will say:

(A) "Let's make a deal,"

(B) "I hope you grade on the curve,"

(C) "I'm an undeserving sinner, but I'm trusting in Jesus to pay for my sin,"

(D) "Can you hear me now?"

QUESTION 6:

Jesus is like a life jacket because:

(A) He is orange and buoyant,

(B) We are sunk without him,

(C) His power is most effective if we keep him close to our hearts,

(D) I'm not sure, but both B & C sound pretty good

QUESTION 7:

What do bread and wine have to do with our redemption?:

(A) Jesus gave his body and blood for us,

(B) Jesus gave his body and blood in our place,

(C) Jesus gave his body and blood to pay for our sin,

(D) All of the above, plus he comes to us again whenever we take Holy Communion

QUESTION 8:

The word "ransom" means:

(A) To release a person in return for payment of a demanded price,

(B) To redeem or buy back,

(C) Both A & B,

(D) The opposite of "walk some"

QUESTION 9:

According to Luther, what did Jesus ransom us from?:

(A) Sin,

(B) Sin and death,

(C) Sin, death, and the power of the devil,

(D) Euclidean geometry

FINKMANIA FINAL QUESTION:

Colossians 1:13-14, the verse of the week, tells us, "He (Jesus) has...":

(A) "...rescued us from the power of darkness and transferred us into the kingdom of his beloved Son,"

(B) "...rescued us from the power of darkness and transferred us to another junior high,"

(C) "...had about enough of our whining,"

(D) None of the above

Play this online game using FINKlink

LL15 @ www.faithink.com

THE WEAKEST FINK

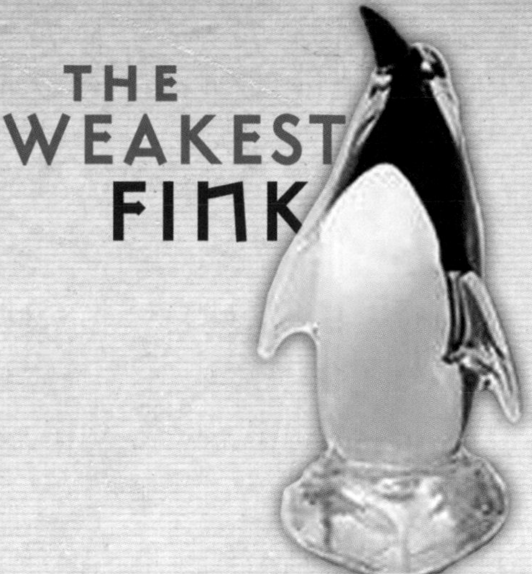

ONE CAN NEVER PAY IN GRATITUDE; ONE CAN ONLY PAY "IN KIND" SOMEWHERE ELSE IN LIFE.

ANNE MORROW LINDBERG

TERMS

WRITE A DEFINITION BELOW.

FORGIVENESS

....

....

RANSOM

....

....

REDEEM

....

....

RESCUE

....

....

SALVATION

....

....

FAITH INKUBATORS

"The Doubt of Thomas" Copyright © Dr. He Qi www.heqigallery.com

"EVERYONE WHO CALLS ON THE NAME OF THE LORD

SHALL BE SAVED."

— JOEL 2:32

Listen to this song using FINKlink

LL16 @ www.faithink.com

You are walking along a stone path through a tropical garden. The humidity makes your clothes stick to your skin and sweat trickles down your face.

Broad palm leaves arch over the path and lush, green ivy crawls up bamboo stalks. Your guide—a sandal-shod, bald-headed monk—leads you into a clearing. At the far end a stone statue of Buddha squats comfortably, smiling down at the jungle. A half dozen monks in red and orange tunics kneel at the impressive statue's base, praying as incense and candles around them lift their prayers into vapor. Standing before the Buddha, you look into his eyes. Cold stone stares back. No words. Not a sound. Just cold stone.

Six months later and a world away, you find yourself walking through the streets of your own hometown. Rain is pouring down in sheets. You see the glowing lights of a church. You try the door. It is open, so you step in to wait out the storm. The place is empty. You walk into the sanctuary and notice a statue of Jesus along the wall. Candles are lit at his feet. You look into his eyes and cold stone stares back at you. No words. Not a sound. Just cold stone.

The rain lets up, and you walk back out into the evening. The air is fresh and clean. Water stands in pools in the dark streets. As you step out the door you nearly trip over a homeless man resting beside an empty bottle. He squints up through bloodshot eyes and smiles through three yellow teeth. You glance around, and suddenly a long-haired, bearded stranger in a robe is standing next to you. He puts his arm around the old drunk. They begin to sing and invite you to join them. They sing a song of love, forgiveness, and peace. These words fill the old man with memories. The stranger prays for you both. Then, as suddenly as he appeared, he is gone. You kneel next to the beggar. A voice inside whispers, "Help him." What will you do?

JESUS TAPPED ME ON THE SHOULDER AND SAID, "BOB, WHY ARE YOU RESISTING ME?" I SAID, "I'M NOT RESISTING YOU!" HE SAID, "YOU GONNA FOLLOW ME?" I SAID, "I'VE NEVER THOUGHT ABOUT THAT BEFORE!" HE SAID, "WHEN YOU'RE NOT FOLLOWING ME, YOU'RE RESISTING ME."

BOB DYLAN

ONLY JESUS

Strange as it may seem, some people in the world today still worship gods of wood and stone. Some follow their horoscopes and let the stars tell them what to do and where to go. Some worship Hollywood stars as gods. Some value their bank accounts above everything else. Some worship status, popularity, clothes, cars, or their own looks. Some let other people lord over them. There is a problem with letting any of these things be your god or guide. Every single one of them is finite. Every single one of them is material. Every single one of them will disappear when you die. Not one earthly god will go with you to the other side of eternity. Only Jesus has gone through the door of death and back. Only Jesus can take you through. Only Jesus is worthy of your worship. Only Jesus is worthy of your ultimate trust. Only Jesus is Lord. And as Lord, he asks you to serve him. So again, what will you do?

Order this art print using FINKlink

LL16 | @ www.faithink.com

IMAGES IN ART

- What do you see in today's painting by Dr. He Qi?
- Where are you in this work of art?
- How do the image and the verse apply to your life today?

So What Does This Mean?

WE ARE ALL IN FAVOR OF HAVING A SAVIOR, BUT THIS "JESUS IS LORD" BUSINESS IS ASKING A BIT MUCH...

"A man who was merely a man and said the sort of things Jesus said would not be a great moral teacher. He would either be a lunatic—on the level with a man who says he is a poached egg—or he would be the devil of hell. You must take your choice. Either this was, and is, the Son of God, or else a madman or something worse. You can shut him up for a fool or you can fall at his feet and call him Lord and God. But let us not come with any patronizing nonsense about his being a great human teacher. He has not left that open to us."

C.S. Lewis (Author of the "Chronicles of Narnia")

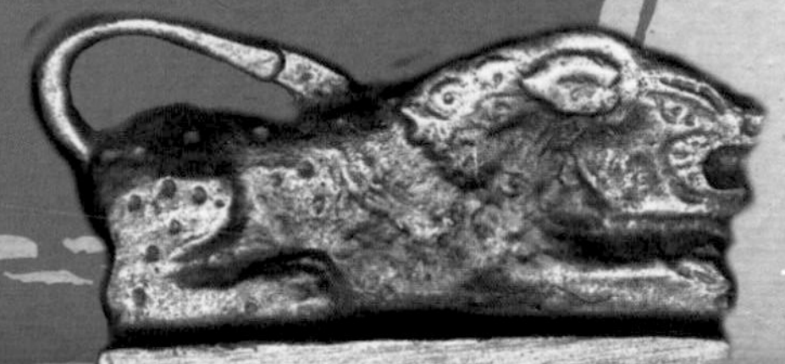

Jesus the Lord

Some say Jesus was a good teacher. Read the C. S. Lewis quotation (left). According to Lewis, you can't say Jesus was simply a good teacher. A good teacher wouldn't claim to be God. If he said he was God but knew it wasn't true, he wasn't good at all. He was a liar. If he said he was God but thought it to be true and wasn't, he was crazy. There are plenty of people locked up in mental institutions who think they are God. When you really think about it, claiming Jesus as simply a good teacher or great religious figure isn't an option. Jesus is either history's greatest liar, history's greatest lunatic, or the Lord of all. The radical nature of Jesus' call is that he asks people to trust their eternity to him. If he was exactly who he said he was—the Lord of all creation—then he confronts you with a life-changing challenge. If Jesus is God and he asks you to serve him by helping others, to love him by loving the unlovable, and to trust your eternity to him and live for God today, what are you going to do?

Who is Jesus to you? A liar? A lunatic? Or the Lord of creation? Your answer to that question is no small matter.

Bible Time

Read and highlight Joel 2:32 and John 6:68b, in your Bible, writing "Lord!" in the margin.

Prayer

Come Lord Jesus, be our guest, let these gifts to us be blessed. Jesus, you are Lord of creation. Be Lord of my life today. In your precious name I pray. Amen.

Catechism Encounter

Scan Luther's explanation of the Second Article of the Apostles' Creed and circle the verbs that show what the Lord Jesus did for you. Write them here:

Questions to Ponder

1. Some cultures still use the title "Lord." What is a Lord?

2. If someone asked you, "Who is the Lord Jesus?" how would you respond?

3. The term "Lord" refers to having power or dominion or rule over something. Over what does Jesus have dominion?

Small Group

share, read, talk, pray, bless

1. **SHARE** your highs and lows of the week one-on-one with another person. Listen carefully and record your friend's thoughts in the space below. Then return to small group and share your friend's highs and lows.

   MY HIGHS + LOWS THIS WEEK WERE:

   ....

   MY FRIEND'S HIGHS + LOWS THIS WEEK WERE:

   ....

2. **READ** and highlight the theme verse in your Bibles. Circle key words and learn the verse in song if time permits.

3. **TALK** about how today's verse relates to your highs and lows. Review the art for today, the Quiz Bowl questions, the terms, and the cartoons. Then write a sentence on each of the following:

   ONE NEW THING I LEARNED TODAY:

   ....

   ONE THING I ALREADY KNEW THAT IS WORTH REPEATING:

   ....

   ONE THING I WOULD LIKE TO KNOW MORE ABOUT:

   ....

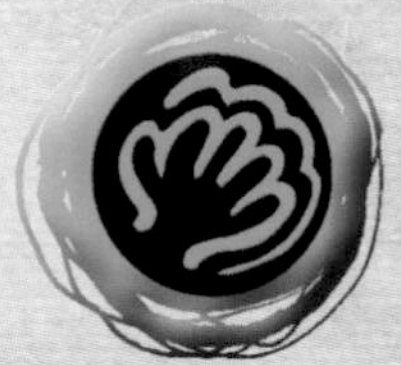

4. **PRAY** for one another, praising and thanking God for your highs, and asking God to be with you in your lows. Include your friend's highs and lows in your prayers.

   A PRAISING PRAYER: ....

   A THANKING PRAYER: ....

   AN ASKING PRAYER: ....

5. **BLESS** one another using the blessing of the week. (right) Mark each person with the sign of the cross as you bless them.

THIS WEEK'S BLESSING
(NAME), CHILD OF GOD, MAY THE RISEN LORD OF HEAVEN AND EARTH BE LORD OF YOUR LIFE THIS DAY. AMEN.

WEEK I

FAITH JOURNAL

Read the full devotions using FINKlink
LL16 @ www.faithink.com

DAY 1

TODAY'S BIBLE VERSE:

JOEL 2:32

Everyone who calls on the name of the Lord shall be saved.

MY HIGH TODAY WAS:

MY LOW TODAY WAS:

MY PRAYER TODAY IS:

DAY 2

TODAY'S BIBLE VERSE:

JOHN 20:27-28

He (Jesus) said to Thomas, "Put your finger here and see my hands. Reach out your hand and put it in my side. Do not doubt but believe." Thomas answered him, "My Lord and my God!"

MY HIGH TODAY WAS:

MY LOW TODAY WAS:

MY PRAYER TODAY IS:

DAY 3

TODAY'S BIBLE VERSE:

Acts 2:36

Therefore let the entire house of Israel know with certainty that God has made him both Lord and Messiah, this Jesus whom you crucified.

MY HIGH TODAY WAS:

MY LOW TODAY WAS:

MY PRAYER TODAY IS:

my HIGH today was:

my LOW today was:

my PRAYER today is:

DAY 4

today's bible verse:

Acts 2:38

Repent, and be baptized every one of you in the name of Jesus Christ so that your sins may be forgiven; and you will receive the gift of the Holy Spirit.

my HIGH today was:

my LOW today was:

my PRAYER today is:

DAY 5

today's bible verse:

Romans 14:9-11

Christ died and lived again, so that he might be Lord of both the dead and the living. For we will all stand before the judgment seat of God... every knee shall bow... every tongue shall confess...

my HIGH today was:

my LOW today was:

my PRAYER today is:

DAY 6

today's bible verse:

Colossians 2:6

As you therefore have received Christ Jesus the Lord, continue to live your lives in him.

my HIGHEST HIGH this week was:

my LOWEST LOW this week was:

my PRAYER for next week is:

DAY 7

this week's blessing

(Name), child of God, may the risen Lord of heaven and earth be Lord of your life this day. Amen.

WEEK 2

FAITH JOURNAL

Read the full devotions using FINKlink LL16 @ www.faithink.com

DAY 1

TODAY'S BIBLE VERSE:

I Chronicles 16:31

Let the heavens be glad, and let the earth rejoice, and let them say among the nations, "The Lord is king!"

MY HIGH TODAY WAS:

MY LOW TODAY WAS:

MY PRAYER TODAY IS:

DAY 2

TODAY'S BIBLE VERSE:

Exodus 15:11

Who is like you, O Lord, among the gods? Who is like you, majestic in holiness, awesome in splendor, doing wonders?

MY HIGH TODAY WAS:

MY LOW TODAY WAS:

MY PRAYER TODAY IS:

DAY 3

TODAY'S BIBLE VERSE:

Deuteronomy 6:4-5

Hear, O Israel: The Lord is our God, the Lord alone. You shall love the Lord your God with all your heart, and with all your soul, and with all your might.

MY HIGH TODAY WAS:

MY LOW TODAY WAS:

MY PRAYER TODAY IS:

2. READ and highlight the verse of the day in your Bibles.

3. TALK about how today's verse relates to your highs & lows.

4. PRAY for your highs & lows, for your family and for the world.

5. BLESS one another using this week's blessing (on the previous page).

my HIGH today was:

my LOW today was:

my PRAYER today is:

DAY 4

today's Bible verse:

Acts 17:24-25

The God who made the world and everything in it, he who is Lord of heaven and earth, does not live in shrines made by human hands, nor is he served by human hands, as though he needed anything.

my HIGH today was:

my LOW today was:

my PRAYER today is:

DAY 5

today's Bible verse:

Philippians 2:10-11

At the name of Jesus every knee should bend, in heaven, on earth and under the earth, and every tongue confess that Jesus Christ is Lord, to the glory of God the Father.

my HIGH today was:

my LOW today was:

my PRAYER today is:

DAY 6

today's Bible verse:

Revelation 19:6

Then I heard what seemed to be the voice of a great multitude, like the sound of may waters... crying out, "Hallelujah! For the Lord our God the Almighty reigns."

S | M | T | W | TH | F | S

THEME IN REVIEW

As you will,
What you will,
When you will.

Thomas a Kempis

DAY 7

my favorite VERSE from the theme was:

....

....

....

....

....

....

....

....

....

looking back on these two weeks, my highest HIGH was:

....

my lowest LOW these past weeks was:

....

one way God answered my PRAYERS was:

....

one way God might use me as a SACRED AGENT to answer these prayers:

....

....

Family Covenant

We have shared *Highs & Lows* this week, read and highlighted the verses assigned in our Bibles, talked about our lives, prayed for one another's highs and lows, and blessed one another.

....	....	....
Parent's Signature	*Teen's Signature*	*Date*

THE FINKMANIA QUIZBOWL

Question 1:

The Second Article of the Apostles' Creed is:

(A) "I believe in God the Father Almighty, Creator of heaven and earth,"

(B) "I believe in Jesus Christ, his only Son, our Lord...,"

(C) "I believe in the Holy Spirit,"

(D) "I believe in music, I believe in love"

Question 2:

The word "Lord" is:

(A) From the Latin *leonardo* meaning "lion of war,"

(B) From the Latin *leonardo* meaning "handsome hunk,"

(C) From the Old English *hlaf* meaning "bread" and *weard* meaning "guardian,"

(D) From the French *lard* meaning "I can't believe it's not butter!"

Question 3:

To say, "Jesus is Lord" is to say:

(A) He is the provider and guardian of my daily bread,

(B) He is Master of the Universe,

(C) He is Master of my life and I owe him my love, obedience, and loyalty in front of my friends,

(D) All of the above and I should consult him on my decisions

Question 4:

When Moses asked God for a name from the burning bush:

(A) God said "I Am,"

(B) God said "I Was,"

(C) God said "Gary"

(D) God said "None of Your Darn Business"

Question 5:

In John's gospel, Jesus said, "I Am the...":

(A) "Way, the Truth and the Life,"

(B) "Bread of Life"

(C) "Eggman, I Am the Eggman, I Am the Walrus"

(D) Both A and B

Question 6:

Jesus lived on earth for:

(A) 3 years,

(B) 30 years,

(C) 33 years,

(D) 333.3 years

Question 7:

Jesus is Lord over:

(A) Sin, the sting of death, and the power of the devil,

(B) Pittsburgh,

(C) A twenty-acre estate in rural Vermont,

(D) Actually, all of the above when you think about it

Question 8:

Why did the Lord Jesus give up his throne of power?:

(A) He saw we were lost and chose to rescue us,

(B) He wanted to visit earth on a thirty-three year vacation,

(C) He was bored in heaven with all those angels singing all the time,

(D) He wanted to visit Vegas before it became too crowded and commercial

Question 9:

Martin Luther said, "All this he (Jesus) has done so that I might..."

(A) "...be his own and live under him in his kingdom,"

(B) "...serve him in everlasting righteousness, innocence and blessedness,"

(C) Both A & B,

(D) "...get off Scott-free on judgment day by claiming him at the last minute like the thief on the cross"

FINKmania Final Question:

Joel 2:32 says, "Everyone who calls on the name of the Lord shall be...":

(A) Smart

(B) Thankful

(C) Saved

(D) Surprised

Play this online game using FINKlink

LL16 @ www.faithink.com

THE WEAKEST FINK

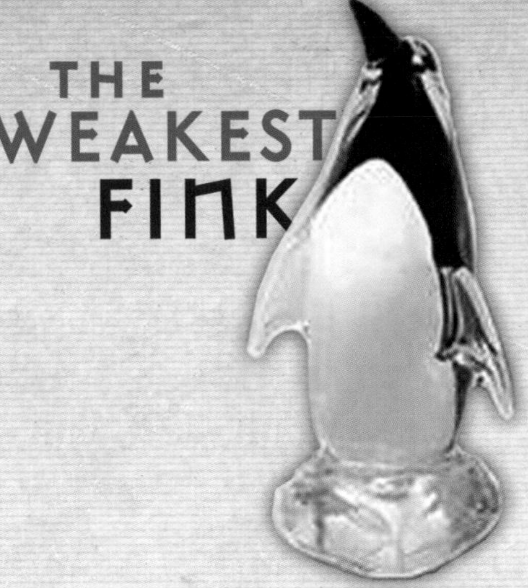

Most people are happy to have a Savior when they're in trouble, but very few want a Lord when they're not.

Rich Melheim

TERMS

Write a definition below.

Christ

....

....

Disciple

....

....

Messiah

....

....

Lord

....

....

Saved

....

....

FAITH INKUBATORS

The Holy Spirit

"Now there are varieties of gifts,

but the same Spirit."

— I Corinthians 12:4

Listen to this song using FINKlink
LL17 @ www.faithink.com

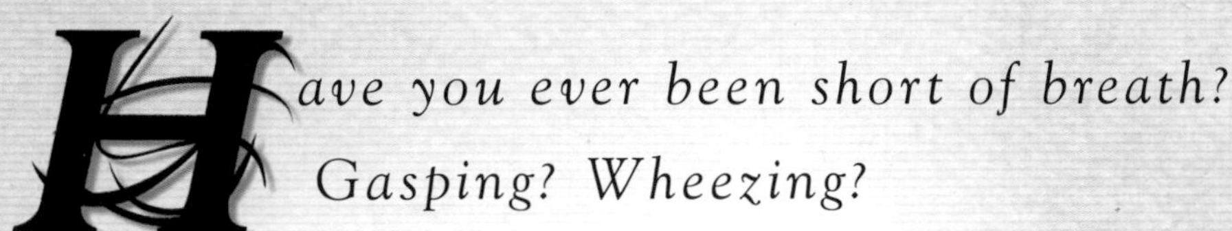

Have you ever been short of breath? Gasping? Wheezing?

Maybe you know the tense feeling of not being able to catch your breath. Maybe you were confined in a tight spot and felt claustrophobic. Maybe you ran too fast in gym class and almost passed out. Maybe you have asthma and forgot your inhaler. What was it like to finally catch your breath? To breathe freely? How necessary was air to you at that moment?

People rarely think about breathing when air is all around them. It is only when air is in short supply that they realize how important it is.

There is an underwater game called "Shark" where you have to swim from one end of a pool to the other before coming up for air. Your lungs may be bursting, but you can't emerge until you touch the edge of other side of the pool. If you've ever played this game, you know what happens in the last few seconds. You feel like you are going to explode. Your mind screams: "Get air, get air!" You wonder if you can make it or if you should just give up. You need to release, so you push yourself faster. Faster. Faster. Finally, you touch the end and shoot upward, gasping. You lift your head above the water, sputter, and literally catch the breath you so desperately needed to survive. Inhale. Exhale. Inhale. Exhale. Air is life.

The Holy Spirit

Spirit, wind, breath. They are all the same word in Hebrew—*Ruah*. Spirit. Wind. Breath.

At the beginning of time, when the Spirit of God brooded over the vast emptiness before anything was called to be, it was the Spirit, wind, breath of God that called it all to life. When God blew into Adam, the breath of life brought a inanimate lump of clay to his feet. It was the Spirit, wind, breath of God that made him a living being. When our Lord Jesus breathed his last and cried out from the cross, "Father, into your hands I commend my spirit," it was his spirit, wind, breath that returned to God. And, on that Pentecost day when the disciples were huddled behind locked doors fearing for their own lives, the sound of a great wind rushed upon them. They were filled with the mighty Spirit, wind, breath of God. This Holy Spirit sent them out with boldness to proclaim Christ to the world!

In essence, we are animated by the very Spirit, wind, breath of God. We carry a small spark of eternity within these frail bodies—a living soul. We carry a small wisp of the very Spirit of the living God.

I believe in the Holy Spirit, the holy catholic (Christian) church, the communion of saints, the forgiveness of sins, the Resurrection of the body and life Everlasting. Amen.

Third Article
Apostles' Creed

Order this art print using FINKlink
LL17 @ www.faithink.com

Images in Art

- What do you see in today's painting by Dr. He Qi?
- Where are you in this work of art?
- How do the image and the verse apply to your life today?

So What Does This Mean?

Bible Time

Read and highlight I Corinthians 12:4 as you think about your spirit today. Is it full of life or a little flat? Think of yourself as a beach ball. Are you inflated with the fullness of God's Spirit? Or are you deflated, feeling empty, and without shape, form, or purpose? Open your Bible to I Corinthians 12. Find and circle the word "spirit" every time you see it between verses 1 and 13. How many times is it used? This chapter is all about the Spirit blowing life in your being by gifting you with purpose. God is as close to you as the air you breathe. Are you inhaling enough of God to keep you full? Are you exhaling God's life-giving love to others? Take a few more deep breaths and pray:

Prayer

God, breathe on me, fill me, and bring me the gifts of your Spirit. In Jesus' name I pray. Amen.

The Holy Spirit has called me through the gospel, enlightened me with his gifts, and sanctified and kept me in true faith.

Martin Luther

Catechism Encounter

Check out Luther's explanation to the Third Article of the Apostles' Creed in the Small Catechism. What is the work of God's Holy Spirit?

Questions to Ponder

1. Do you believe in ghosts? Why or why not? The Holy Spirit is sometimes called the Holy Ghost. How is God's Spirit like a ghost? Unlike a ghost?

2. How is living without God's Holy Spirit like living without enough air?

3. "We've got spirit, yes we do! We've got spirit how about you?" What does it mean to say a team has spirit?

4. What does it mean to say a person has the Holy Spirit?

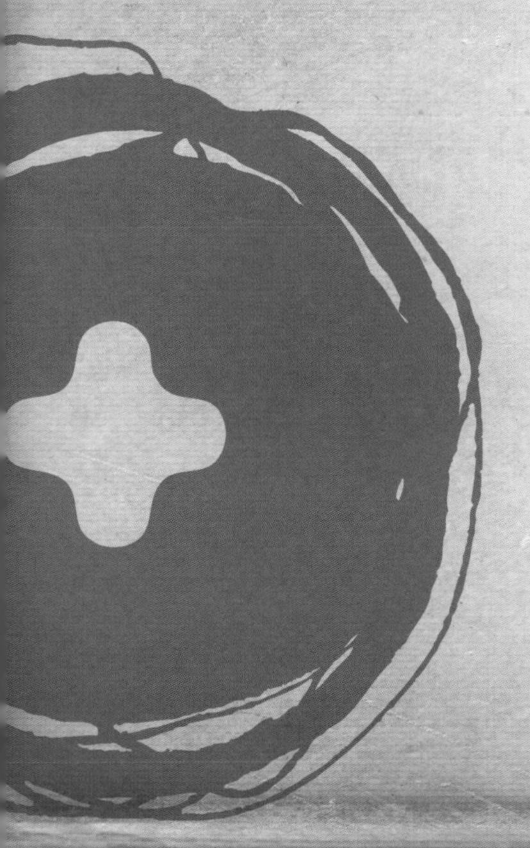

Small Group
share, read, talk, pray, bless

1. SHARE your highs and lows of the week one-on-one with another person. Listen carefully and record your friend's thoughts in the space below. Then return to small group and share your friend's highs and lows.

MY HIGHS + LOWS THIS WEEK WERE:

....

MY FRIEND'S HIGHS + LOWS THIS WEEK WERE:

....

2. READ and highlight the theme verse in your Bibles. Circle key words and learn the verse in song if time permits.

3. TALK about how today's verse relates to your highs and lows. Review the art for today, the Quiz Bowl questions, the terms, and the cartoons. Then write a sentence on each of the following:

ONE NEW THING I LEARNED TODAY:

....

ONE THING I ALREADY KNEW THAT IS WORTH REPEATING:

....

ONE THING I WOULD LIKE TO KNOW MORE ABOUT:

....

4. PRAY for one another, praising and thanking God for your highs, and asking God to be with you in your lows. Include your friend's highs and lows in your prayers.

A PRAISING PRAYER: ....

A THANKING PRAYER: ....

AN ASKING PRAYER: ....

5. BLESS one another using the blessing of the week. (right) Mark each person with the sign of the cross as you bless them.

THIS WEEK'S BLESSING

(NAME), CHILD OF GOD, MAY THE FIRE OF THE HOLY SPIRIT BURN IN YOUR SOUL THIS DAY.

WEEK 1

THE FAITH 5 JOURNAL

Read the full devotions using FINKlink LL17 @ www.faithink.com

DAY 1

TODAY'S BIBLE VERSE:

1 Corinthians 12:4

Now there are varieties of gifts, but the same Spirit.

MY HIGH TODAY WAS:

MY LOW TODAY WAS:

MY PRAYER TODAY IS:

DAY 2

TODAY'S BIBLE VERSE:

Genesis 1:1-2

In the beginning when God created the heavens and the earth, the earth was a formless void and darkness covered the face of the deep, while a wind from God swept over the face of the waters.

MY HIGH TODAY WAS:

MY LOW TODAY WAS:

MY PRAYER TODAY IS:

DAY 3

TODAY'S BIBLE VERSE:

Psalm 42:1

As a deer longs for flowing streams, so my soul longs for you, O God.

MY HIGH TODAY WAS:

MY LOW TODAY WAS:

MY PRAYER TODAY IS:

my HIGH today was:

my LOW today was:

my PRAYER today is:

DAY 4

today's bible verse:

Isaiah 61:1-2

The spirit of the Lord God is upon me, because the Lord has anointed me, he has sent me to bring good news to the oppressed, to bind up the brokenhearted, to proclaim liberty to the captives...

my HIGH today was:

my LOW today was:

my PRAYER today is:

DAY 5

today's bible verse:

John 14:26

The Advocate, the Holy Spirit, whom the Father will send in my name, will teach you everything, and remind you of all that I have said to you.

my HIGH today was:

my LOW today was:

my PRAYER today is:

DAY 6

today's bible verse:

Acts 1:8

But you will receive power when the Holy Spirit has come upon you; and you will be my witnesses in Jerusalem, in all Judea and Samaria, and to the ends of the earth.

my HIGHEST HIGH this week was:

my LOWEST LOW this week was:

my PRAYER for next week is:

DAY 7

this week's blessing

(NAME), CHILD OF GOD, MAY THE FIRE OF THE HOLY SPIRIT BURN IN YOUR SOUL THIS DAY.

WEEK 2

THE FAITH 5 JOURNAL

Read the full devotions using FINKlink LL17 @ www.faithink.com

DAY 1

TODAY'S BIBLE VERSE:

Acts 2:1-2

When the day of Pentecost had come, they were all together in one place. And suddenly from heaven there came a sound like a rush of a violent wind, and it filled the entire house where they were sitting.

MY HIGH TODAY WAS:

MY LOW TODAY WAS:

MY PRAYER TODAY IS:

DAY 2

TODAY'S BIBLE VERSE:

Acts 2:3-4

Divided tongues, as of fire, appeared among them, and a tongue rested on each of them. All of them were filled with the Holy Spirit and began to speak in other languages, as the Spirit gave them the ability.

MY HIGH TODAY WAS:

MY LOW TODAY WAS:

MY PRAYER TODAY IS:

DAY 3

TODAY'S BIBLE VERSE:

I Kings 19:12(RSV)

There was a great wind... but the Lord was not in the wind... and after the wind an earthquake, but the Lord was not in the earthquake; and after the earthquake a fire, but the Lord was not in the fire; and after the fire a still small voice.

MY HIGH TODAY WAS:

MY LOW TODAY WAS:

MY PRAYER TODAY IS:

my HIGH today was:

my LOW today was:

my PRAYER today is:

DAY 4

today's bible verse:

II Corinthians 13:13

The grace of our Lord Jesus Christ, the love of God and the communion of the Holy Spirit be with you.

my HIGH today was:

my LOW today was:

my PRAYER today is:

DAY 5

today's bible verse:

I Corinthians 12:3b

No one can say "Jesus is Lord," except by the Holy Spirit.

my HIGH today was:

my LOW today was:

my PRAYER today is:

DAY 6

today's bible verse:

Galatians 5:22-23

The fruit of the Spirit is love, joy, peace, patience, kindness, generosity, faithfulness, gentleness and self control.

S | M | T | W | TH | F | S

THEME IN REVIEW

People are like stained-glass windows. They sparkle and shine when the sun is out, but when the darkness sets in, their true beauty is revealed only if there is a light from within.

Maggie Kuhn

DAY 7

My favorite VERSE from the theme was:

Looking back on these two weeks, my highest HIGH was:

My lowest LOW these past weeks was:

One way God answered my PRAYERS was:

One way God might use me as a SACRED AGENT to answer these prayers:

Family Covenant

We have shared *Highs & Lows* this week, read and highlighted the verses assigned in our Bible talked about our lives, prayed for one another's highs and lows, and blessed one another.

Parent's Signature | *Teen's Signature* | *Date*

THE FINKMANIA QUIZBOWL

QUESTION 1:

The Third Article of the Apostles' Creed is:

(A) "Remember the Sabbath,"
(B) "Your will be done, on earth as in heaven,"
(C) "I believe in the Holy Spirit, the holy catholic church, the communion of saints, the forgiveness of sins, the resurrection of the body and the life everlasting,"
(D) None of the above

QUESTION 2:

The Holy Spirit is:

(A) A holiday drink,
(B) A ghost that comes out of the television,
(C) A good feeling,
(D) God's living Spirit and presence in the hearts and lives of God's people

QUESTION 3:

Martin Luther said "I cannot by my own understanding or effort...":

(A) "...believe in Jesus Christ my Lord,"
(B) "...come to him (Jesus),"
(C) "...get an A in algebra,"
(D) A and B, although C is probably true but we have no record of Luther ever saying it

QUESTION 4:

What does God's Holy Spirit do?:

(A) Gets us out of trouble,
(B) Gets us into trouble,
(C) Calls, gathers, enlightens, sanctifies and keeps us in the true faith,
(D) All of the above could be true when you really think about it

QUESTION 5:

How does the Holy Spirit call people?:

(A) Through the Verizon IN Network,
(B) Through Instant Messaging,
(C) Through the Gospel,
(D) Through a Mountain Dew and M & M induced stupor

QUESTION 6:

How does the Holy Spirit enlighten people?:

(A) With Weight Watchers,
(B) With GE Soft White 120 watt bulbs,
(C) With God's gifts,
(D) Mostly through FOX News

QUESTION 7:

What does it mean when we say the Holy Spirit "sanctifies" us?:

(A) It makes us coffee,
(B) It makes us perfect,
(C) It makes us sacred, holy, pure and set apart for God's use,
(D) It makes us scared and scarred

QUESTION 8:

The Hebrew word "ruah" means:

(A) Earth, wind, and fire,
(B) Earth, wind, and spirit,
(C) Wind, breath and spirit,
(D) Wind, breath, fire, and baking soda

QUESTION 9:

What do the Holy Spirit and your conscience have in common?:

(A) Nothing,
(B) They are the same thing,
(C) They are of equal value,
(D) The Holy Spirit sometimes comes as a still, small voice that speaks to your conscience and guides you

FINKMANIA FINAL QUESTION:

I Corinthians 12:4 says, "There are varieties of gifts, but..."

(A) "...many Spirits,"
(B) "...the same Spirit,"
(C) "...you don't deserve them,"
(D) "...the Geeks will inherit the earth"

Play this online game using FINKlink
LL17 | @ www.faithink.com

THE WEAKEST FINK

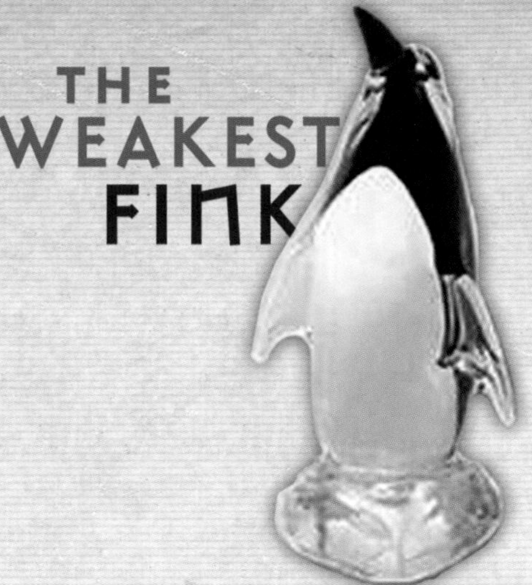

ALL THAT IS TRUE, BY WHOMSOEVER IT HAS BEEN SAID, IS BY THE HOLY SPIRIT.

THOMAS AQUINAS

TERMS

WRITE A DEFINITION BELOW.

BREATH

GIFTS

HOLY SPIRIT

PENTECOST

RUAH

FAITH INKUBATORS

The Church and the Saints

"For as in one body we have many members, and not all the members have the same function, so we, who are many, are one body in Christ, and individually we are members one of another."

— Romans 12:4-5

Listen to this song using FINKlink
LL18 @ www.faithink.com

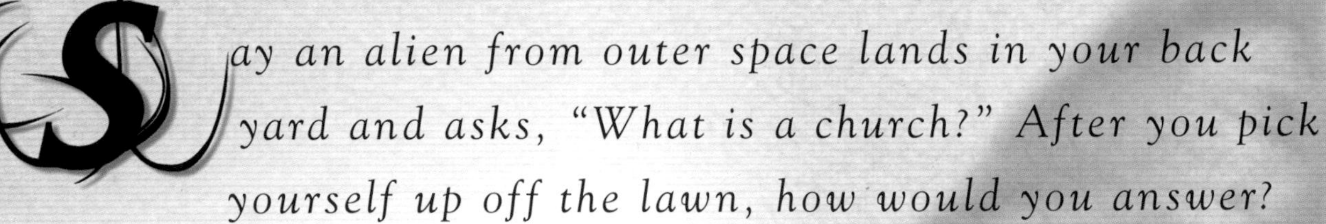

Say an alien from outer space lands in your back yard and asks, "What is a church?" After you pick yourself up off the lawn, how would you answer?

Would you say the church is a building? A group of people? A pastor? God's presence? God's work in human hands? A parking lot? A youth group? A mission project? A funteral? A baptism? A pot luck supper? Pizza night? If the alien asked, "When does church happen?" What would you say? On Sundays? Wednesday nights? When someone dies? When a baby is born?

Try this: Stand in front of a full-length mirror and look at yourself. Go ahead. Do it! What do you see? Place your hand to your throat and feel your heart beating. Examine your fingers. Picture red and white blood cells speeding through your veins like a billion tiny trucks down a superhighway. They branch off to major roads, then again to tiny capillary streets to deliver their goods and take away the trash. Run in place for 60 seconds and watch how all the parts of your body work together to make movement possible. Now stand quietly and think about your breath. Inhale slowly, thinking of all the fresh, clean oxygen moving to every cell in your body. Exhale slowly, imagining all of the poisons leaving your body. Now wiggle your nose, your ears, your fingers and your toes all at the same time. What do you see in your body? What are you thinking? What are you feeling? Can you hear yourself breathing? How do you move each muscle?

Amazing.

Your body works as a unit. Most of what you do—breathing, digesting, heating and cooling, pumping blood—doesn't even take conscious thought. Can you comprehend how wonderfully everything works together to make you you?

The Church and the Saints

Some call the church a body. Like you, this body is made up of many parts working together. Some of these parts are close by. Some are spread all over the world. Think about the world-wide body of Christ for a moment. How many parts do you think there are? There are 2.1 billion Christians living around the world. They practice all manner of worship. How are the other parts like you? How are they different? How does what they do and who they are affect what you do and who you are? Isn't it amazing? No matter what part of the body of Christ you are, you are called to work together with the other parts—other Christians—to build up the body and do God's good work on earth. Every part of the body is important. Every part has gifts and talents to share to keep the whole body healthy and alive. This may sound a bit alien, but you are the church. The church is not a building. We are the church, not separately, but together.

The church is not a building, a committee or a board, it's not a corporation for the business of the Lord.

We are the church.

Jay Beech

Order this art print using FINKlink
LL18
@ www.faithink.com

Images in Art

- What do you see in today's painting by Dr. He Qi?
- Where are you in this work of art?
- How do the image and the verse apply to your life today?

So What Does This Mean?

I HAVE ALWAYS THOUGHT THAT THE MIRACLE OF THE RESURRECTION PALES IN COMPARISON TO THE MIRACLE THAT THE CHURCH IS STILL IN EXISTENCE 2000 YEARS LATER MADE UP OF THE LIKES OF US...

To gather with God's people in united adoration of the Father is as necessary to the Christian life as prayer.

Martin Luther

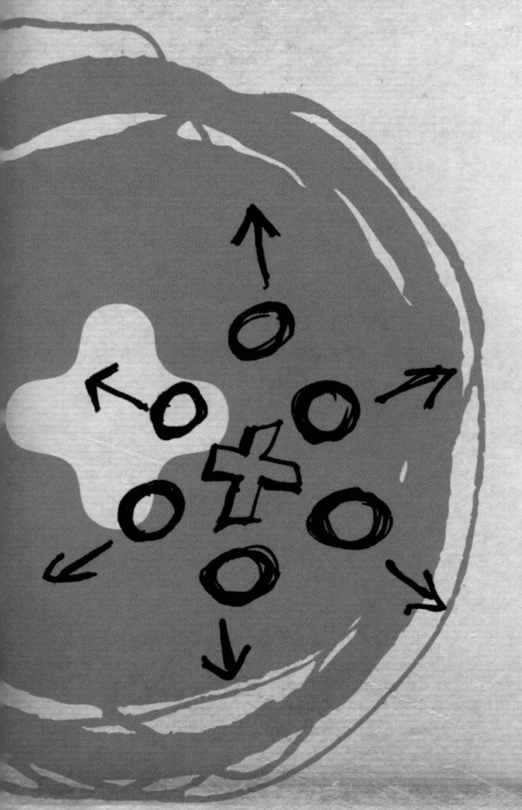

Bible Time

All parts of a body work together for the good of the body. If any part is missing, the body is in trouble! Read and highlight Romans 12:4-5. What does this verse tell you about being part of the body of Christ?

Look at yourself in the mirror once again. How might your hands be used to further God's work on earth? Your feet? Your mouth? Your heart? What could you do to spread God's love and God's word at your school? What could you do with your close friends to make your church healthier and more alive? What could you do at home tonight? In your community tomorrow? In the world this year? Will you do it?

Prayer

Light of the World, make me a candle to spread your light and love. Creator of all, I want to be all you created me to be. Keep me connected to your body, so together in love and unity we can take your message of love and forgiveness to this hurting world! In Jesus' name I pray. Amen.

Catechism Encounter

Scan Luther's Small Catechism looking for words that might describe the work of the church. Circle them and write five of the best words here:

Questions to Ponder

1. What is one thing you love to do? What is one talent or gift you possess?

2. How might you use the passions and gifts above to strengthen the church? To bring God's love to the world?

3. What are three different functions and systems of a human body?

4. How are these functions like functions of a church?

SMALL GROUP

SHARE, READ, TALK, PRAY, BLESS

1. **SHARE** your highs and lows of the week one-on-one with another person. Listen carefully and record your friend's thoughts in the space below. Then return to small group and share your friend's highs and lows.

   MY HIGHS + LOWS THIS WEEK WERE:

   ....

   MY FRIEND'S HIGHS + LOWS THIS WEEK WERE:

   ....

2. **READ** and highlight the theme verse in your Bibles. Circle key words and learn the verse in song if time permits.

3. **TALK** about how today's verse relates to your highs and lows. Review the art for today, the Quiz Bowl questions, the terms, and the cartoons. Then write a sentence on each of the following:

   ONE NEW THING I LEARNED TODAY:

   ....

   ONE THING I ALREADY KNEW THAT IS WORTH REPEATING:

   ....

   ONE THING I WOULD LIKE TO KNOW MORE ABOUT:

   ....

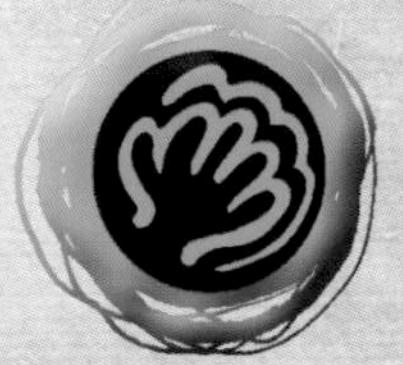

4. **PRAY** for one another, praising and thanking God for your highs, and asking God to be with you in your lows. Include your friend's highs and lows in your prayers.

   A PRAISING PRAYER: ....

   A THANKING PRAYER: ....

   AN ASKING PRAYER: ....

5. **BLESS** one another using the blessing of the week. (right) Mark each person with the sign of the cross as you bless them.

THIS WEEK'S BLESSING

(NAME), CHILD OF GOD, MAY YOU BE THE CHURCH TODAY IN EVERY WORD AND EVERY WAY.

WEEK 1

FAITH JOURNAL

Read the full devotions using FINKlink LL18 @ www.faithink.com

DAY 1

TODAY'S BIBLE VERSE:

Romans 12:4-5

For as in one body we have many members, and not all the members have the same function, so we, who are many, are one body in Christ, and individually we are members one of another.

MY HIGH TODAY WAS:

MY LOW TODAY WAS:

MY PRAYER TODAY IS:

DAY 2

TODAY'S BIBLE VERSE:

Ephesians 4:3-6

...making every effort to maintain the unity of the Spirit in the bond of peace. There is one body and one Spirit...

MY HIGH TODAY WAS:

MY LOW TODAY WAS:

MY PRAYER TODAY IS:

DAY 3

TODAY'S BIBLE VERSE:

Acts 2:38-39

Repent, and be baptized every one of you in the name of Jesus Christ so your sins may be forgiven; and you will receive the gift of the Holy Spirit. For the promise is for you, for your children....

MY HIGH TODAY WAS:

MY LOW TODAY WAS:

MY PRAYER TODAY IS:

my HIGH today was:

my LOW today was:

my PRAYER today is:

DAY 4

today's bible verse:

Acts 2:44-45

All who believed were together and had all things in common; they would sell their possessions and goods and distribute the proceeds to all, as any had need.

my HIGH today was:

my LOW today was:

my PRAYER today is:

DAY 5

today's bible verse:

Acts 2:46-47a

Day by day, as they spent much time together in the temple, they broke bread at home and ate their food with glad and generous hearts, praising God and having the goodwill of all the people.

my HIGH today was:

my LOW today was:

my PRAYER today is:

DAY 6

today's bible verse:

Acts 2:47b

And day by day the Lord added to their number those who were being saved.

my HIGHEST HIGH this week was:

my LOWEST LOW this week was:

my PRAYER for next week is:

DAY 7

this week's blessing

(NAME), CHILD OF GOD, MAY YOU BE THE CHURCH TODAY IN EVERY WORD AND EVERY WAY.

WEEK 2

FAITH

Read the full devotions using FINKlink LL18 @ www.faithink.com

FAITH JOURNAL

DAY 1

TODAY'S BIBLE VERSE:

Matthew 16:18

And I tell you, you are Peter, and on this rock I will build my church, and the gates of Hades will not prevail against it.

MY HIGH TODAY WAS:

MY LOW TODAY WAS:

MY PRAYER TODAY IS:

DAY 2

TODAY'S BIBLE VERSE:

Matthew 18:15

If another member of the church sins against you, go and point out the fault when the two of you are alone. If the member listens to you, you have regained that one.

MY HIGH TODAY WAS:

MY LOW TODAY WAS:

MY PRAYER TODAY IS:

DAY 3

TODAY'S BIBLE VERSE:

James 5:14

Are any among you sick? They should call for the elders of the church and have them pray over them, anointing them with oil in the name of the Lord.

MY HIGH TODAY WAS:

MY LOW TODAY WAS:

MY PRAYER TODAY IS:

1. SHARE HIGHS & LOWS OF THE DAY.

2. READ AND HIGHLIGHT THE VERSE OF THE DAY IN YOUR BIBLES.

3. TALK ABOUT HOW TODAY'S VERSE RELATES TO YOUR HIGHS & LOWS.

4. PRAY FOR YOUR HIGHS & LOWS, FOR YOUR FAMILY AND FOR THE WORLD.

5. BLESS ONE ANOTHER USING THIS WEEK'S BLESSING (ON THE PREVIOUS PAGE).

DAY 4

TODAY'S BIBLE VERSE:

I Corinthians 12:21

The eye cannot say to the hand, "I have no need of you," nor again the head to the feet, "I have no need of you."

MY HIGH TODAY WAS:

MY LOW TODAY WAS:

MY PRAYER TODAY IS:

DAY 5

TODAY'S BIBLE VERSE:

Hebrews 10:24-25

And let us consider how to provoke one another to love and good deeds, not neglecting to meet together, as is the habit of some, but encouraging one another, and all the more as you see the Day approaching.

MY HIGH TODAY WAS:

MY LOW TODAY WAS:

MY PRAYER TODAY IS:

DAY 6

TODAY'S BIBLE VERSE:

I John 1:7

But if we walk in the light as he himself is in the light, we have fellowship with one another, and the blood of Jesus his Son cleanses us from all sin.

MY HIGH TODAY WAS:

MY LOW TODAY WAS:

MY PRAYER TODAY IS:

CREED no 9

The Forgiveness of Sins

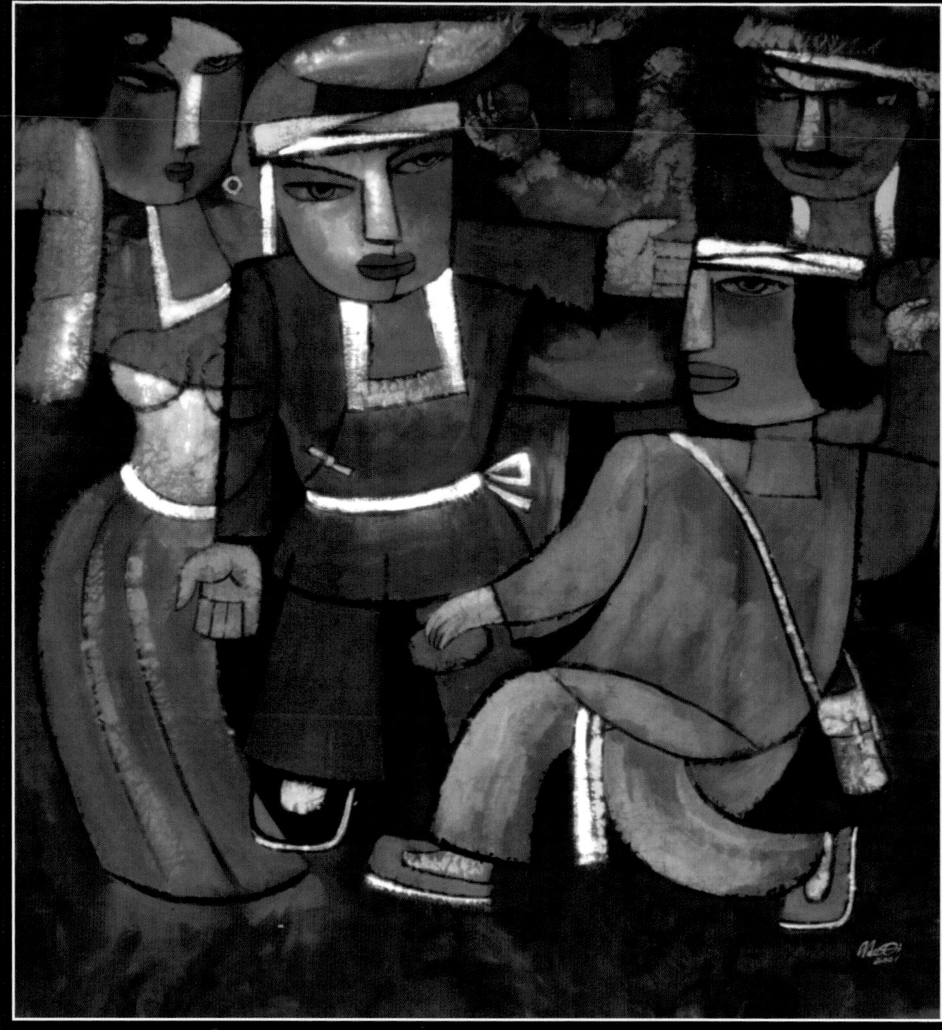

"Woman Caught in Adultery" Copyright © Dr. He Qi www.heqigallery.com

"If we say that we have no sin, we deceive ourselves, and the truth is not in us. If we confess our sins, he who is faithful and just will forgive us our sins and cleanse us from all unrighteousness."

— I John 1:9

Listen to this song using FINKlink LL19 @ www.faithink.com

The woman deserved what she was about to get. She had been caught in the act of adultery, and according to the laws of Moses, she was to be stoned.

They dragged her to Jesus and threw her into the dirt at his feet. What would the rabbi do? Would he follow the letter of the law and condemn her to death? Would he pardon her and set her free? Either way the religious leaders could use this test to get Jesus into trouble with someone.

Rather than playing into their trap, Jesus revealed something about the law, himself, and the true nature of God. First he knelt down to the woman's level and wrote something in the sand with his finger. We don't know what he wrote. Maybe it was a Bible verse. Maybe it was a symbol. Maybe it was the names of all the men in the crowd holding stones who had also slept with this woman. Then he said something brilliant, "Let whoever has no sin cast the first stone."

One by one the murderous posse dropped their stones and trudged away. Finally alone, Jesus turned and asked the woman where her judge, jury, and executioners had gone. "They have left, sir," said the woman. Then he said, "Neither do I condemn you. Go and sin no more."

PEOPLE WHO LIVE IN GLASS HOUSES SHOULDN'T THROW STONES.

ANCIENT PROVERB

THE FORGIVENESS OF SINS

Have you ever messed up? You're in good company. Have you ever sinned, broken a law, or hurt someone? Join the club.

The Bible says everyone has sinned. The Bible says we live in a fallen world. St. Paul wrote, "The good that I want to do, I don't. The evil that I don't want to do, I do. O wretched man that I am, who can save me from this body of death?" If the most famous saint in the Bible also knew he was a major league sinner, there's hope for everyone.

Martin Luther knew he was a sinner, too. He knew he didn't measure up to the demands of God's Law. Young Martin grew up picturing God as a vengeful judge, just waiting to send him to hell if he wasn't perfect. How did Luther find peace with God? He found it in the grace and love of Jesus. He found it in a Savior who took his punishment for him; in a Lord who took his sins to the cross. In the cross of Jesus, Luther found a God of love—not a God of vengeance. This God didn't desire the death of sinners, but desired their salvation and a life together with them in eternity.

If you want to know the true nature of God, don't look at yourself. Don't look at the Law. Don't look at the preacher, the pope, or the saints. You don't have to look any further than Jesus. In him you are forgiven.

Order this art print using FINKlink LL19 @ www.faithink.com

IMAGES IN ART

- What do you see in today's painting by Dr. He Qi?
- Where are you in this work of art?
- How do the image and the verse apply to your life today?

So What Does This Mean?

FORGIVE AND FORGET? I CAN FORGET THAT SERMON, BUT I'M NEVER GOING TO FORGIVE YOU FOR IT!

An eye for an eye only makes the whole world blind.

Gandhi

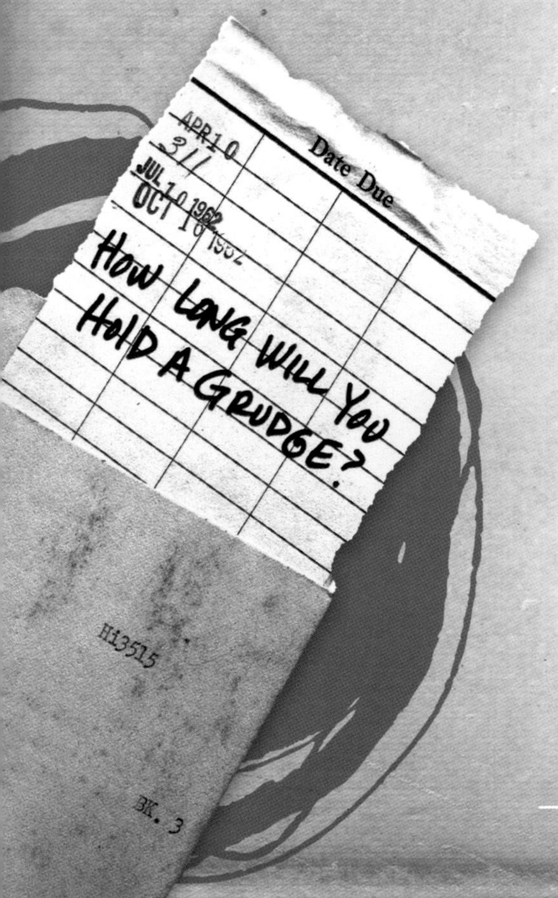

HOW LONG WILL YOU HOLD A GRUDGE?

Bible Time

Sin can be like dirt. It clings to you. Christ's forgiveness is like soap. It's stronger than dirt! It takes honesty and courage to admit what you've done wrong, how you've failed, and how you've hurt others. It takes a big person to say "I'm sorry" for sins and to make amends.

Where do you need forgiveness today? Write a sentence here asking God for forgiveness for something specific, then take a moment and make your confession.

It isn't always easy to confess, but the promise comes if you do. God will forgive, cleanse, and start the process of restoring you to right relationships. Once you confess, you can leave it all behind and make a fresh start. Whew!

Prayer

God, I'm sorry for all the times I have messed up. Only you can make it right for me. Forgive me. Wash me. Make me clean again through Jesus. Amen.

Catechism Encounter

Scan Luther's Small Catechism for the words "forgive" and "forgiveness." Circle them every time they appear. How many times can you find them? What does this tell you?

Questions to Ponder

1. Talk about a time when you experienced forgiveness or offered it to someone recently.

2. What happens when you forgive a person? What happens when you don't forgive?

3. Why is forgiveness important for relationships? For your family? For the world?

4. In the Lord's Prayer, Jesus asks God, "Forgive our debts, as we also have forgiven our debtors." Why is it important to forgive if you want to be forgiven?

Small Group

share, read, talk, pray, bless

1. **SHARE** your highs and lows of the week one-on-one with another person. Listen carefully and record your friend's thoughts in the space below. Then return to small group and share your friend's highs and lows.

   MY HIGHS + LOWS THIS WEEK WERE:

   ....

   MY FRIEND'S HIGHS + LOWS THIS WEEK WERE:

   ....

2. **READ** and highlight the theme verse in your Bibles. Circle key words and learn the verse in song if time permits.

3. **TALK** about how today's verse relates to your highs and lows. Review the art for today, the Quiz Bowl questions, the terms, and the cartoons. Then write a sentence on each of the following:

   ONE NEW THING I LEARNED TODAY:

   ....

   ONE THING I ALREADY KNEW THAT IS WORTH REPEATING:

   ....

   ONE THING I WOULD LIKE TO KNOW MORE ABOUT:

   ....

4. **PRAY** for one another, praising and thanking God for your highs, and asking God to be with you in your lows. Include your friend's highs and lows in your prayers.

   A PRAISING PRAYER: ....

   A THANKING PRAYER: ....

   AN ASKING PRAYER: ....

5. **BLESS** one another using the blessing of the week. (right) Mark each person with the sign of the cross as you bless them.

THIS WEEK'S BLESSING

(NAME), CHILD OF GOD, MAY YOU BE A FORGIVEN, FORGIVING PERSON THIS DAY.

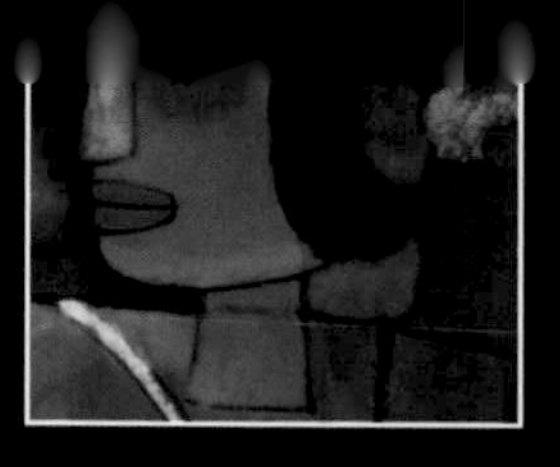

THE FAITH JOURNAL

Read the full devotions using FINKlink LL19 @ www.faithink.com

WEEK 1

DAY 1

TODAY'S BIBLE VERSE:

I JOHN 1:8-9

If we say that we have no sin, we deceive ourselves, and the truth is not in us. If we confess our sins, God who is faithful and just will forgive us our sins and cleanse us from all unrighteousness.

MY HIGH TODAY WAS:

MY LOW TODAY WAS:

MY PRAYER TODAY IS:

DAY 2

TODAY'S BIBLE VERSE:

MATTHEW 6:12, 15

And forgive us our debts, as we also have forgiven our debtors. If you do not forgive others, neither will your Father forgive your trespasses.

MY HIGH TODAY WAS:

MY LOW TODAY WAS:

MY PRAYER TODAY IS:

DAY 3

TODAY'S BIBLE VERSE:

MATTHEW 18:21

Then Peter came and said to him, "Lord, if another member of the church sins against me, how often should I forgive? As many as seven times?"

MY HIGH TODAY WAS:

MY LOW TODAY WAS:

MY PRAYER TODAY IS:

my HIGH today was:

my LOW today was:

my PRAYER today is:

DAY 4

today's bible verse:

MARK 2:10

But so that you may know that the Son of Man has authority on earth to forgive sins...

my HIGH today was:

my LOW today was:

my PRAYER today is:

DAY 5

today's bible verse:

LUKE 23:34

Father, forgive them; for they do not know what they are doing.

my HIGH today was:

my LOW today was:

my PRAYER today is:

DAY 6

today's bible verse:

JOHN 20:23

If you forgive the sins of any, they are forgiven them; if you retain the sins of any, they are retained.

my HIGHEST HIGH this week was:

my LOWEST LOW this week was:

my PRAYER for next week is:

DAY 7

this week's blessing

(NAME), CHILD OF GOD, MAY YOU BE A FORGIVEN, FORGIVING PERSON THIS DAY.

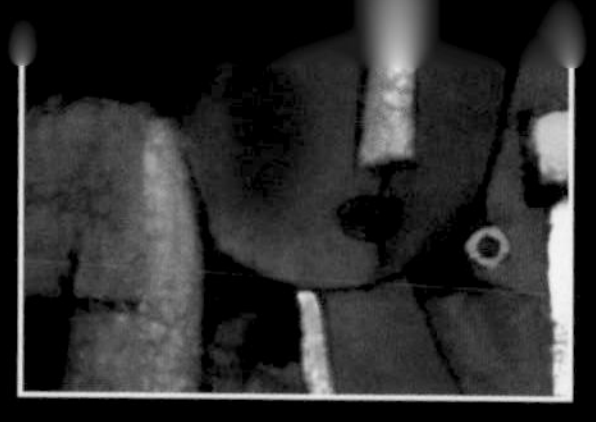

WEEK 2

FAITH JOURNAL

Read the full devotions using FINKlink
LL19 @ www.faithink.com

DAY 1

TODAY'S BIBLE VERSE:

Genesis 18:24

Suppose there are fifty righteous within the city; will you then sweep away the place and not forgive it for the fifty righteous who are in it?

my HIGH today was:

my LOW today was:

my PRAYER today is:

DAY 2

TODAY'S BIBLE VERSE:

I Kings 8:30

Hear the plea of your servant and of your people Israel when they pray toward this place; O hear in heaven your dwelling place; heed and forgive.

my HIGH today was:

my LOW today was:

my PRAYER today is:

DAY 3

TODAY'S BIBLE VERSE:

Nehemiah 9:17

But you are a God ready to forgive, gracious and merciful, slow to anger and abounding in steadfast love...

my HIGH today was:

my LOW today was:

my PRAYER today is:

1. SHARE highs & lows of the day.

2. READ and highlight the verse of the day in your bibles.

3. TALK about how today's verse relates to your highs & lows.

4. PRAY for your highs & lows, for your family and for the world.

5. BLESS one another using this week's blessing (on the previous page).

my HIGH today was: ……………………………………

my LOW today was: ……………………………………

my PRAYER today is: ……………………………………

……………………………………

DAY 4

today's bible verse:

Psalm 51:9

Hide your face from my sins, and blot out all my iniquities.

Sorry

my HIGH today was: ……………………………………

my LOW today was: ……………………………………

my PRAYER today is: ……………………………………

……………………………………

DAY 5

today's bible verse:

Psalm 79:9

Help us, O God of our salvation, for the glory of your name; deliver us, and forgive our sins, for your name's sake.

my HIGH today was: ……………………………………

my LOW today was: ……………………………………

my PRAYER today is: ……………………………………

……………………………………

DAY 6

today's bible verse:

Jeremiah 31:34

No longer shall they teach one another, or say to each other, "Know the Lord," for they shall all know me, from the least of them to the greatest, says the Lord; for I will forgive their iniquity, and remember their sin no more.

S | M | T | W | TH | F | S

THEME IN REVIEW

BLAME KEEPS WOUNDS OPEN. ONLY FORGIVENESS HEALS.

WILLA CATHER

DAY 7

MY FAVORITE VERSE FROM THE THEME WAS:

SOME SAY WE ARE BECOMING MORE AND MORE THE PEOPLE GOD WANTS US TO BE...
YES... WELL...
FOR SOME REASON I DON'T FIND THAT THOUGHT ALL THAT COMFORTING...
SYNOD CONVO

LOOKING BACK ON THESE TWO WEEKS, MY HIGHEST HIGH WAS:

MY LOWEST LOW THESE PAST WEEKS WAS:

ONE WAY GOD ANSWERED MY PRAYERS WAS:

ONE WAY GOD MIGHT USE ME AS A SACRED AGENT TO ANSWER THESE PRAYERS:

FAMILY COVENANT

We have shared *Highs & Lows* this week, read and highlighted the verses assigned in our Bibles, talked about our lives, prayed for one another's highs and lows, and blessed one another.

Parent's Signature | *Teen's Signature* | *Date*

THE FINKMANIA QUIZ BOWL

Question 1:

According to Webster Online, the word "forgive" comes from the:

(A) Latin *forgifan*, meaning to present a gift,

(B) Old English *forgifan*, meaning to give up,

(C) Greek *forgiuos*, meaning stand before holding a gift,

(D) Norwegian *forgrugeun*, meaning to pretend to give up but continue to hold a grudge

Question 2:

Webster Online defines the word "forgive" as:

(A) To give up resentment of or claim for an insult or injury,

(B) To grant relief from payment,

(C) To cease to feel resentment against an offender,

(D) All of the above

Question 3:

In the Apostles' Creed, "I believe in the forgiveness of sins" refers to:

(A) God's forgiveness of us in Christ,

(B) Our forgiveness of others for Christ's sake,

(C) Both A and B,

(D) Neither A nor B

Question 4:

Why should we forgive others?:

(A) Jesus tells us to,

(B) Jesus tells us to,

(C) Jesus tells us to,

(D) All of the above, and it's a lot healthier way to live

Question 5:

People who don't forgive:

(A) Should not expect God to forgive them,

(B) Don't understand grace,

(C) Get more headaches, ulcers and hemorrhoids than people who do,

(D) A and B and sometimes C

Question 6:

In the Lord's Prayer, Jesus taught his disciples to pray: "Forgive us our sins...":

(A) "... because we deserve it,"

(B) "...as we forgive those who sin against us and are truly sorry,"

(C) "...as we forgive those who sin against us and pay us back,"

(D) "...as we forgive those who sin against us"

Question 7:

Jesus once saved a woman caught in adultery from being stoned to death. He told her:

(A) "Go and sin no more,"

(B) "Go and don't get caught again,"

(C) "Go and use protection,"

(D) "Just go"

Question 8:

According to I John 1:9, if we say we have no sin:

(A) We deceive ourselves,

(B) The truth is not in us,

(C) Both A and B,

(D) We should run for president

Question 9:

Mahatma Gandhi said, "An eye for an eye...":

(A) "...is what justice is all about,"

(B) "...makes the whole world see better,"

(C) "...makes the whole world blind,"

(D) "...is the American way"

FINKmania Final Question:

According to I John 1:9, if we confess our sins...:

(A) God will forgive us our sins,

(B) God will cleanse us from all unrighteousness,

(C) Both A and B,

(D) God will pretend they didn't happen

Play this online game using **FINKlink**

LL19 | @ www.faithink.com

THE WEAKEST FINK

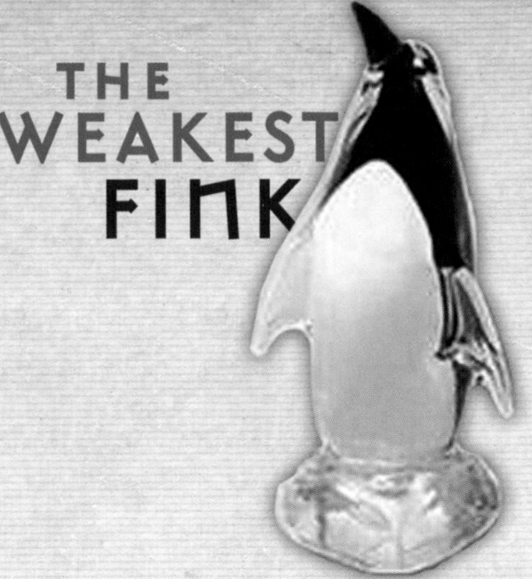

Always forgive your enemies. Nothing annoys them so much.

Oscar Wilde

TERMS

WRITE A DEFINITION BELOW.

Absolution

....

....

Confession

....

....

Forgiveness

....

....

Law

....

....

Sins

....

....

FAITH INKUBATORS

Resurrection and Eternal Life

"If we live, we live to the Lord, and if we die, we die to the Lord; so then, whether we live or whether we die, we are the Lord's. Listen, I will tell you a mystery! We will not all die, but we will all be changed, in a moment, in the twinkling of an eye, at the last trumpet. For the trumpet will sound, and the dead will be raised imperishable."

— Romans 14:8, I Corinthians 15:51–52

Listen to this song using FINKlink

LL20 @ www.faithink.com

Imagine what it would be like to be a caterpillar. You inch along in search of tender leaves. You munch away the day eating double your weight. Fat. Happy. Content.

Slowly you chew your food, oblivious to the future as your many legs pull you forward. You eat and eat and eat. Munch and munch and munch. Suddenly, a huge, black shadow crashes violently onto your branch, knocking some of your friends off. You can barely hang on. The crow pecks at the underside of your leaf, nabbing a fat green caterpillar just like you—swallowing him whole. Hanging on with only a few of your sticky feet, you are petrified by the thought of what might happen next. The crow hops toward you. He's seen you. He hops again. This time as he lands on the branch, the force of his weight shakes you loose. Just as he stabs at your body, you drop. Down you go, down, down. You land on top of a thistle plant. Feeling safer, you shake off the fall and glance around. To your amazement, you are surrounded by hundreds of silky grey pouches hanging from the underside of the leaves. What are they?

Crawling closer, you notice something move inside. Your eyes rivet onto the beings behind the cocoons. Soon one heaves outward, splitting the cloudy veil of woven webs lengthwise. A most beautiful winged creature struggles to emerge. The butterfly unfolds her wings and flaps them dry in the summer air. Then she flaps again, launching herself into the sunlight. She is big and colorful and lighter than the breeze. She soars high above the predators. Her only question is, "How high?" Now you start to feel an itching. Somewhere deep inside you know you'll soon join her. You will have to give up the life you know for the grander one that is to come. You must leave the earth, the crawling, the slow plodding body behind. You must be encased in this home-made box. You must die to the old ways and sleep. Then, and only then, will you emerge and become what you were meant to be. You will fly.

LIFE IS A GREAT SURPRISE. I DO NOT SEE WHY DEATH SHOULD BE AN EVEN GREATER ONE.

VLADIMIR NABOKOV

Resurrection and Eternal Life

Most people fear death. It is natural to be afraid of the unknown. Jesus promised he was preparing a place for his followers on the other side of the grave. He told the thief on the cross, "Truly I tell you, today you will be with me in Paradise." He taught that a grain of wheat must fall to the ground and be buried for it to rise in a new and wonderful form. He wept when his friend Lazarus died, but he didn't leave it at that. Jesus called the dead man back to life. Then, when all of his teaching on earth was done, he gave us the most powerful, world-changing example of all. He suffered. He died. He rose. And he broke the powerful chains of death forever. We don't know what the journey of death will be like, but we have a wonderful friend who has been there and come back to take us through.

Images in Art

- What do you see in today's painting by Dr. He Qi?
- Where are you in this work of art?
- How do the image and the verse apply to your life today?

So What Does This Mean?

IF IT'S TRUE THAT THE DEAD IN CHRIST WILL RISE FIRST THEN I HAVE A FEELING THAT THIS CONGREGATION IS GOING TO BE IN THE FRONT OF THE LINE...

I'm not afraid of death. I just don't want to be there when it happens.

Woody Allen

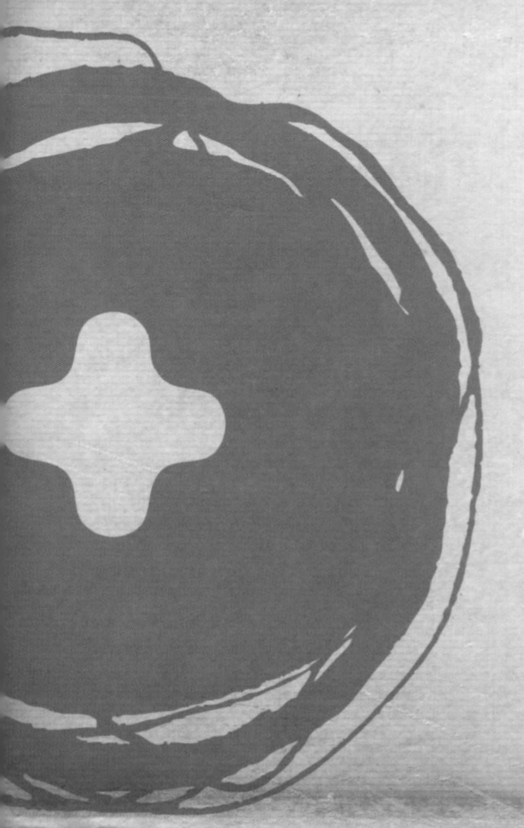

Bible Time

Jesus promises eternal life. He said he is preparing a place for you. You need not fear death. Your friend awaits you on the other side to bring you life. Read and highlight the following verses about life, death, and God's promises in your Bible, writing the word "resurrection" in the margin:

Job 19:25-26

Luke 24:1-12

Luke 24:44-49

Romans 14:8

I Corinthians 15:51-52

Catechism Encounter

Find Luther's explanation for the Third Article of the Apostles' Creed in your Small Catechism. What does Luther say Christ will do on the last day?

Questions to Ponder

1. How have you experienced the death of someone close to you? A relative? A friend? A pet? Write about your experience:

2. What do you believe happens after you die? On what do you base that belief?

3. What does the resurrection of Jesus mean to you? Why is it important?

4. How do you know Christ's promise of eternal life is true?

SMALL GROUP

SHARE, READ, TALK, PRAY, BLESS

1. **SHARE** your highs and lows of the week one-on-one with another person. Listen carefully and record your friend's thoughts in the space below. Then return to small group and share your friend's highs and lows.

   MY HIGHS + LOWS THIS WEEK WERE:

   ....

   MY FRIEND'S HIGHS + LOWS THIS WEEK WERE:

   ....

2. **READ** and highlight the theme verse in your Bibles. Circle key words and learn the verse in song if time permits.

3. **TALK** about how today's verse relates to your highs and lows. Review the art for today, the Quiz Bowl questions, the terms, and the cartoons. Then write a sentence on each of the following:

   ONE NEW THING I LEARNED TODAY:

   ....

   ONE THING I ALREADY KNEW THAT IS WORTH REPEATING:

   ....

   ONE THING I WOULD LIKE TO KNOW MORE ABOUT:

   ....

4. **PRAY** for one another, praising and thanking God for your highs, and asking God to be with you in your lows. Include your friend's highs and lows in your prayers.

   A PRAISING PRAYER: ....

   A THANKING PRAYER: ....

   AN ASKING PRAYER: ....

5. **BLESS** one another using the blessing of the week. (right) Mark each person with the sign of the cross as you bless them.

THIS WEEK'S BLESSING

(NAME), CHILD OF DUST: DUST YOU ARE AND TO DUST YOU SHALL RETURN. BUT MAY YOU DIE WITH THE WHISPER, "SURPRISE ME, JESUS," ON YOUR LIPS.

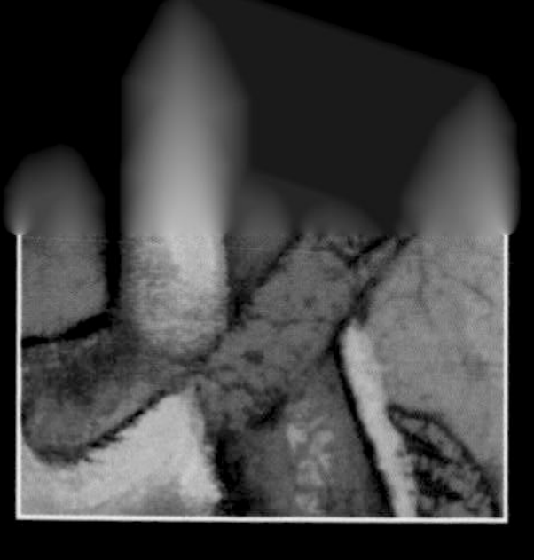

WEEK 1

FAITH JOURNAL

Read the full devotions using FINKlink
LL20 @ www.faithink.com

ADMIT ONE 566570

DAY 1

TODAY'S BIBLE VERSE:

Romans 14:8

If we live, we live to the Lord, and if we die, we die to the Lord; so then, whether we live or whether we die, we are the Lord's.

MY HIGH TODAY WAS:

MY LOW TODAY WAS:

MY PRAYER TODAY IS:

DAY 2

TODAY'S BIBLE VERSE:

1 Corinthians 15:51-52

Listen, I will tell you a mystery! We will not all die, but we will all be changed, in a moment, in the twinkling of an eye, at the last trumpet.

MY HIGH TODAY WAS:

MY LOW TODAY WAS:

MY PRAYER TODAY IS:

DAY 3

TODAY'S BIBLE VERSE:

Job 19:25-26

For I know that my Redeemer lives, and that at the last he will stand upon the earth; and after my skin has been thus destroyed, then in my flesh I shall see God.

MY HIGH TODAY WAS:

MY LOW TODAY WAS:

MY PRAYER TODAY IS:

my HIGH today was:

my LOW today was:

my PRAYER today is:

DAY 4

today's bible verse:

John 14:1-3

In my Father's house there are many dwelling places. If it were not so, would I have told you that I go to prepare a place for you? And if I go and prepare a place for you, I will come again and will take you to myself...

my HIGH today was:

my LOW today was:

my PRAYER today is:

DAY 5

today's bible verse:

Acts 10:40-41

God raised him on the third day and allowed him to appear, not to all the people but to us who were chosen by God as witnesses, and who ate and drank with him after he rose from the dead.

my HIGH today was:

my LOW today was:

my PRAYER today is:

DAY 6

today's bible verse:

Revelation 22:13

I am the Alpha and the Omega, the first and the last, the beginning and the end.

my HIGHEST HIGH this week was:

my LOWEST LOW this week was:

my PRAYER for next week is:

DAY 7

this week's blessing

(NAME), CHILD OF DUST: DUST YOU ARE AND TO DUST YOU SHALL RETURN. BUT MAY YOU DIE WITH THE WHISPER, "SURPRISE ME, JESUS," ON YOUR LIPS.

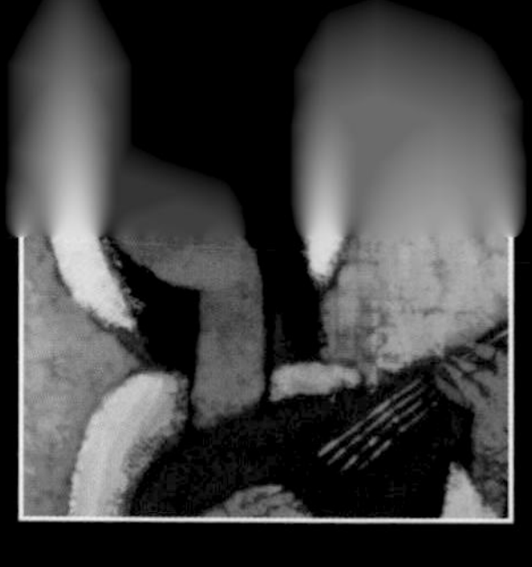

WEEK 2

FAITH JOURNAL

Read the full devotions using FINKlink
LL20 @ www.faithink.com

DAY 1

TODAY'S BIBLE VERSE:

MATTHEW 28:5-7

Do not be afraid; I know that you are looking for Jesus who was crucified. He is not here; for he has been raised, as he said. Come, see the place where he lay. Then go quickly and tell his disciples, "He has been raised from the dead…"

MY HIGH TODAY WAS:

MY LOW TODAY WAS:

MY PRAYER TODAY IS:

DAY 2

TODAY'S BIBLE VERSE:

JOHN 6:40

This is indeed the will of my Father, that all who see the Son and believe in him may have eternal life; and I will raise them up on the last day.

MY HIGH TODAY WAS:

MY LOW TODAY WAS:

MY PRAYER TODAY IS:

DAY 3

TODAY'S BIBLE VERSE:

JOHN 11:25-26

I am the resurrection and the life. Those who believe in me, even though they die, will live, and everyone who lives and believes in me will never die. Do you believe this?

MY HIGH TODAY WAS:

MY LOW TODAY WAS:

MY PRAYER TODAY IS:

1. SHARE highs & lows of the day.

2. READ and highlight the verse of the day in your bibles.

3. TALK about how today's verse relates to your highs & lows.

4. PRAY for your highs & lows, for your family and for the world.

5. BLESS one another using this week's blessing (on the previous page).

DAY 4

today's bible verse:

Psalm 118:22

The stone that the builders rejected has become the chief cornerstone.

my HIGH today was:

my LOW today was:

my PRAYER today is:

DAY 5

today's bible verse:

Isaiah 53:12b

He poured out himself to death, and was numbered with the transgressors; yet he bore the sin of many, and made intercession for the transgressors.

my HIGH today was:

my LOW today was:

my PRAYER today is:

DAY 6

today's bible verse:

Revelation 21:4

He will wipe every tear from their eyes. Death will be no more; mourning and crying and pain will be no more, for the first things have passed away.

my HIGH today was:

my LOW today was:

my PRAYER today is:

S | M | T | W | TH | F | S

THEME IN REVIEW

All people should strive to learn before they die what they are running from, and to, and why.

James Thurber

DAY 7

MY FAVORITE VERSE FROM THE THEME WAS:

Da Da Da Da Da Da
JESUS ROCKS!
YEA YEA YEA!
IF ETERNITY WITH JESUS IS ALREADY UNDERWAY, WHY WAIT UNTIL YOU'RE DEAD TO START THE PARTY?
YOU YOUNG PEOPLE ARE HAVING WAY TOO MUCH FUN FOR THIS TO BE WORSHIP!
HEY!
JC ROCKS
Melheim

LOOKING BACK ON THESE TWO WEEK, MY HIGHEST HIGH WAS:

MY LOWEST LOW THESE PAST WEEKS WAS:

ONE WAY GOD ANSWERED MY PRAYERS WAS:

ONE WAY GOD MIGHT USE ME AS A SACRED AGENT TO ANSWER THESE PRAYERS:

FAMILY COVENANT

We have shared *Highs & Lows* this week, read and highlighted the verses assigned in our Bible, talked about our lives, prayed for one another's highs and lows, and blessed one another.

Parent's Signature | *Teen's Signature* | *Date*

THE FINKMANIA QUIZ BOWL

QUESTION 1:

The Third Article of the Apostles' Creed is:

(A) "I believe in the Holy Spirit,"

(B) "I believe in the Holy Spirit and the holy catholic (Christian) church,"

(C) "I believe in the Holy Spirit and the holy catholic (Christian) church, the communion of saints, the forgiveness of sins,"

(D) C, plus "the resurrection of the body and life everlasting"

QUESTION 2:

We can count on God's promise of eternal life because:

(A) We have a signed and notarized document on file,

(B) Our pastor tells us so,

(C) God sealed this promise with the blood Jesus and the power of his resurrection,

(D) It was on Oprah

QUESTION 3:

When Jesus rose on Easter, he defeated:

(A) A Roman betting pool,

(B) Death,

(C) The Pittsburgh Steelers,

(D) None of the above

QUESTION 4:

Jesus is different from all other great religious teachers because:

(A) He was the smartest,

(B) He was a better teacher,

(C) He had better-looking disciples,

(D) He rose from death, proving he was God's only Son

QUESTION 5:

The change from death to life is called the:

(A) Election of the Dead,

(B) Resurrection of the Dead,

(C) Reflection of the Dead,

(D) Grateful Dead

QUESTION 6:

Death is often frightening because:

(A) It is unknown,

(B) It is the end of our earthly bodies,

(C) It is often associated with pain and suffering,

(D) All of the above and then some

QUESTION 7:

The reason Christians don't need to fear death is because:

(A) Christ's love and power are stronger than death,

(B) Jesus is waiting on the other side of death to take care of us,

(C) Losing 70 years is nothing compared to gaining eternity,

(D) All of the above and then some

QUESTION 8:

Because of Jesus' resurrection, you get:

(A) A "Get out of Hell" card,

(B) Free Parking (in heaven),

(C) A hotel on St. James Place,

(D) When you think about it, both A & B are pretty good answers

QUESTION 9:

Without the promise of the resurrection:

(A) Life would be empty, frightening, and meaningless for most people,

(B) Death would be empty, frightening, and meaningless for most people,

(C) Both A & B,

(D) My pastor would be out of work

FINKMANIA FINAL QUESTION:

In Romans 14:8, St. Paul writes, "If we live, we live to the Lord, and if we die...":

(A) "...we turn to dust,"

(B) "...we die to the Lord,"

(C) "...we sleep with the Saints,"

(D) "...that's it, but it was a nice run while it lasted"

Play this online game using **FINKlink**

LL20 | **@ www.faithink.com**

THE WEAKEST FINK

WHAT IF YOU'RE A REALLY GOOD PERSON, BUT YOU GET INTO A REALLY, REALLY BAD FIGHT AND YOUR LEG GETS GANGRENE AND IT HAS TO BE AMPUTATED. WILL IT BE WAITING FOR YOU IN HEAVEN?

BART SIMPSON

TERMS

WRITE A DEFINITION BELOW.

DEATH

....

....

ETERNAL LIFE

....

....

ETERNITY

....

....

PROMISE

....

....

RESURRECTION

....

....

FAITH INKUBATORS

LUTHERAN LIFE

1. ONE LORD, FAITH AND BAPTISM
2. NEWNESS OF LIFE
3. PASSOVER TO LAST SUPPER
4. TASTE AND SEE
5. WORSHIP: THE GATHERING
6. WORSHIP: THE WORD
7. WORSHIP: MEAL AND SENDING
8. CONFESSING MY FAITH
9. CONFIRMING MY CONVICTIONS
10. CLAIMING MY CALLING

One Lord, Faith and Baptism

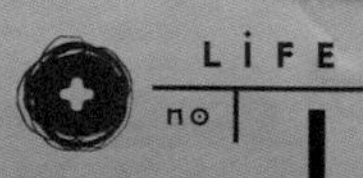

"Baptism of Jesus (2004)" Copyright © Dr. He Qi www.heqigallery.com

"There is one body and one Spirit, just as you were called to the one hope of your calling, one Lord, one faith, one baptism, one God and Father of all, who is above all and through all and in all."

— Ephesians 4:4-6

Listen to this song using FINKlink LL21 @ www.faithink.com

Anne, Cole, Elizabeth, Tyronne, Jeremy, Brody, Cameron, McKenna, Mikayla, Ellie, Hanna, Blake, Madeline, Shantelle, Erik, Nicholas, Andrew, Julianna, Song...

Do you know what your name means? Do you know who chose your name for you and why they chose it? Are you named after a famous person, an ancestor, or a family friend? People sometimes run into problems when naming babies. Can they give a child the same name they gave their dog? What if a new mother finds a baby name she loves, but the initials spell a bad word?

What's in a name? Does the name you give a baby matter? Does it set a boy up for success if you give him a power name like Daunte or Duke or Washington? Does it change a girl's personality and future if you name her Queen or Sissy or Patsy? Sometimes a name expresses family loyalty and tradition. Sometimes a name can show flare and originality. Some names convey subtle messages about who we are and what we want. Sometimes a name says more about the parent than the child. Experts who research such matters are unclear about whether a name actually influences a person's success. Some believe names are more an indicator of one's family and economic circumstances than a predictor of the child's future. Some say the name will change a child's future and become part of their identity. It may affect or alter the face they present to the world, the way people treat them, and how they think of themselves.

There was once a day when you were not my child, but from this day on—no matter what you do—there will never be a day that you will not be mine.

Dick Lowey
(To his adopted son)

One Lord, Faith, Baptism

In baptism, God gave you a new name: Christian! Although you were always precious to your Creator, on that day you were claimed and named by God in a special way. Just as a last name connects you with a family, a history, and a heritage, the name Christian connects you with a new family—the church. Just as an adopted child inherits a new family along with the new name, in baptism you inherited aunts, uncles, and cousins who all bear that same name and all pledge to be part of your future.

Even more important than the new family, in baptism, you are connected to Christ. In Christ, God begins something new in you! A new heart. A new spirit. A new hope and calling. A new name. And with it all, a new identity.

Although there are millions of names in the world and billions of people, there is only one you. Even if someone else claims your same name, you are unique, special, precious, and known by God. More than that: you are God's child.

Hey you... what's your name?

Order this art print using FINKlink
LL21
@ www.faithink.com

Images in Art

- What do you see in today's painting by Dr. He Qi?
- Where are you in this work of art?
- How do the image and the verse apply to your life today?

So What Does This Mean?

THAT'S "THE GREAT COMMISSION," FENSTER.
NOT "THE GREAT OMISSION."
YOU OBVIOUSLY DON'T KNOW MUCH ABOUT THIS HERE CHURCH, DO YOU?

Baptizing Babies?

Some churches practice "believer baptism" and say a person must be old enough to reject sin and choose Christ in order to be baptized. This is John the Baptist's type of baptism—a baptism of repentance to prepare the way for Jesus. Since babies can't repent or choose Jesus, these churches don't baptize babies. Lutherans see baptism in a different light. From the earliest accounts of the church in the book of Acts, whole families were baptized into Christ. The earliest Christian art in the Catacombs of Rome showed the first followers of Jesus baptizing both adults and infants. The important thing was not how old one was, but plugging into the body of Christ—the church—where a child could grow in faith, hope, love and obedience to the Word of God.

Bible Time

Read and highlight Ephesians 4:6. Underline all of the "one" words in the verses, and circle all of the words that follow the "one" word. What do the circled words tell you about who you are as a baptized member of the body of Christ?

Read and highlight Ezekiel 36:24-28. Circle all of the action words. Every one of these words has a promise. What are some of the promises?

1.

2.

3.

Prayer

Dear God, I am glad you know my name. Thank you for claiming me, naming me and bringing me into your forever family. In Jesus' name. Amen.

Catechism Encounter

Scan Luther's explanation of the Sacrament of Holy Baptism. What happens in Baptism according to Luther?

Questions to Ponder

1. Do you know what your name means? Do you know who named you and why your name was chosen?

2. What words are spoken at baptism in the Lutheran church? Does it matter what words are spoken at a Christian baptism? Why or why not?

3. A friend says, "You can't baptize babies because they are not old enough to repent and accept Jesus." How do you answer?

Small Group

share, read, talk, pray, bless

1. **SHARE** your highs and lows of the week one-on-one with another person. Listen carefully and record your friend's thoughts in the space below. Then return to small group and share your friend's highs and lows.

my highs + lows this week were:

....

my friend's highs + lows this week were:

....

2. **READ** and highlight the theme verse in your Bibles. Circle key words and learn the verse in song.

3. **TALK** about how today's verse relates to your highs and lows. Review the art for today, the Quiz Bowl questions, the terms, and the cartoons. Then write a sentence on each of the following:

one new thing i learned today:

....

one thing i already knew that is worth repeating:

....

one thing i would like to know more about:

....

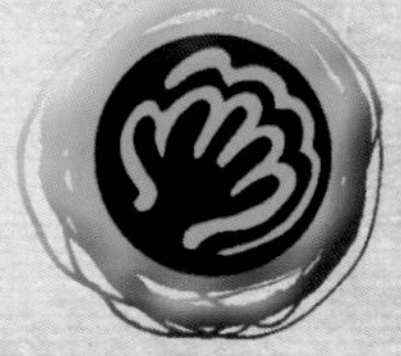

4. **PRAY** for one another, praising and thanking God for your highs, and asking God to be with you in your lows. Include your friend's highs and lows in your prayers.

a praising prayer: ....

a thanking prayer: ....

an asking prayer: ....

5. **BLESS** one another using the blessing of the week. (right) Mark each person with the sign of the cross as you bless them.

this week's blessing

(Name), child of God, you have been sealed by the Holy Spirit and marked with the cross of Christ forever.

WEEK 1

THE FAITH 5 JOURNAL

Read the full devotions using FINKlink LL21 @ www.faithink.com

DAY 1

TODAY'S BIBLE VERSE:

Ephesians 4:4-6

There is one body and one Spirit, just as you were called to the one hope of your calling, one Lord, one faith, one baptism, one God and Father of all, who is above all and through all and in all.

MY HIGH TODAY WAS:

MY LOW TODAY WAS:

MY PRAYER TODAY IS:

DAY 2

TODAY'S BIBLE VERSE:

Luke 3:16

(John said) "I baptize you with water; but one who is more powerful than I is coming; I am not worthy to untie the thong of his sandals. He will baptize you with the Holy Spirit and fire."

MY HIGH TODAY WAS:

MY LOW TODAY WAS:

MY PRAYER TODAY IS:

DAY 3

TODAY'S BIBLE VERSE:

Matthew 3:13-14

Then Jesus came from Galilee to John at the Jordan, to be baptized by him. John would have prevented him, saying, "I need to be baptized by you, and do you come to me?"

MY HIGH TODAY WAS:

MY LOW TODAY WAS:

MY PRAYER TODAY IS:

my HIGH today was:

my LOW today was:

my PRAYER today is:

DAY 4

today's bible verse:

Matthew 3:15

Jesus answered him (John), "Let it be so now; for it is proper for us in this way to fulfill all righteousness."

my HIGH today was:

my LOW today was:

my PRAYER today is:

DAY 5

today's bible verse:

Matthew 3:16

And when Jesus had been baptized, just as he came up from the water, suddenly the heavens were opened to him and he saw the Spirit of God descending like a dove and alighting on him.

my HIGH today was:

my LOW today was:

my PRAYER today is:

DAY 6

today's bible verse:

Matthew 3:17

And a voice from heaven said, "This is my Son, the Beloved, with whom I am well pleased."

my HIGH today was:

OW today was:

PRAYER today is:

DAY 7

this week's blessing

(NAME), CHILD OF GOD, YOU HAVE BEEN SEALED BY THE HOLY SPIRIT AND MARKED WITH THE CROSS OF CHRIST FOREVER.

THE FAITH5

Read the full devotions using FINKlink
LL21 @ www.faithink.com

JOURNAL

WEEK 2

DAY 1

TODAY'S BIBLE VERSE:

JEREMIAH 1:5

Before I formed you in the womb I knew you, and before you were born I consecrated you; I appointed you a prophet to the nations.

MY HIGH TODAY WAS:

MY LOW TODAY WAS:

MY PRAYER TODAY IS:

DAY 2

TODAY'S BIBLE VERSE:

MARK 10:14

Let the little children come to me; do not stop them; for it is to such as these that the kingdom of God belongs.

MY HIGH TODAY WAS:

MY LOW TODAY WAS:

MY PRAYER TODAY IS:

DAY 3

TODAY'S BIBLE VERSE:

MARK 10:15

Truly I tell you, whoever does not receive the kingdom of God as a little child will never enter it.

MY HIGH TODAY WAS:

MY LOW TODAY WAS:

MY PRAYER TODAY IS:

1. SHARE HIGHS & LOWS OF THE DAY.
2. READ AND HIGHLIGHT THE VERSE OF THE DAY IN YOUR BIBLES.
3. TALK ABOUT HOW TODAY'S VERSE RELATES TO YOUR HIGHS & LOWS.
4. PRAY FOR YOUR HIGHS & LOWS, FOR YOUR FAMILY AND FOR THE WORLD.
5. BLESS ONE ANOTHER USING THIS WEEK'S BLESSING (ON THE PREVIOUS PAGE).

DAY 4

TODAY'S BIBLE VERSE:

PROVERBS 22:6

Train children in the right way, and when old, they will not stray.

MY HIGH TODAY WAS:

MY LOW TODAY WAS:

MY PRAYER TODAY IS:

DAY 5

TODAY'S BIBLE VERSE:

Acts 16:33

At the same hour of the night he took them and washed their wounds; then he and his entire family were baptized without delay.

MY HIGH TODAY WAS:

MY LOW TODAY WAS:

MY PRAYER TODAY IS:

DAY 6

TODAY'S BIBLE VERSE:

I CORINTHIANS 12:13

For in the one Spirit we were all baptized into one body—Jews or Greeks, slaves or free—and we were all made to drink of one Spirit.

MY HIGH TODAY WAS:

MY LOW TODAY WAS:

MY PRAYER TODAY IS:

S | M | T | W | TH | F | S

THEME IN REVIEW

JOHN SAID "I BAPTIZE YOU WITH WATER BUT THERE IS ONE COMING AFTER ME WHO WILL BAPTIZE YOU WITH THE HOLY SPIRIT AND FIRE.

WHOA. FIRE

SURF

FINK FACTOID

TOP BABY NAMES IN USA:

EMMA & AIDAN

TOP BABY NAMES IN ENGLAND:

CHLOE & JACK

DAY 7

MY FAVORITE VERSE FROM THE THEME WAS:

....

....

....

....

....

....

....

....

LOOKING BACK ON THESE TWO WEEKS, MY HIGHEST HIGH WAS:

....

MY LOWEST LOW THESE PAST WEEKS WAS:

....

ONE WAY GOD ANSWERED MY PRAYERS WAS:

....

ONE WAY GOD MIGHT USE ME AS A SACRED AGENT TO ANSWER THESE PRAYERS:

....

....

FAMILY COVENANT

We have shared *Highs & Lows* this week, read and highlighted the verses assigned in our Bibles talked about our lives, prayed for one another's highs and lows, and blessed one another.

....	....	....
Parent's Signature	*Teen's Signature*	*Date*

THE FINKMANIA QUIZBOWL

QUESTION 1:

A disciple is:

(A) A person who sells Frisbee discs,
(B) A person who likes disco,
(C) A faithful follower,
(D) A person who puts others down

QUESTION 2:

Jesus commanded his followers to:

(A) Sit and wait,
(B) Baptize and teach,
(C) Stand up and cheer,
(D) Be quiet and listen to the lecture

QUESTION 3:

Jesus promised his followers:

(A) I will be back next Tuesday,
(B) I will miss you,
(C) I will make you financially better off,
(D) I will be with you always

QUESTION 4:

We become disciples of Christ by:

(A) Loving Jesus and living the way Jesus taught,
(B) Trying to be perfect,
(C) Entering a "Holiest Person" contest,
(D) Winning the lottery

QUESTION 5:

Baptism is necessary because:

(A) It keeps pastors employed,
(B) It keeps churches busy,
(C) Jesus commanded it and said it was even necessary for himself,
(D) It uses up extra water

QUESTION 6:

You can "baptize and teach" if you're not a pastor by:

(A) Becoming ordained,
(B) Getting a special permit,
(C) Watching pastors and being perfect like they are,
(D) Bringing friends to Christ, inviting them to church and living a Christ-like example

QUESTION 7:

We can make use of our baptism:

(A) By remembering God's grace and living a forgiving, forgiven lifestyle,
(B) By auctioning it on eBay,
(C) As a "get out of hell" free card,
(D) None of the above

QUESTION 8:

To be "called" by God means:

(A) To be chosen for a purpose,
(B) To be a good listener, but nothing else,
(C) To be perfect,
(D) None of the above

QUESTION 9:

The Great Commission is:

(A) The Supreme Court,
(B) The United Nations,
(C) The Christian's job to go out into the world and tell all nations about Jesus,
(D) The extra price people pay on cars to the salespeople

FINKMANIA FINAL QUESTION:

Ephesians 4:6 tells us:

(A) There is one body of Christ,
(B) There is one Lord, one faith and one baptism,
(C) There is one God and father of all,
(D) All of the above

Play this online game using **FINKlink**
LL21 @ www.faithink.com

THE WEAKEST FINK

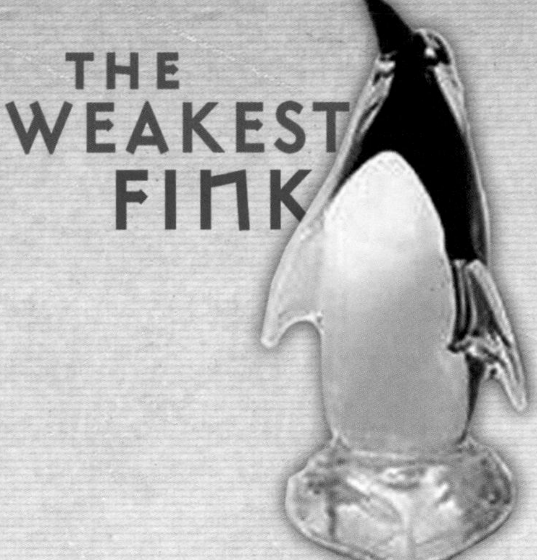

LIFE IS EASIER THAN YOU'D THINK; ALL THAT IS NECESSARY IS TO ACCEPT THE IMPOSSIBLE, DO WITHOUT THE INDISPENSABLE, AND BEAR THE INTOLERABLE.

KATHLEEN NORRIS

TERMS

WRITE A DEFINITION BELOW.

ADOPTION

....

....

BAPTISM

....

....

CHRISTIAN

....

....

INHERIT

....

....

PROMISE

....

....

LIFE no 2

Newness of Life

"Jonah and the Whale" Copyright © Dr. He Qi www.heqigallery.com

"Do you not know that all of us who have been baptized into Christ Jesus were baptized into his death? Therefore we have been buried with him by baptism into death, so that, just as Christ was raised from the dead by the glory of the Father, so we too might walk in newness of life."

— Romans 6:3-4

Listen to this song using FINKlink LL22 @ www.faithink.com

The sun is blocked by a dense cover of clouds. It begins to drizzle. Soon the drizzle turns to rain. The jungle path becomes mud under your feet. Cold greenish-brown muck.

Now the rain turns to a down-pour. It hits you in sheets, then waves. You slosh along, then stop. Slowly you realize the path beneath you is beginning to sink. You step off the path onto a dead tree, but the rotting trunk gives way and you sink knee deep in the slop. You tear at your legs to free them. One foot comes loose, but your boot remains buried below. You fall head-first into the slime, flailing frantically, but there is nothing solid to hold. You are sinking, sinking, sinking into the watery coffin. Past your waist. Past your shoulders. In one frantic moment you realize this could be the end. Your chin is covered. The ooze is pulling you down. The more you fight, the faster you sink. You take a deep breath, gasping as your head goes under. One last breath. Your body struggles until it can struggle no more. Your groping fingers go limp.

Suddenly, a strong arm digs into the mud and snatches your wrist. It pulls and pulls. You feel yourself rising beyond the powerful suction of the pit. You draw your first erratic breath, coughing and spitting. You struggle to open your clouded, muddied eyes, but you cannot see your savior. You collapse in strong arms, your body too weak to move, and pass out. As you come slowly to consciousness, you are aware that you are being carried down a path. A warm, gentle rain washes you clean. You look up into a face and see the silhouette of a man eclipsed by a halo of sunlight. You are placed gently down into a warm, clear stream. Cleansing waters rush over you and the mud washes away. In the back of your mind you hear these words:

"I waited patiently for the Lord; he inclined to me and heard my cry. He drew me up from the desolate pit, out of the miry bog, and set my feet upon a rock, making my steps secure" (Psalm 40). You fade away, then back, but your savior is gone. All that is left is the echo of the words, "Walk in newness of life!"

Newness of Life

The Bible calls baptism many things. It is a washing. It is a "regeneration" (making something new again). It is a burial and a death of the old, sinful self and a rising to new life. It is God reaching out to us with the long arms of love, pulling us out of the old mire of our original sin and drawing us into new life in Christ!

Drown the old, rise to the new! Have you experienced the daily rising to new life? Every morning you can trace the sign of the cross on your forehead, for you have new life in Christ!

To put it most simply, the power, effect, benefit, fruit and purpose of Baptism is to save.

To be saved, we know, is nothing else than to be delivered from sin, death, and the devil and to enter into the kingdom of Christ and to live with him forever.

Martin Luther
The Large Catechism

Order this art print using FINKlink
LL22 @ www.faithink.com

Images in Art

- What do you see in today's painting by Dr. He Qi?
- Where are you in this work of art?
- How do the image and the verse apply to your life today?

So What Does This Mean?

I'M ALL FOR THE "NEWNESS OF LIFE" BUSINESS, BUT COULDN'T WE JUST SKIP THE "DYING TO SIN" PART?

Immersion vs Sprinkling?

In some Christian traditions, people are dunked under water during baptism to symbolize the drowning of the old ways and rising to new life. This can be a beautiful and meaningful practice. Lutherans can baptise in this way if they wish, but do not see it as necessary for baptism to be valid. It is not the amount of water used or the symbolic ritual of immersion that counts. We aren't the primary actors in Baptism—God is! Lutherans believe it is not our actions, motions, or correctness in the ceremony that count. God is the Giver. We are the receivers of the gift. God is the adopter. We are the children brought into the family. Like an adopted child, we grow to understand our inheritance and acceptance into the family over time.

Bible Time

Most people love to get presents. On our baptism day, we probably received many gifts from friends and family celebrating the joyous celebration! What is often forgotten are the gifts that are ours every day. Read and highlight Romans 6:3-4, writing "Newness" in the margin. Next, read and highlight the verses below. By each verse, write the gift that is given through baptism. Is this a gift you have received?

John 3:5
John 15:5
Acts 22:16
2 Corinthians 1: 21-22
Galatians 3: 27-28
Ephesians 1: 3-5
Colossians 1: 13-14

Prayer

Dear Jesus, thank you for pulling me out of the muck of my sin and saving me. Help me to die to sin and rise to newness of life this day and every day. Amen.

Catechism Encounter

Scan Luther's explanation of the Sacrament of Holy Baptism. What are the benefits of Baptism according to Luther?:

Questions to Ponder

1. How is sin like mud? How is sin like quicksand?

2. There are seven different meanings for the word "baptize" in Greek (the New Testament language). They include to dip, to submerge, to wash and to sprinkle. Can any or all of these be used for a baptism? Why or why not?

3. A friend says, "If you aren't totally immersed under water, you aren't really baptized." How do you answer?

Small Group

Share, Read, Talk, Pray, Bless

1. **SHARE** your highs and lows of the week one-on-one with another person. Listen carefully and record your friend's thoughts in the space below. Then return to small group and share your friend's highs and lows.

   MY HIGHS + LOWS THIS WEEK WERE:

   ....

   MY FRIEND'S HIGHS + LOWS THIS WEEK WERE:

   ....

2. **READ** and highlight the theme verse in your Bibles. Circle key words and learn the verse in song.

3. **TALK** about how today's verse relates to your highs and lows. Review the art for today, the Quiz Bowl questions, the terms, and the cartoons. Then write a sentence on each of the following:

   ONE NEW THING I LEARNED TODAY:

   ....

   ONE THING I ALREADY KNEW THAT IS WORTH REPEATING:

   ....

   ONE THING I WOULD LIKE TO KNOW MORE ABOUT:

   ....

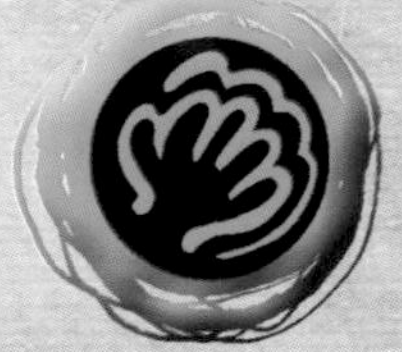

4. **PRAY** for one another, praising and thanking God for your highs, and asking God to be with you in your lows. Include your friend's highs and lows in your prayers.

   A PRAISING PRAYER: ....

   A THANKING PRAYER: ....

   AN ASKING PRAYER: ....

5. **BLESS** one another using the blessing of the week. (right) Mark each person with the sign of the cross as you bless them.

THIS WEEK'S BLESSING

(NAME), CHILD OF GOD, MAY YOU DIE TO SIN AND RISE TO NEWNESS OF LIFE THIS DAY.

THE FAITH5 JOURNAL

WEEK 1

Read the full devotions using FINKlink LL22 @ www.faithink.com

DAY 1

TODAY'S BIBLE VERSE:

Romans 6:3

Do you not know that all of us who have been baptized into Christ Jesus were baptized into his death?

MY HIGH TODAY WAS:

MY LOW TODAY WAS:

MY PRAYER TODAY IS:

DAY 2

TODAY'S BIBLE VERSE:

Romans 6:4

Therefore we have been buried with him by baptism into death, so that, just as Christ was raised from the dead by the glory of the Father, so we too might walk in newness of life.

MY HIGH TODAY WAS:

MY LOW TODAY WAS:

MY PRAYER TODAY IS:

DAY 3

TODAY'S BIBLE VERSE:

Isaiah 53:6

All we like sheep have gone astray; we have all turned to our own way, and the Lord has laid on him the iniquity of us all.

MY HIGH TODAY WAS:

MY LOW TODAY WAS:

MY PRAYER TODAY IS:

my HIGH today was:

my LOW today was:

my PRAYER today is:

DAY 4

today's bible verse:

Acts 2:38

Repent, and be baptized every one of you in the name of Jesus Christ so that your sins may be forgiven; and you will receive the gift of the Holy Spirit.

my HIGH today was:

my LOW today was:

my PRAYER today is:

DAY 5

today's bible verse:

Ephesians 5:25b-26

Christ loved the church and gave himself up for her, in order to make her holy by cleansing her with the washing of water by the word.

my HIGH today was:

my LOW today was:

my PRAYER today is:

DAY 6

today's bible verse:

1 Peter 3:21-22

And baptism, which this prefigured, now saves you—not as a removal of dirt from the body, but as an appeal to God for a good conscience, through the resurrection of Jesus Christ.

my HIGH today was:

my LOW today was:

my PRAYER today is:

DAY 7

this week's blessing

(NAME), CHILD OF GOD, MAY YOU DIE TO SIN AND RISE TO NEWNESS OF LIFE THIS DAY.

Read the full devotions using FINKlink
LL22 @ www.faithink.com

FAITH JOURNAL

WEEK 2

DAY 1

TODAY'S BIBLE VERSE:

JOHN 3:5-6

Very truly, I tell you, no one can enter the kingdom of God without being born of water and Spirit. What is born of the flesh is flesh, and what is born of the Spirit is spirit.

MY HIGH TODAY WAS:

MY LOW TODAY WAS:

MY PRAYER TODAY IS:

DAY 2

TODAY'S BIBLE VERSE:

JOHN 15:5

I am the vine, you are the branches. Those who abide in me and I in them bear much fruit, because apart from me you can do nothing.

MY HIGH TODAY WAS:

MY LOW TODAY WAS:

MY PRAYER TODAY IS:

DAY 3

TODAY'S BIBLE VERSE:

Acts 16:30

Then he brought them outside and said, "Sirs, what must I do to be saved?"

MY HIGH TODAY WAS:

MY LOW TODAY WAS:

MY PRAYER TODAY IS:

1. SHARE highs & lows of the day.

2. READ and highlight the verse of the day in your bibles.

3. TALK about how today's verse relates to your highs & lows.

4. PRAY for your highs & lows, for your family and for the world.

5. BLESS one another using this week's blessing (on the previous page).

DAY 4

today's bible verse:

Acts 22:16

And now why do you delay? Get up, be baptized, and have your sins washed away, calling on his name.

my HIGH today was:

my LOW today was:

my PRAYER today is:

DAY 5

today's bible verse:

Ephesians 1:15-16

I have heard of your faith in the Lord Jesus and your love toward all the saints, and for this reason I do not cease to give thanks for you as I remember you in my prayers.

my HIGH today was:

my LOW today was:

my PRAYER today is:

DAY 6

today's bible verse:

Ephesians 1:17-18

The God of our Lord Jesus... give you a spirit of wisdom and revelation as you come to know him, so that, with the eyes of your heart enlightened, you may know what is the hope to which he has called you...

my HIGH today was:

my LOW today was:

my PRAYER today is:

S | M | T | W | TH | F | S

THEME IN REVIEW

Baptism is not a bath, but a funeral bier. If it were a bath, you would need it again and again. But since it is a death and new life, it is a once for all picture of the transformation that has taken place in our lives.

Anders

DAY 7

My favorite VERSE from the theme was:

....

....

....

....

....

....

....

....

....

Looking back on these two weeks, my highest HIGH was:

....

My lowest LOW these past weeks was:

....

One way God answered my PRAYERS was:

....

One way God might use me as a SACRED AGENT to answer these prayers:

....

....

Family Covenant

We have shared *Highs & Lows* this week, read and highlighted the verses assigned in our Bibles, talked about our lives, prayed for one another's highs and lows, and blessed one another.

....

Parent's Signature *Teen's Signature* *Date*

The Finkmania Quiz Bowl

Question 1:

The gifts we receive on our baptism day are:

(A) Liberation from sin and death and and a new adopted family (the church),
(B) New car and a year's supply of gas,
(C) New shoes and a sweater,
(D) A pair of socks and a T-shirt

Question 2:

We remember our baptism because:

(A) It helps us remember that we have been claimed by Christ,
(B) If we don't, no one will,
(C) Our pastor tells us to,
(D) It's better than remembering how dorky we looked in grade school

Question 3:

Baptism like shedding skin because:

(A) We get baptized while crawling on our bellies like a snake,
(B) We "shed" our sinful selves for new life,
(C) We sometimes wear a robe which we take off later,
(D) We lose a good chunk of skin afterwards

Question 4:

A major benefit of baptism is:

(A) New life in Christ,
(B) Money,
(C) Applause from the congregation,
(D) Free 8x10 glossies

Question 5:

Words are spoken over the water in baptism because:

(A) We don't like silence,
(B) Pastors are paid by the number of words they speak,
(C) God's word is the sign and holy seal of baptism,
(D) A good speaking voice is pleasing to God

Question 6:

We baptize babies:

(A) Because the first disciples of Jesus baptized whole households,
(B) Because Jesus said, "let the little children come to me,"
(C) A and B,
(D) Good question. Ask your pastor

Question 7:

"Newness of life" means:

(A) In baptism we are cleansed and reborn to live our life in Christ,
(B) Once we are baptized we'll never sin again,
(C) We need to always use new water in a baptism,
(D) None of the above

Question 8:

"Original sin" is:

(A) Like KFC's "Original Recipe,"
(B) The first sin you commit after turning 18,
(C) The sinful nature we are born with as humans,
(D) A new dance club

Question 9:

The resurrection is:

(A) A new movie starring Brad Pitt,
(B) The event of Easter morning where Jesus rose from the dead,
(C) What the lunch lady does with last week's meat loaf,
(D) All of the above

Finkmania Final Question:

Romans 6:3-4, the verse of the week tells us:

(A) Being buried can be fun,
(B) We should walk a mile everyday,
(C) Jesus buries us in paperwork during confirmation,
(D) Just as Christ died and rose again, through baptism we die to the old sinful self and rise to newness of life

Play this online game using FINKlink
LL22
@ www.faithink.com

The Weakest Fink

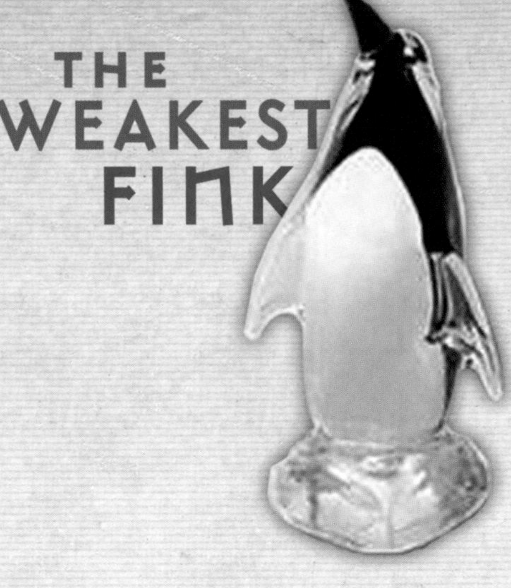

My Baptism was a Wash & Wear Event.

Bumper Sticker

Terms

Write a definition below.

Baptism

....

....

Believer Baptism

....

....

Immersion

....

....

New Life

....

....

Repentance

....

....

LiFE no 3

Passover to Last Supper

"Gideon and the Angel" Copyright © Dr. He Qi www.heqigallery.com

"The cup of blessing that we bless, is it not a sharing in the blood of Christ? The bread that we break, is it not a sharing in the body of Christ? Because there is one bread, we who are many are one body, for we all partake of the one bread."

— I Corinthians 10:16-17

Listen to this song using FINKlink
LL23 @ www.faithink.com

They huddled in their slave quarters on the darkest night of the year behind locked, blood-stained doors. At midnight the shrieks and cries began. First from one house, then to another.

Something terrible was happening. Something terrible and wonderful that would soon buy them their freedom. The Angel of Death was passing over the land. In the homes of the faithful who had covered their door posts with the blood of a sacrificial lamb, all of the children were spared. In the homes that laughed at God—those who had not made the sacrifice—the first-born sons were dying. Soon they would be granted their freedom. Soon they would make their exodus into the wilderness. Soon all would know their God was the one true God. Soon they would return to the land promised their ancestor Abraham. But for now they waited and wondered and prayed in terror and hope. The sacrifice had been made. Their freedom was at hand.

Passover to Last Supper

It was another Passover night over a millennium later. All through the land faithful Jews were gathering with family and friends to share a special meal and celebrate the central saving act in their history. Jesus, knowing his time on earth was short, asked his disciples to find a place they could share this one last supper together. They reserved an upper room and arranged for the traditional meal of unleavened (flat) bread, roast lamb, bitter herbs and wine. At one point in the meal, as they reclined around the customary low table, Jesus rose, took the bread, broke it, and departed from the Passover script. "This is my body, broken for you," he said. "Do this in remembrance of me." What could he mean? How would his body be broken? His disciples each took a piece and ate, wondering. Then he raised the cup, blessed it and gave thanks saying something even more strange. "This cup is the new testament in my blood shed for you and for many for the forgiveness of sins. Do this in remembrance of me."

They had no way of knowing, but their Lord knew. Hours later his body would be broken for them. His blood would be spilled for the sin of the world. Soon he would be taken. Soon he would be beaten and bloodied. Soon he would be whipped beyond recognition and nailed to a criminal's cross. Soon the Lamb of God who came to take away the sin of the world would be sacrificed. And the blood of that spotless lamb would not be smeared on the door posts of a thousand homes, but on the door post of a cross.

A wooden cross would be the door that opened the world to forgiveness, freedom and life.

2000 Years have come and gone. Today 2.2 billion people kneel in humble thanks and joy to celebrate the new Passover we call Holy Communion. We kneel as slaves, waiting for freedom. No Angel of Death appears, but an Angel of Life! Christ, himself, comes to bring us forgiveness. We kneel as disciples, waiting for a gift from our Master. No simple symbol is presented, but a living symbol and more! Christ, himself, comes to us in, with, and under the bread and wine to give us life .

Images in Art

- What do you see in today's painting by Dr. He Qi?
- Where are you in this work of art?
- How do the image and the verse apply to your life today?

So What Does This Mean?

THINK OF IT THIS WAY, REV.: THE DISCIPLES DID NOT KNOW THE WORDS OF INSTITUTION ON THE NIGHT HE WAS BETRAYED BUT HE GAVE THEM COMMUNION ANYWAY!

My Passover Things

Sing this to the tune of "My Favorite Things" from The Sound of Music)

Cleaning and cooking and so many dishes
Out with the hametz, no pasta, no knishes
Fish that's gefiltered, horseradish that stings
These are a few of our Passover things.

Matzoh and karpas and chopped up haroset
Shankbones and kidish and Yiddish neuroses
Tante who kvetches and uncle who sings
These are a few of our Passover things.

Motzi and maror and trouble with Pharoahs
Famines and locust and slaves with wheelbarrows
Matzoh balls floating and eggshell that clings
These are a few of our Passover things.

When the plagues strike
When the lice bite
When we're feeling sad
We simply remember our Passover things
And then we don't feel so bad!

Now look up all the words you don't recognize. What do they have to do with Passover?

Bible Time

Read and highlight the theme verse, I Corinthians 10:16-17. Write "Passover Event, see Exodus 12:1-14" in the margin of your Bible. Next, find the Exodus text and write "Passover: See Matthew 26:26-28" in the margin. Finally, find the Matthew text and write "The Final Passover: See Exodus 12:14" in the margin.

Catechism Encounter

Open your Small Catechism and search the Holy Communion section for Luther's answers to the question, "What are the benefits of Holy Communion?"

Prayer

Lamb of God, you take away the sins of the world. Thanks for taking away my sins. You passed over the homes sprinkled in the sacrificial blood. By your blood, pass over my sins, too. Holy Spirit of the Living God, deepen my understanding of who Jesus is and what he did for me. God of power and might, I need your forgiveness. I need your strength, I want to receive you again and again. Be with me now in a real way. In Jesus' name I pray. Amen.

Questions to Ponder

1. List five kinds of addictions people your age can have. What advice would you give to a friend who confessed an addiction to you and asked for help? What part can Christ play in their freedom?

2. What does Holy Communion have to do with Passover?

3. What does taking Holy Communion have to do with freedom?

SMALL GROUP

SHARE, READ, TALK, PRAY, BLESS

1. **SHARE** your highs and lows of the week one-on-one with another person. Listen carefully and record your friend's thoughts in the space below. Then return to small group and share your friend's highs and lows.

   MY HIGHS + LOWS THIS WEEK WERE:

   ....

   MY FRIEND'S HIGHS + LOWS THIS WEEK WERE:

   ....

2. **READ** and highlight the theme verse in your Bibles. Circle key words and learn the verse in song.

3. **TALK** about how today's verse relates to your highs and lows. Review the art for today, the Quiz Bowl questions, the terms, and the cartoons. Then write a sentence on each of the following:

   ONE NEW THING I LEARNED TODAY:

   ....

   ONE THING I ALREADY KNEW THAT IS WORTH REPEATING:

   ....

   ONE THING I WOULD LIKE TO KNOW MORE ABOUT:

   ....

4. **PRAY** for one another, praising and thanking God for your highs, and asking God to be with you in your lows. Include your friend's highs and lows in your prayers.

   A PRAISING PRAYER: ....

   A THANKING PRAYER: ....

   AN ASKING PRAYER: ....

5. **BLESS** one another using the blessing of the week. (right) Mark each person with the sign of the cross as you bless them.

THIS WEEK'S BLESSING

MAY THE PRESENCE OF THE LIVING CHRIST BE REAL TO YOU THIS DAY AND GIVE YOU FORGIVENESS, POWER AND PEACE. IN HIS NAME. AMEN.

Read the full devotions using FINKlink LL23 @ www.faithink.com

WEEK 1

FAITH JOURNAL

DAY 1

TODAY'S BIBLE VERSE:

1 Corinthians 10:16a

The cup of blessing that we bless, is it not a sharing in the blood of Christ?

MY HIGH TODAY WAS:

MY LOW TODAY WAS:

MY PRAYER TODAY IS:

DAY 2

TODAY'S BIBLE VERSE:

1 Corinthians 10:16b

The bread that we break, is it not a sharing in the body of Christ?

MY HIGH TODAY WAS:

MY LOW TODAY WAS:

MY PRAYER TODAY IS:

DAY 3

TODAY'S BIBLE VERSE:

1 Corinthians 10:17

Because there is one bread, we who are many are one body, for we all partake of the one bread.

MY HIGH TODAY WAS:

MY LOW TODAY WAS:

MY PRAYER TODAY IS:

my HIGH today was:

my LOW today was:

my PRAYER today is:

DAY 4

TODAY'S BIBLE VERSE:

Exodus 12:3, 5a, 6b

Tell the whole congregation of Israel... they are to take a lamb... Your lamb shall be without blemish... you shall slaughter it at twilight...

my HIGH today was:

my LOW today was:

my PRAYER today is:

DAY 5

TODAY'S BIBLE VERSE:

Exodus 12: 7, 13

Take some of the blood and put it on the two door posts and the lintel of the houses. The blood shall be a sign for you... when I see the blood I will pass over you, and no plague shall destroy you.

my HIGH today was:

my LOW today was:

my PRAYER today is:

DAY 6

TODAY'S BIBLE VERSE:

Exodus 12:14

This day shall be a day of remembrance for you. You shall celebrate it as a festival of the Lord; throughout your generations you shall observe it...

my HIGH today was:

my LOW today was:

my PRAYER today is:

DAY 7

THIS WEEK'S BLESSING

MAY THE PRESENCE OF THE LIVING CHRIST BE REAL TO YOU THIS DAY AND GIVE YOU FORGIVENESS, POWER AND PEACE. IN HIS NAME. AMEN.

THE FAITH 5

Read the full devotions using FINKlink LL23 @ www.faithink.com

WEEK 2

JOURNAL

DAY 1

TODAY'S BIBLE VERSE:

Matthew 26:17

On the first day of Unleavened Bread the disciples came to Jesus, saying, "Where do you want us to make the preparations for you to eat the Passover?"

MY HIGH TODAY WAS:

MY LOW TODAY WAS:

MY PRAYER TODAY IS:

DAY 2

TODAY'S BIBLE VERSE:

Matthew 26:18

He (Jesus) said, "Go into the city to a certain man, and say to him, 'The Teacher says, My time is near; I will keep the Passover at your house with my disciples.' "

MY HIGH TODAY WAS:

MY LOW TODAY WAS:

MY PRAYER TODAY IS:

DAY 3

TODAY'S BIBLE VERSE:

Matthew 26:19-20

So the disciples did as Jesus had directed them, and they prepared the Passover meal. When it was evening, he took his place with the twelve.

MY HIGH TODAY WAS:

MY LOW TODAY WAS:

MY PRAYER TODAY IS:

1. **SHARE** HIGHS & LOWS OF THE DAY.
2. **READ** AND HIGHLIGHT THE VERSE OF THE DAY IN YOUR BIBLES.
3. **TALK** ABOUT HOW TODAY'S VERSE RELATES TO YOUR HIGHS & LOWS.
4. **PRAY** FOR YOUR HIGHS & LOWS, FOR YOUR FAMILY AND FOR THE WORLD.
5. **BLESS** ONE ANOTHER USING THIS WEEK'S BLESSING (ON THE PREVIOUS PAGE).

DAY 4

TODAY'S BIBLE VERSE:

MATTHEW 26:26

While they were eating, Jesus took a loaf of bread, and after blessing it he broke it, gave it to the disciples, and said, "Take, eat; this is my body."

MY HIGH TODAY WAS:

MY LOW TODAY WAS:

MY PRAYER TODAY IS:

DAY 5

TODAY'S BIBLE VERSE:

MATTHEW 26:27

Then he took a cup, and after giving thanks he gave it to them, saying, "Drink from it, all of you..."

MY HIGH TODAY WAS:

MY LOW TODAY WAS:

MY PRAYER TODAY IS:

DAY 6

TODAY'S BIBLE VERSE:

MATTHEW 26:28

"This is my blood of the covenant, which is poured out for many for the forgiveness of sins."

MY HIGH TODAY WAS:

MY LOW TODAY WAS:

MY PRAYER TODAY IS:

THEME IN REVIEW

Re = Again + Member. To remember Christ in this meal is to become a member with him again and again and again.

Rich Melheim

DAY 7

My favorite VERSE from the theme was:

....

....

....

....

....

....

....

....

....

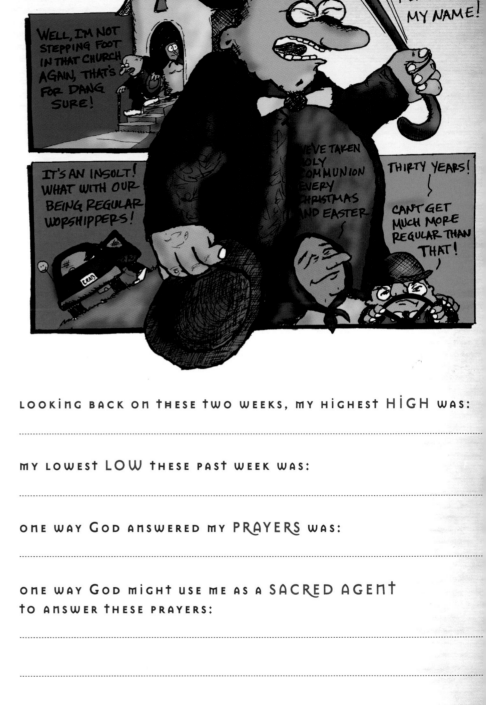

Looking back on these two weeks, my highest HIGH was:

....

My lowest LOW these past week was:

....

One way God answered my PRAYERS was:

....

One way God might use me as a SACRED AGENT to answer these prayers:

....

....

Family Covenant

We have shared *Highs & Lows* this week, read and highlighted the verses assigned in our Bible, talked about our lives, prayed for one another's highs and lows, and blessed one another.

....	....	....
Parent's Signature	*Teen's Signature*	*Date*

THE FINKMANIA QUIZ BOWL

Question 1:

A sacrifice is:

(A) Giving up something of value for another's well-being,
(B) Someone or something that takes the place and the punishment for someone else,
(C) An "out" that allows the advance of the runner,
(D) All of the above

Question 2:

Communion is meant to be done:

(A) Only on Sunday,
(B) With pizza and Coke as the elements,
(C) With others as part of a community,
(D) Quickly

Question 3:

What did the people of the Old Testament do to show sorrow for sins?:

(A) Interpretive dance,
(B) Animal sacrifice,
(C) Yodeling,
(D) Sermon notes

Question 4:

We should prepare for Holy Communion by:

(A) Confessing our sins,
(B) Making amends,
(C) Seeking forgiveness,
(D) All of the above

Question 5:

The Last Supper was held at a home and not at a temple because:

(A) The temple was booked for a wedding,
(B) A dinner at the temple would have included a hot dish,
(C) Passover was always a time for families to remember God's saving acts,
(D) Health codes

Question 6:

The gifts of Holy Communion include:

(A) Forgiveness of sin,
(B) Life,
(C) Salvation,
(D) All of the above

Question 7:

A sacrament is:

(A) An after dinner mint,
(B) A type of fancy sack used by pastors,
(C) A gift of God's grace, commanded by Christ with a physical element attached,
(D) None of the above

Question 8:

The event that finally set Israel free from slavery is called:

(A) The Passport,
(B) The Passkey,
(C) The Forward Pass,
(D) The Passover

Question 9:

A declaration of forgiveness and release from penalty is called:

(A) An absolutely,
(B) An absolution,
(C) An abdominal crunch,
(D) An abomination

FINKmania Final Question:

I Corinthians 10:16-17, the verse of the week, tells us:

(A) The communion cup is Christ's blood,
(B) The bread is Christ's body,
(C) We are one Body in Christ,
(D) All of the above

Play this online game using FINKlink
LL23 @ www.faithink.com

THE WEAKEST FINK

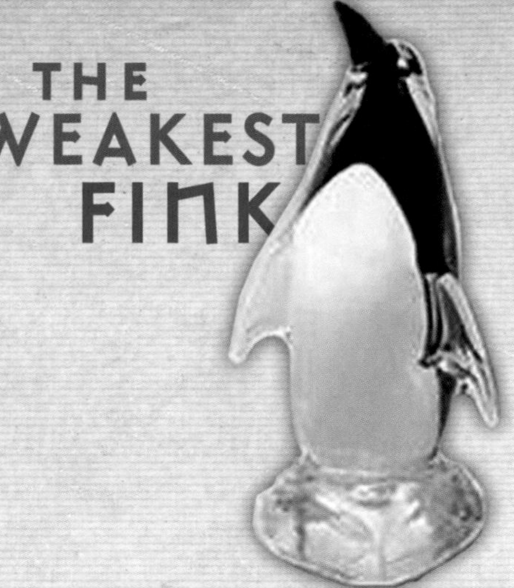

PASSOVER? I'M COUNTING ON JESUS PASSING OVER A LOT OF THINGS.

ANONYMOUS 7TH GRADER

TERMS

WRITE A DEFINITION BELOW.

ANGEL OF DEATH

LAMB OF GOD

MOSES

PASSOVER

REMEMBRANCE

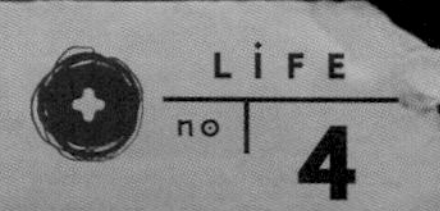

Taste and See

"The Spies Return from Canaan" Copyright © Dr. He Qi www.heqigallery.com

"I will bless the LORD at all times; his praise shall continually be in my mouth. My soul makes its boast in the LORD; let the humble hear and be glad. O magnify the LORD with me, and let us exalt his name together. I sought the LORD, and he answered me, and delivered me from all my fears. Look to him, and be radiant; so your faces shall never be ashamed. This poor soul cried, and was heard by the LORD, and was saved from every trouble. The angel of the LORD encamps around those who fear him, and delivers them. O taste and see that the LORD is good." — Psalm 34:1-8

Listen to this song using FINKlink LL24 @ www.faithink.com

ave you ever felt full and still empty? Have you ever sat beneath a loaded Christmas tree an hour after opening presents and wondered, "Is that all there is?"

Have you ever sensed you had a full house but an empty home? A full schedule, but an empty life? If you were merely a physical being, food, drink, sleep, warmth and shelter would be all you needed to survive. But you aren't simply the sum of your physical parts. There is more to you than flesh and bones, organs and nerve cells, blood and hair and skin tissue. The Bible says God created you as a spiritual being. There is another part of you—another dimension—that must be nurtured and fed. You can fill a spiritual being's stomach with cheeseburgers and Doritos and they will still be hungry. You can drown them in Gatorade and Mountain Dew and they will still be thirsty.

On the night he was betrayed, Jesus knew he was soon to be snatched away from his friends and crucified. He took the ancient Passover meal and transformed it into a gift that would give them strength even after he was gone. First he took bread—the symbol for life—and told them "this is my body." Bread was central to nutrition in that culture. By using bread for this meal, Jesus told his followers that he was to be their sustenance and strength from that night on. Next Jesus took a cup of wine and said, "this is my blood." In the ancient world, the blood of an animal was thought to hold its living essence. The blood of a spotless animal was often used as a sacrifice to show sorrow and pay the price for sin. When Jesus called the wine his blood, our Lord was telling his friends that he was to be the final sacrifice for their sin. His blood would pay the price. His power would now be available to his followers. Just as bread and wine gave physical strength, in this new meal Jesus would become the spiritual food to go with them and keep them alive in the days to come.

WHAT CAN WASH AWAY MY SIN?

NOTHING BUT THE BLOOD OF JESUS;

WHAT CAN MAKE ME WHOLE AGAIN?

NOTHING BUT THE BLOOD OF JESUS.

ROBERT LOWRY

THE MEANING OF THE MEAL

Some call this new meal Holy Communion. In it, we find unity with God through the real presence of Christ and the forgiveness he brings. Some call this meal the Last Supper. This term reminds us of the last meal Jesus shared with his followers. Some call the meal the Lord's Supper. It was our Lord who gave us the meal. Some call the celebration Eucharist. This is the Greek word for the "good grace" that comes to us in the bread, wine, and presence of Christ to fill us. Whatever you call it, this meal is more than a symbol, more than a memorial, more than the physical eating of bread and drinking of wine. In it, the one who said, "I am the bread of life" is feeding your spirit what it needs to survive. In, with, and under this gift God is waiting to give the gifts of forgiveness of sins, life and salvation.

Taste and see that the Lord is good!

Order this art print using FINKlink LL24 @ www.faithink.com

IMAGES IN ART

- What do you see in today's painting by Dr. He Qi?
- Where are you in this work of art?
- How do the image and the verse apply to your life today?

So What Does This Mean?

Psssт. It's been a rough week. I wonder if we could talk seconds?

We sing "Make a Joyful Noise Unto the Lord" while our faces reflect the sadness of one who has just buried a rich aunt who left everything to her pregnant hamster.

Erma Bombeck

The word "Companion" comes from the Latin "Com" = With, and "Pan" = Bread. In Holy Communion Jesus is our true companion in every sense of the word.

Bible Time

Open your Bible and read Psalm 34:1-10. Find and highlight the words taste, hunger and seek. What does it mean to "taste and see" the Lord is good?

Read and highlight Matthew 5:6. What happens when you seek the Lord?

What happens to those who hunger and thirst after righteousness?

Catechism Encounter

Open your Small Catechism and search the Holy Communion section for Martin Luther's answer to the question: "When is a person rightly prepared to take the meal?"

Prayer

Dear Jesus, may I taste on my lips and hold in my hands what my heart and mind cannot understand. Come Lord Jesus. Amen.

Questions to Ponder

1. A friend says, "The bread and wine actually turn into flesh and blood in communion. You just can't see it." How do you answer them?

2. A friend says, "The bread and wine are simply a symbol of Jesus. Jesus isn't really there." How do you answer?

3. Does it matter what kind of bread and wine are used for communion? Would potato chips and grape juice work just as well?

Small Group

share, read, talk, pray, bless

1. **SHARE** your highs and lows of the week one-on-one with another person. Listen carefully and record your friend's thoughts in the space below. Then return to small group and share your friend's highs and lows.

   MY HIGHS + LOWS THIS WEEK WERE:

   ....

   MY FRIEND'S HIGHS + LOWS THIS WEEK WERE:

   ....

2. **READ** and highlight the theme verse in your Bibles. Circle key words and learn the verse in song.

3. **TALK** about how today's verse relates to your highs and lows. Review the art for today, the Quiz Bowl questions, the terms, and the cartoons. Then write a sentence on each of the following:

   ONE NEW THING I LEARNED TODAY:

   ....

   ONE THING I ALREADY KNEW THAT IS WORTH REPEATING:

   ....

   ONE THING I WOULD LIKE TO KNOW MORE ABOUT:

   ....

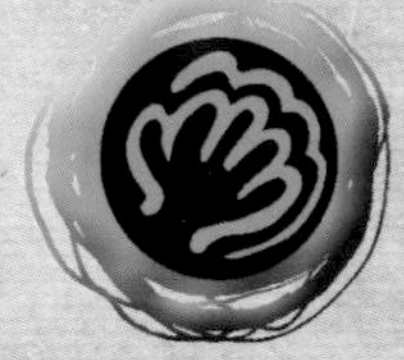

4. **PRAY** for one another, praising and thanking God for your highs, and asking God to be with you in your lows. Include your friend's highs and lows in your prayers.

   A PRAISING PRAYER: ....

   A THANKING PRAYER: ....

   AN ASKING PRAYER: ....

5. **BLESS** one another using the blessing of the week. (right) Mark each person with the sign of the cross as you bless them.

THIS WEEK'S BLESSING

(NAME), CHILD OF GOD, MAY CHRIST'S BODY GIVE YOU STRENGTH AND HIS BLOOD WASH YOU CLEAN. AMEN.

WEEK 1

THE FAITH5 JOURNAL

Read the full devotions using FINKlink
LL24 @ www.faithink.com

DAY 1

TODAY'S BIBLE VERSE:

Psalm 34:1b, 2

I will bless the Lord at all times; his praise shall continually be in my mouth. My soul makes its boast in the Lord; let the humble hear and be glad.

MY HIGH TODAY WAS:

MY LOW TODAY WAS:

MY PRAYER TODAY IS:

DAY 2

TODAY'S BIBLE VERSE:

Psalm 34:3-4

O magnify the Lord with me, and let us exalt his name together! I sought the Lord, and he answered me, and delivered me from all my fears.

MY HIGH TODAY WAS:

MY LOW TODAY WAS:

MY PRAYER TODAY IS:

DAY 3

TODAY'S BIBLE VERSE:

Psalm 34:5

Look to him, and be radiant; so your faces shall never be ashamed.

MY HIGH TODAY WAS:

MY LOW TODAY WAS:

MY PRAYER TODAY IS:

my HIGH today was:

my LOW today was:

my PRAYER today is:

DAY 4

today's bible verse:

Psalm 34:6

This poor soul cried, and was heard by the Lord, and was saved from every trouble.

my HIGH today was:

my LOW today was:

my PRAYER today is:

DAY 5

today's bible verse:

Psalm 34:7

The angel of the Lord encamps around those who fear him, and delivers them.

my HIGH today was:

my LOW today was:

my PRAYER today is:

DAY 6

today's bible verse:

Psalm 34:8

O taste and see that the Lord is good; happy are those who take refuge in him.

my HIGH today was:

my LOW today was:

my PRAYER today is:

DAY 7

this week's blessing

(NAME), CHILD OF GOD, MAY CHRIST'S BODY GIVE YOU STRENGTH AND HIS BLOOD WASH YOU CLEAN. AMEN.

Read the full devotions using FINKlink
LL24 @ www.faithink.com

WEEK 2

FAITH JOURNAL

DAY 1

TODAY'S BIBLE VERSE:

JOHN 6:32-33

Very truly, I tell you, it was not Moses who gave you the bread from heaven, but it is my Father who gives you the true bread from heaven. For the bread of God is that which comes down from heaven and gives life to the world.

MY HIGH TODAY WAS:

MY LOW TODAY WAS:

MY PRAYER TODAY IS:

DAY 2

TODAY'S BIBLE VERSE:

JOHN 6:35

Jesus said to them, "I am the bread of life. Whoever comes to me will never be hungry, and whoever believes in me will never be thirsty."

MY HIGH TODAY WAS:

MY LOW TODAY WAS:

MY PRAYER TODAY IS:

DAY 3

TODAY'S BIBLE VERSE:

JOHN 6:54-55

Those who eat my flesh and drink my blood have eternal life, and I will raise them up on the last day; for my flesh is true food and my blood is true drink.

MY HIGH TODAY WAS:

MY LOW TODAY WAS:

MY PRAYER TODAY IS:

2. READ AND HIGHLIGHT THE VERSE OF THE DAY IN YOUR BIBLES.

3. TALK ABOUT HOW TODAY'S VERSE RELATES TO YOUR HIGHS & LOWS.

4. PRAY FOR YOUR HIGHS & LOWS, FOR YOUR FAMILY AND FOR THE WORLD.

5. BLESS ONE ANOTHER USING THIS WEEK'S BLESSING (ON THE PREVIOUS PAGE).

my HIGH today was:

my LOW today was:

my PRAYER today is:

DAY 4

today's bible verse:

Ephesians 2:13

But now in Christ Jesus you who once were far off have been brought near by the blood of Christ.

my HIGH today was:

my LOW today was:

my PRAYER today is:

DAY 5

today's bible verse:

Hebrews 13:12

Therefore Jesus also suffered outside the city gate in order to sanctify the people by his own blood.

GOT ANY STAIN REMOVER?

my HIGH today was:

my LOW today was:

my PRAYER today is:

DAY 6

today's bible verse:

I John 1:7

If we walk in the light as he himself is in the light, we have fellowship with one another, and the blood of Jesus his Son cleanses us from all sin.

S | M | T | W | TH | F | S

THEME IN REVIEW

FORGIVENESS IS GOD'S COMMAND.

THE GIFTS OF THIS SACRAMENT ARE FORGIVENESS OF SIN, LIFE, AND SALVATION. FOR WHERE THERE IS FORGIVENESS OF SIN, THERE IS ALSO LIFE AND SALVATION.

MARTIN LUTHER

DAY 7

MY FAVORITE VERSE FROM THE THEME WAS:

....

....

....

....

....

....

....

....

....

REVEREND FINK! DO YOU MEAN TO TELL ME THAT THIS CHURCH IS CONSIDERING GIVING COMMUNION TO CHILDREN WHO CAN'T EVEN ARTICULATE THE FAITH?
HUH?

LOOKING BACK ON THESE TWO WEEKS, MY HIGHEST HIGH WAS:

....

MY LOWEST LOW THESE PAST WEEKS WAS:

....

ONE WAY GOD ANSWERED MY PRAYERS WAS:

....

ONE WAY GOD MIGHT USE ME AS A SACRED AGENT TO ANSWER THESE PRAYERS:

....

....

FAMILY COVENANT

We have shared *Highs & Lows* this week, read and highlighted the verses assigned in our Bibles, talked about our lives, prayed for one another's highs and lows, and blessed one another.

....	....	....
Parent's Signature	*Teen's Signature*	*Date*

THE FINKMANIA QUIZ BOWL

Question 1:

The very first enactment of communion came at:

(A) 7th inning of a Yankees-Orioles game,
(B) Maundy (command) Thursday,
(C) A celebration of the Passover,
(D) B & C

Question 2:

Jesus used bread and wine for Holy Communion because:

(A) Bread and wine give life, just like Jesus gives life,
(B) They were common elements from the Passover that reminded people of a miraculous act of God,
(C) Both A & B,
(D) He was out of grape juice

Question 3:

"Holy" means:

(A) See-through,
(B) Special,
(C) Sacred,
(D) B & C

Question 4:

We no longer have animal sacrifice for forgiveness as in the Old Testament because:

(A) Animals got smart and hired bodyguards,
(B) Animals are too expensive,
(C) In Jesus, God supplied the perfect sacrifice once and for all,
(D) PETA stepped in

Question 5:

Holy Communion is also called:

(A) Eucharist,
(B) Ukulele,
(C) Europe,
(D) None of the above

Question 6:

An agreement binding two parties together is called a:

(A) Convent,
(B) Corvette,
(C) Con man,
(D) Covenant

Question 7:

The Words of Institution are:

(A) The oath you give before you join a college,
(B) Marriage vows,
(C) The words Jesus used to start the gift of communion,
(D) The Declaration of Independence

Question 8:

The Greek word "eucharist" translates as:

(A) Good grace,
(B) Good grief,
(C) Good golly Miss Molly,
(D) Good night

Question 9:

The belief that Jesus is really present in, with and under the bread and wine at communion is called:

(A) The Real World,
(B) The Real Deal Meal,
(C) The Real Thing,
(D) The Real Presence

FINKmania Final Question:

Psalm 34:1-8, the verse of the week, tells us, "Taste and see the Lord is...":

(A) "...Good,"
(B) "...Good,"
(C) "...Good,"
(D) All of the above, and God is good all the time

Play this online game using FINKlink
LL24 @ www.faithink.com

THE WEAKEST FINK

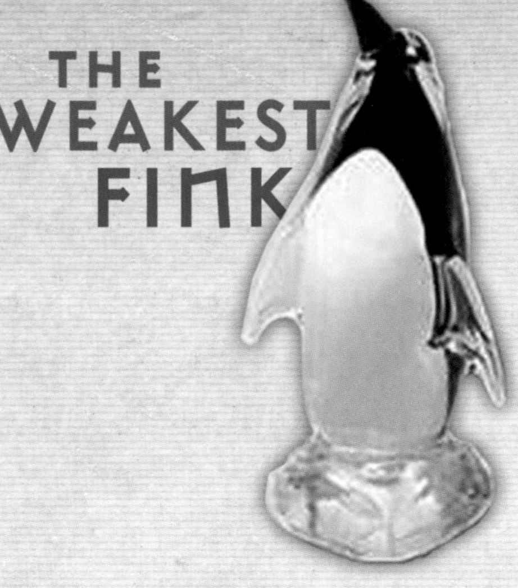

Forgiveness is not an occasional act: it is an attitude.

Martin Luther King, Jr

TERMS

Write a definition below.

Eucharist

Forgiveness

Holy Communion

The Last Supper

The Lord's Supper

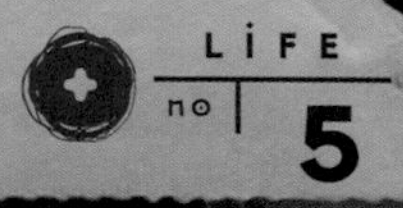

Worship: The Gathering

"Glory to God in the Highest" Copyright © Dr. He Qi www.heqigallery.com

"But the Lord is in his holy temple;

let all the earth keep silence before him!"

— Habakkuk 2:20

Listen to this song using FINKlink
LL25 @ www.faithink.com

SMALL GROUP

SHARE, READ, TALK, PRAY, BLESS

1. **SHARE** your highs and lows of the week one-on-one with another person. Listen carefully and record your friend's thoughts in the space below. Then return to small group and share your friend's highs and lows.

   MY HIGHS + LOWS THIS WEEK WERE:

   ....

   MY FRIEND'S HIGHS + LOWS THIS WEEK WERE:

   ....

2. **READ** and highlight the theme verse in your Bibles. Circle key words and learn the verse in song.

3. **TALK** about how today's verse relates to your highs and lows. Review the art for today, the Quiz Bowl questions, the terms, and the cartoons. Then write a sentence on each of the following:

   ONE NEW THING I LEARNED TODAY:

   ....

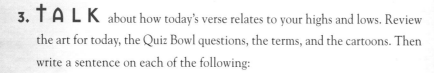

   ONE THING I ALREADY KNEW THAT IS WORTH REPEATING:

   ....

   ONE THING I WOULD LIKE TO KNOW MORE ABOUT:

   ....

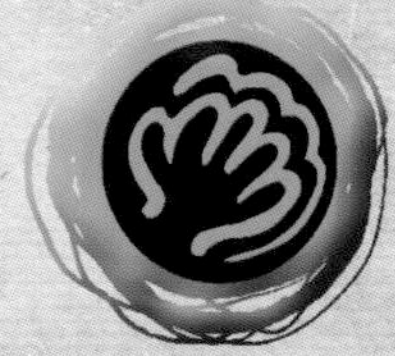

4. **PRAY** for one another, praising and thanking God for your highs, and asking God to be with you in your lows. Include your friend's highs and lows in your prayers.

   A PRAISING PRAYER: ....

   A THANKING PRAYER: ....

   AN ASKING PRAYER: ....

5. **BLESS** one another using the blessing of the week. (right) Mark each person with the sign of the cross as you bless them.

THIS WEEK'S BLESSING

(NAME), CHILD OF GOD, MAY GOD BE PRESENT IN YOUR WORDS AND THOUGHTS THIS DAY.

FAITH JOURNAL

WEEK 1

Read the full devotions using FINKlink

LL25 @ www.faithink.com

DAY 1

TODAY'S BIBLE VERSE:

Habakkuk 2:20

But the Lord is in his holy temple; let all the earth keep silence before him.

my HIGH today was:

my LOW today was:

my PRAYER today is:

DAY 2

TODAY'S BIBLE VERSE:

Exodus 34:14

You shall not worship any other god, for the Lord, whose name is Jealous, is a jealous God.

my HIGH today was:

my LOW today was:

my PRAYER today is:

DAY 3

TODAY'S BIBLE VERSE:

1 Chronicles 16:29

Ascribe to the Lord the glory due his name; Bring an offering, and come before him; Worship the Lord in holy splendor.

my HIGH today was:

my LOW today was:

my PRAYER today is:

my HIGH today was:

my LOW today was:

my PRAYER today is:

DAY 4

today's bible verse:

Psalm 95:6

Come, let us worship and bow down, let us kneel before the Lord, our Maker.

my HIGH today was:

my LOW today was:

my PRAYER today is:

DAY 5

today's bible verse:

Psalm 115:1

Not to us, O Lord, not to us, but to your name give glory, for the sake of your steadfast love and your truthfullness.

my HIGH today was:

my LOW today was:

my PRAYER today is:

DAY 6

today's bible verse:

Psalm 122:1

I was glad when they said to me, "Let us go to the house of the Lord."

my HIGH today was:

my LOW today was:

my PRAYER today is:

DAY 7

this week's blessing

(NAME), CHILD OF GOD, MAY GOD BE PRESENT IN YOUR WORDS AND THOUGHTS THIS DAY.

THE FAITH 5

Read the full devotions using FINKlink LL25 @ www.faithink.com

JOURNAL

WEEK 2

DAY 1

TODAY'S BIBLE VERSE:

JOHN 4:23

But the hour is coming, and is now here, when the true worshipers will worship the Father in spirit and truth, for the Father seeks such as these to worship him.

MY HIGH TODAY WAS:

MY LOW TODAY WAS:

MY PRAYER TODAY IS:

DAY 2

TODAY'S BIBLE VERSE:

JOHN 4:24

God is spirit, and those who worship him must worship in spirit and truth.

MY HIGH TODAY WAS:

MY LOW TODAY WAS:

MY PRAYER TODAY IS:

DAY 3

TODAY'S BIBLE VERSE:

HEBREWS 12:28

Therefore, since we are receiving a kingdom that cannot be shaken, let us give thanks, by which we offer to God an acceptable worship with reverence and awe.

MY HIGH TODAY WAS:

MY LOW TODAY WAS:

MY PRAYER TODAY IS:

1. SHARE HIGHS & LOWS OF THE DAY.
2. READ AND HIGHLIGHT THE VERSE OF THE DAY IN YOUR BIBLES.
3. TALK ABOUT HOW TODAY'S VERSE RELATES TO YOUR HIGHS & LOWS.
4. PRAY FOR YOUR HIGHS & LOWS, FOR YOUR FAMILY AND FOR THE WORLD.
5. BLESS ONE ANOTHER USING THIS WEEK'S BLESSING (ON THE PREVIOUS PAGE).

DAY 4

TODAY'S BIBLE VERSE:

Revelation 7:12

Blessing and glory and wisdom and thanksgiving and honor and power and might be to our God forever and ever! Amen.

MY HIGH TODAY WAS:

MY LOW TODAY WAS:

MY PRAYER TODAY IS:

DAY 5

TODAY'S BIBLE VERSE:

Revelation 15:4

Lord, who will not fear and glorify your name? For you alone are holy. All nations will come and worship before you, for your judgments have been revealed.

MY HIGH TODAY WAS:

MY LOW TODAY WAS:

MY PRAYER TODAY IS:

DAY 6

TODAY'S BIBLE VERSE:

Revelation 19:5, 6b

Praise our God, all you servants, and all who fear him, small and great. Hallelujah! For the Lord our God the Almighty reigns. Let us rejoice and exult and give him the glory...

MY HIGH TODAY WAS:

MY LOW TODAY WAS:

MY PRAYER TODAY IS:

S | M | T | W | TH | F | S

THEME IN REVIEW

IT IS ONLY WHEN PEOPLE BEGIN TO WORSHIP THAT THEY BEGIN TO GROW.

CALVIN COOLIDGE

WELCOME TO BUSTERCHURCH

THE VERY FIRST CHURCH WHICH OUR DENOMINATION (NEVER AGAIN TO BE MENTIONED) HAS SANCTIONED AS A MISSION OUTPOST FOR THE LOST GENERATION XERS. MY NAME IS MICHAEL AND I'LL BE YOUR SERVER TODAY...

Our Communion wine will be a 1992 Cotê du Rhone. We do have sparkling cider made from fresh Washington apples for those to whom wine is not an option.

Two kinds of bread are featured today: a sun dried tomato and pesto foccacia and a stone ground seven grain from the heartland.

You may pay your server on the way out. Mastercard and Visa are, of course, accepted.

DAY 7

MY FAVORITE VERSE FROM THE THEME WAS:

LOOKING BACK ON THESE TWO WEEKS, MY HIGHEST HIGH WAS:

MY LOWEST LOW THESE PAST WEEKS WAS:

ONE WAY GOD ANSWERED MY PRAYERS WAS:

ONE WAY GOD MIGHT USE ME AS A SACRED AGENT TO ANSWER THESE PRAYERS:

FAMILY COVENANT

We have shared *Highs & Lows* this week, read and highlighted the verses assigned in our Bible talked about our lives, prayed for one another's highs and lows, and blessed one another.

Parent's Signature | *Teen's Signature* | *Date*

THE FINKMANIA QUIZBOWL

Question 1:

At the beginning of Lutheran worship, most churches include:

(A) The Invocation, Confession of Sins, Absolution, and the Kyrie,

(B) The Invocation, Confession of Sins, Absolution, and Holy Communion,

(C) The Invocation, Confession of Sins and an offering,

(D) 62 announcements

Question 2:

The word "invocation" comes from the Latin:

(A) Invoice,

(B) *In*, as in "in" and *vox* as in "voice,"

(C) *In*, as in "in" and *vaccione* as in "vacation,"

(D) I haven't the foggiest

Question 3:

At the beginning of worship, Lutherans and other Christians use the Invocation to:

(A) Invite the presence of God,

(B) Begin in the name of the Father/Creator, Son/Savior and Holy Spirit,

(C) Proclaim to the triune God to the world,

(D) A, B, and maybe C

Question 4:

Why invoke the presence of God? Isn't God already there?:

(A) Yes, God is already there, but it helps worshippers to realize God's presence more fully,

(B) No, God doesn't show up until we call,

(C) Yes, but it gets God's attention,

(D) I don't know. Go ask my pastor

Question 5:

Following the Invocation, Lutherans usually do what in worship?:

(A) Confess their sins and receive the absolution,

(B) Confess their sins and receive the offering,

(C) Confess their absolutions and receive their sins,

(D) Fall immediately into a sound and restful sleep until the sermon is over

Question 6:

Confession of sins is usually done:

(A) Privately and quietly in the heart,

(B) Open and publicly with other worshippers,

(C) Both A and B,

(D) Only after getting caught

Question 7:

Confession is good for the:

(A) Wallet,

(B) Soul,

(C) Other sinners, but not me,

(D) Duration (do it once and you'll never have to do it again because all of your other sins are grandfathered in)

Question 8:

The pastor or worship leader proclaims God's forgiveness of sins in a statement called:

(A) The Absolution,

(B) The AB Solution,

(C) The Absolutely,

(D) The Indulgence

Question 9:

Kyrie Elesion is a Latin phrase meaning:

(A) Lord have elation,

(B) Lord have mercy,

(C) Lord have money,

(D) None of the above

FINKmania Final Question:

Habakkuk 2:20 says, "But the Lord is in his holy temple; let all the earth keep...":

(A) "...silence before him!"

(B) "...their hearts and minds on Christ Jesus!"

(C) "...their hands out of the offering plate!"

(D) "...their children quietly in the nursery!"

Play this online game using FINKlink

LL25 @ www.faithink.com

THE WEAKEST FINK

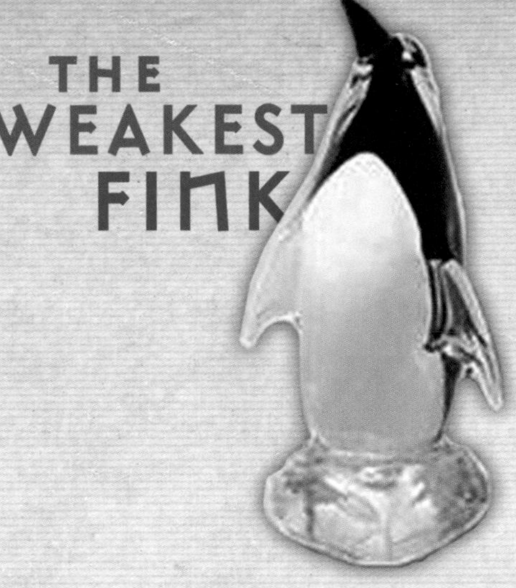

THERE MAY BE WORSHIP WITHOUT WORDS.

JAMES RUSSELL LOWELL

TERMS

WRITE A DEFINITION BELOW.

Absolution

....

....

Confession

....

....

Invocation

....

....

Kyrie

....

....

Worship

....

....

FAITH INKUBATORS

Worship: The Word

"Boy Jesus in the Temple" Copyright © Dr. He Qi www.heqigallery.com

"For as the rain and the snow come down from heaven, and do not return there until they have watered the earth, making it bring forth and sprout, giving seed to the sower and bread to the eater, so shall my word be that goes out from my mouth; it shall not return to me empty, but it shall accomplish that which I purpose, and succeed in the thing for which I sent it." — Isaiah 55:10-11

Listen to this verse using FINKlink
LL26 @ www.faithink.com

Are we all alone in the universe? Is there a possibility intelligent life exists somewhere out there? If it does, could we ever hope to communicate with it?

Imagine getting a radio signal from outer space. Imagine deciphering a code or communication from another intelligent being out there somewhere! The news would make and break history. It would change everything. In recent years scientists at the SETI (Search for Extra-Terrestrial Intelligence) Institute have spent over $150 million aiming telescopes and powerful microphones at the night sky in search of alien intelligence. Sad to say, in spite of all the money and decades of searching by hundreds of scientists, all they've ever managed to come up with is static. White noise. No codes. No communication. No messages.

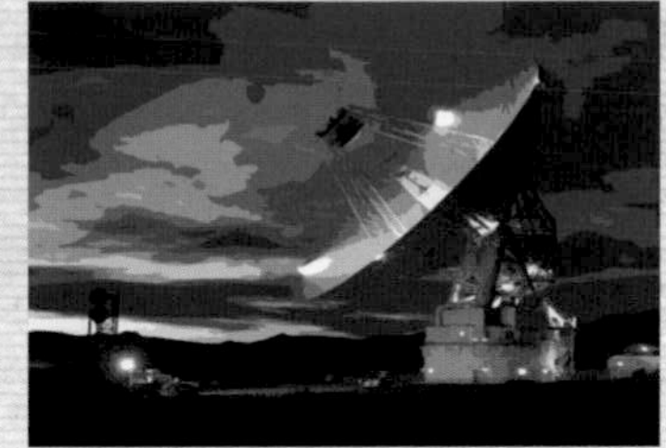

Sometimes I think the surest sign that intelligent life exists elsewhere in the universe is that none of it has tried to contact us.

Calvin & Hobbes

Any Given Sunday

On any given Sunday, a billion people around the world will gather together, sing some songs, and open the same ancient book. They will listen to words read and proclaimed, firmly believing they are receiving a message from a great being from beyond the galaxies. They will then actually communicate with that being, listen to words from that being, and search for a personal message which they believe can shape and transform their lives.

Stranger than fiction? No. It's true.

Lutheran Worship & the Word

Christians believe the Creator of the Universe—an intelligence beyond anything we could ever comprehend—has chosen to speak directly to us, reveal truth, and give us a wisdom we could never find on our own. Lutherans believe God speaks in many ways. God speaks to us in the beauty of nature, the wisdom of friends, and the still, small voice of the Holy Spirit in our consciences. God speaks to us clearly and powerfully in the Holy Bible. God also speaks through the proclamation of the word (preaching). Finally, God has also spoken to us most profoundly and miraculously in the Living Word—Jesus Christ.

Lutherans gather as a body every Sunday to hear God's word and share in Christ's supper. We listen first to stories, wisdom, and truths from the Old Testament. This reading tells of how God chose a people—the Jews—and trained them in righteousness to prepare the world for Christ. Next a Psalm is often read. Psalms are songs and prayers from the worship book of Israel. Many were written or collected by King David. A third reading from the Epistles (Letters) of Paul or another letter from the New Testament is usually read next. These letters give advice, insight, and council to the church. The crown of the readings, which most preachers use for most sermons, comes from one of the four Gospels. These books tell the story of Jesus' life and ministry on earth.

Order this art print using **FINKlink**

LL26 @ www.faithink.com

Images in Art

- What do you see in today's painting by Dr. He Qi?
- Where are you in this work of art?
- How do the image and the verse apply to your life today?

So What Does This Mean?

I DIDN'T APPRECIATE ANY OF THAT SO CALLED "WORSHIP AND PRAISE" MUSIC YOU SANG TODAY, REV.
THAT'S OKAY. WE WEREN'T SINGING IT TO YOU.

Proclaiming the Word

Preaching wasn't always a big deal in Christian worship. Martin Luther lived during a time when worship for the masses centered mainly around the Mass—Holy Communion. In his day, few people had access to a Bible. Most couldn't read. Fewer still owned any books. (Luther didn't see his first Bible until he was 20!) Since Bibles were only printed in Hebrew, Latin and Greek, they were only read by scholars. Luther wanted everyone to know God's will, so he translated the Bible into the language of the common people.

When the Reformation took hold, its leaders elevated the reading of the Bible and preaching to a central place in the weekly gathering. They wanted all to hear and consider God's word for themselves. Today, preaching continues to hold a central position in Protestant worship. Through hearing God's word and listening to a preacher interpret it, we can come to know God's good and gracious will for our lives more completely every time we gather.

Bible Time

Read and highlight Isaiah 55:10-11, writing "God's Word Works!" in the margin. Next, what does each verse below say is a benefit of knowing God's word?

Isaiah 40:8b

Psalm 119:105

John 8:31

II Timothy 3:16-17

Prayer

Jesus, may the power and truth of your word shine into my head, heart, and home this week. Show me the way. Show me your way. Today. Amen.

Questions to Ponder

1. Recall the best sermon you have ever heard. What made it memorable? How could preaching in our church be improved?

2. How do you think a sermon is written? How does it come together? If you were asked to write a sermon, where would you start?

3. A friend asks, "What is the Word of God?" How do you answer?

Our concern is not how to worship in the catacombs, but rather how to remain human in the skyscrapers.

Abraham Joshua Heschel

Small Group

share, read, talk, pray, bless

1. **SHARE** your highs and lows of the week one-on-one with another person. Listen carefully and record your friend's thoughts in the space below. Then return to small group and share your friend's highs and lows.

   my highs + lows this week were:

   ....

   my friend's highs + lows this week were:

   ....

2. **READ** and highlight the theme verse in your Bibles. Circle key words and learn the verse in song.

3. **TALK** about how today's verse relates to your highs and lows. Review the art for today, the Quiz Bowl questions, the terms, and the cartoons. Then write a sentence on each of the following:

   one new thing i learned today:

   ....

   one thing i already knew that is worth repeating:

   ....

   one thing i would like to know more about:

   ....

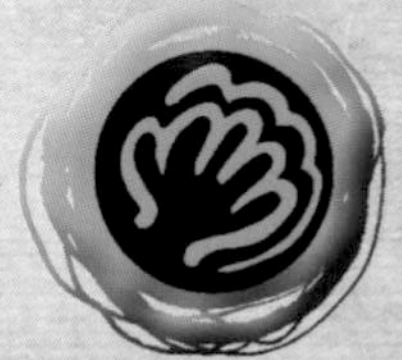

4. **PRAY** for one another, praising and thanking God for your highs, and asking God to be with you in your lows. Include your friend's highs and lows in your prayers.

   a praising prayer: ....

   a thanking prayer: ....

   an asking prayer: ....

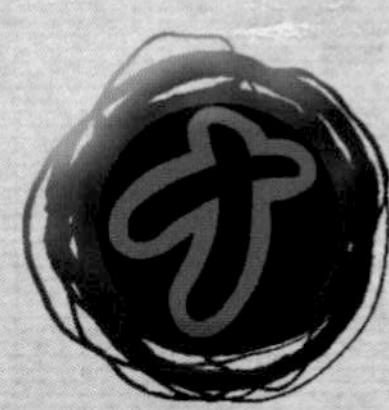

5. **BLESS** one another using the blessing of the week. (right) Mark each person with the sign of the cross as you bless them.

this week's blessing

(NAME), child of God, may the power and truth of God's Word shine in your head, heart and home.

THE FAITH 5

Read the full devotions using FINKlink LL26 @ www.faithink.com

WEEK 1

JOURNAL

DAY 1

TODAY'S BIBLE VERSE:

ISAIAH 55:10

For as the rain and the snow come down from heaven, and do not return there until they have watered the earth, making it bring forth and sprout, giving seed to the sower and bread to the eater, so shall my word be...

MY HIGH TODAY WAS:

MY LOW TODAY WAS:

MY PRAYER TODAY IS:

DAY 2

TODAY'S BIBLE VERSE:

ISAIAH 55:11

It shall not return to me empty, but it shall accomplish that which I purpose, and succeed in the thing for which I sent it.

MY HIGH TODAY WAS:

MY LOW TODAY WAS:

MY PRAYER TODAY IS:

DAY 3

TODAY'S BIBLE VERSE:

NUMBERS 11:23

The Lord said to Moses, "Is the Lord's power limited? Now you shall see whether my word will come true for you or not."

MY HIGH TODAY WAS:

MY LOW TODAY WAS:

MY PRAYER TODAY IS:

my HIGH today was:

my LOW today was:

my PRAYER today is:

DAY 4

today's bible verse:

Deuteronomy 8:3

One does not live by bread alone, but by every word that comes from the mouth of the Lord.

my HIGH today was:

my LOW today was:

my PRAYER today is:

DAY 5

today's bible verse:

Psalm 119:9

How can young people keep their way pure? By guarding it according to your word.

my HIGH today was:

my LOW today was:

my PRAYER today is:

DAY 6

today's bible verse:

Psalm 119:11

I treasure your word in my heart, so that I may not sin against you.

my HIGH today was:

my LOW today was:

my PRAYER today is:

DAY 7

this week's blessing

(NAME), CHILD OF GOD, MAY THE POWER AND TRUTH OF GOD'S WORD SHINE IN YOUR HEAD, HEART AND HOME.

Read the full devotions using FINKlink LL26 @ www.faithink.com

FAITH JOURNAL

WEEK 2

DAY 1

TODAY'S BIBLE VERSE:

MATTHEW 13:23

But as for what was sown on good soil, this is the one who hears the word and understands it, who indeed bears fruit and yields, in one case a hundredfold, in another sixty, and in another thirty.

MY HIGH TODAY WAS:

MY LOW TODAY WAS:

MY PRAYER TODAY IS:

DAY 2

TODAY'S BIBLE VERSE:

MARK 4:14

The sower sows the word.

MY HIGH TODAY WAS:

MY LOW TODAY WAS:

MY PRAYER TODAY IS:

DAY 3

TODAY'S BIBLE VERSE:

LUKE 5:1

Once while Jesus was standing beside the lake of Gennesaret, and the crowd was pressing in on him to hear the word of God...

MY HIGH TODAY WAS:

MY LOW TODAY WAS:

MY PRAYER TODAY IS:

1. SHARE HIGHS & LOWS OF THE DAY.
2. READ AND HIGHLIGHT THE VERSE OF THE DAY IN YOUR BIBLES.
3. TALK ABOUT HOW TODAY'S VERSE RELATES TO YOUR HIGHS & LOWS.
4. PRAY FOR YOUR HIGHS & LOWS, FOR YOUR FAMILY AND FOR THE WORLD.
5. BLESS ONE ANOTHER USING THIS WEEK'S BLESSING (ON THE PREVIOUS PAGE).

DAY 4

TODAY'S BIBLE VERSE:

LUKE 8:21

But he (Jesus) said to them, "My mother and my brothers are those who hear the word of God and do it."

MY HIGH TODAY WAS:

MY LOW TODAY WAS:

MY PRAYER TODAY IS:

DAY 5

TODAY'S BIBLE VERSE:

JOHN 5:24

Very truly, I tell you, anyone who hears my word and believes him who sent me has eternal life, and does not come under judgment, but has passed from death to life.

MY HIGH TODAY WAS:

MY LOW TODAY WAS:

MY PRAYER TODAY IS:

DAY 6

TODAY'S BIBLE VERSE:

JOHN 8:31-32

Then Jesus said to the Jews who had believed in him, "If you continue in my word, you are truly my disciples; and you will know the truth, and the truth will make you free."

MY HIGH TODAY WAS:

MY LOW TODAY WAS:

MY PRAYER TODAY IS:

S | M | T | W | TH | F | S

THEME IN REVIEW

GOD DID NOT WRITE A BOOK AND SEND IT BY MESSENGER TO BE READ AT A DISTANCE BY UNAIDED MINDS. GOD SPOKE A BOOK AND LIVES IN THE SPOKEN WORDS, CONSTANTLY SPEAKING GOD'S WORDS AND CAUSING THE POWER OF THEM TO PERSIST ACROSS THE YEARS.

A. W. TOZER

DAY 7

MY FAVORITE VERSE FROM THE THEME WAS:

....

....

....

....

....

....

....

....

....

THE WORD "WORSHIP" COMES FROM THE OLD ENGLISH "WOERTH" AND "SCHIPPE." IT IS THE SHIP OR VEHICLE THAT BRINGS WORTH TO GOD.

HOW WAS WORSHIP TODAY?

LET'S JUST SAY THE BOAT NEVER LEFT THE DOCK.

LOOKING BACK ON THESE TWO WEEKS, MY HIGHEST HIGH WAS:

....

MY LOWEST LOW THESE PAST WEEKS WAS:

....

ONE WAY GOD ANSWERED MY PRAYERS WAS:

....

ONE WAY GOD MIGHT USE ME AS A SACRED AGENT TO ANSWER THESE PRAYERS:

....

....

FAMILY COVENANT

We have shared *Highs & Lows* this week, read and highlighted the verses assigned in our Bibles, talked about our lives, prayed for one another's highs and lows, and blessed one another.

....	....	....
Parent's Signature	*Teen's Signature*	*Date*

THE FINKMANIA QUIZBOWL

Question 1:

In Lutheran worship, what usually follows directly after the Invocation, Confession, Absolution, and Kyrie?:

(A) The Dismissal,

(B) The Benediction,

(C) Readings from the Old Testament, Psalm, New Testament, and Gospels,

(D) C, plus a proclamation of God's word in the form of a sermon

Question 2:

The standard order for reading the Bible texts in worship usually is:

(A) Gospel, New Testament lesson, Old Testament lesson, Psalm,

(B) Psalm, Old Testament lesson, New Testament lesson, Gospel,

(C) Old Testament lesson, Psalm, New Testament lesson, Gospel,

(D) Watch, bulletin, watch

Question 3:

The Old Testament lesson each Sunday usually:

(A) Tells a story or truth about what God did with the Children of Israel,

(B) Connects with the theme of the Gospel for the day,

(C) Both A and B,

(D) Neither A nor B

Question 4:

The Psalms:

(A) Come from the song book of ancient Israel,

(B) Were written and collected mostly by King David,

(C) Contain songs, prayers, laments, coronation services, and a rich variety of worship poems,

(D) All of the above and then some

Question 5:

The New Testament lesson each week usually:

(A) Comes from one of the Epistles (letters) of Paul or a smaller letter,

(B) Connects with the theme of the Gospel for the day,

(C) Both A and B,

(D) Neither A nor B

Question 6:

The word "Epistle" means:

(A) Guided Missile,

(B) A small furry creature related to an Apostle,

(C) Bathroom,

(D) Letter

Question 7:

The text most preachers focus on each week is:

(A) The Gospel,

(B) The Psalm,

(C) The Old Testament lesson,

(D) The stewardship announcements

Question 8:

The Word "Gospel" comes from:

(A) The Greek *Godspeilein* meaning "God's speech,"

(B) The German *Godsprecke* meaning "God spoke,"

(C) The Old English *God's Spell* meaning God's special magic that sets the world free in Christ,

(D) The Old English *God's Spell* meaning Good News

Question 9:

Other terms for the preacher's main talk during a worship service include:

(A) Homily, sermon and proclamation,

(B) Homonym, service and procrastination,

(C) Harmony, surplus and propitiation,

(D) Snooze time

FINKmania Final Question:

Isaiah 55:10-11 tells us that God's word comes down like:

(A) Good news from the mountains,

(B) Rains and snows from the heavens,

(C) A ton of bricks upon the heads of sinners,

(D) B, and it will accomplish that which God wants it to

Play this online game using FINKlink LL26 @ www.faithink.com

THE WEAKEST FINK

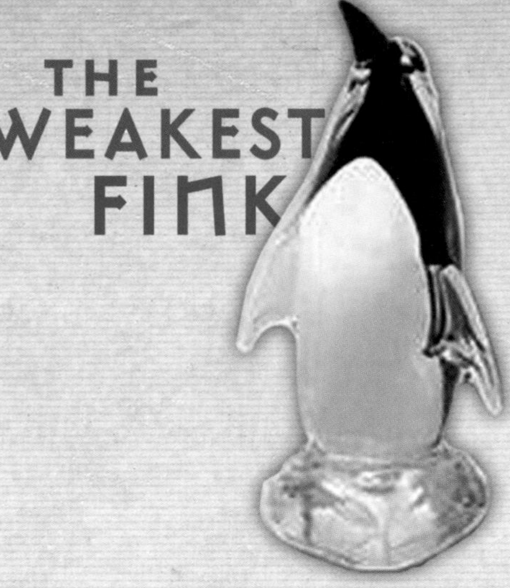

It is impossible to enslave mentally or socially a Bible-reading people.

Horace Greeley

TERMS

Write a definition below.

Epistle

....

....

Gospel

....

....

New Testament

....

....

Old Testament

....

....

Psalms

....

....

FAITH INKUBATORS

Worship: Meal and Sending

"Moses Blesses Israel" Copyright © Dr. He Qi www.heqigallery.com

"The Lord bless you and keep you; the Lord make his face to shine upon you, and be gracious to you; the Lord lift up his countenance upon you, and give you peace."

— Numbers 6:24–26

Listen to this song using FINKlink
LL27 @ www.faithink.com

Most people fed the bums out the back kitchen door. They would sit on the steps, out of sight and out of contact with the family. Rarely would they be invited into the house.

It just wasn't proper. A former Governor and US Senator grew up during the Great Depression. At this time in American history, millions of homeless men were on the move, traveling from town to town on freight trains, looking for work, food, and a place to stay. The unwritten rule in the midwest farming communities was to give these "hobos" a hot meal in exchange for work.

Most farmers and townsfolk would tell the men what to do, then watch them from the kitchen window, and finally feed them a hot plate of food on the back steps. This politician's father, however, regularly broke the rules. He felt it was his Christian duty to welcome strangers into his home. Instead of sliding a plate of food out the back door when an out-of-luck drifter showed up on his property, his dad would welcome the vagabonds into their home. They would be ushered into the dining room, seated at the family table and treated like a long-lost relative or an honored guest.

His father welcomed these strangers like he was welcoming Christ, himself. They would talk, laugh, and share the best of food. The drifters were strengthened by both food and fellowship. Then they were sent out the front door, parting in friendship with a prayer and a blessing. When he became Governor, he never forgot it.

The Gospel declares that no matter how dutiful or prayerful we are, we can't save ourselves... but when we acknowledge that we are paupers at the door of God's mercy, then God can make something beautiful of us.

Brennan Manning

Lutheran Worship: The Meal and the Sending

In a sense, we are all drifters. We are all traveling the train of time between this life and the next. We come as beggars to the back door and are invited inside to the feast at Christ's table. We come with no rights, no claims, nothing to bring to the meal but our ragged and sinful selves. The table is filled with other beggars, yet the host welcomes us all like family. We come as strangers, yet our Lord invites us all to share an event of deeper friendship—a true communion—with him and with our brothers and sisters in Christ.

In this meal Jesus is both the host and the guest. He is both the giver and the gift. Sharing this supper, we share in Christ's life, suffering, death, and resurrection. We come confessing our sins and unworthiness. We kneel with other travelers to take Christ's body and blood. We rise anew to live forgiven, forgiving lives. Then we part as friends with a prayer and a blessing. Christ sends us into the world to find, feed, heal and bless the other hungry drifters in God's name. He calls us to point them all to the open door and the feast that is waiting for them in Christ's church now and in heaven forever.

Images in Art

- What do you see in today's painting by Dr. He Qi?
- Where are you in this work of art?
- How do the image and the verse apply to your life today?

So What Does This Mean?

IN MY CHURCH THEY SAY "THANKS BE TO GOD" AT THE CLOSE OF EVERY SERVICE

THAT'S NOTHING. IN MY CHURCH THEY SAY IT AS SOON AS I STOP PREACHING!

Lord, I am a drifter
You invite me to dine
I am a beggar
You offer me wine
I am so hungry
You give me your bread
I am so weary
You offer a bed
I don't deserve it
I live with my shame
But bless me and send me
To bless in your Name.

Rich Melheim

The Meal & the Sending

When Lutherans gather to worship, there is time to feed the mind and body as well as the soul. Following an engagement with God's word, the service shifts to focus on Holy Communion. Another ancient prayer song, the Great Thanksgiving, is often sung. Christ's Words of Institution are read. The Lord's Prayer is commonly recited. All of these help prepare worshippers to meet and dine with Christ as all are invited to the feast of Holy Communion. Martin Luther claimed the meaning of this meal is "forgiveness of sins, life and salvation." These gifts are not to be kept to yourself. Forgiveness is to be shared. Life is to be lived. Salvation is to be proclaimed to all through all you say and do. In Lutheran worship, after everyone is fed, we move quickly into the world to share what we have been given. Before we go, we receive the blessing of God. This blessing, sometimes called a Benediction, reminds us that God goes with us out the door and into the week. We are invited to go in peace and serve the Lord.

So it comes full circle. We are gathered together in worship in order to be scattered in service. We are gathered to be fed and strengthened so we might go into the world and share our food and strength. The sending in worship lets us loose as drifters again—not as purposeless drifters without a mission or a clue—but as messengers and missionaries who spread out like seeds on the wind to plant God's love and grace wherever we go.

Bible Time

Read and highlight Numbers 6:24-26 in your Bible. In the margin write "Aaron's Blessing." Read and highlight the following verses. Why does God want to bless you?

Genesis 1:22 — I Chronicles 4:10

Jeremiah 29:11 — Hebrews 6:14

Questions to Ponder

1. Who is the last person in the world you would expect to see in church next Sunday?

2. What would it take for you to get them there with you? Would you dare invite them?

3. What do you think about when you kneel at the altar to receive Holy Communion?

SMALL GROUP

SHARE, READ, TALK, PRAY, BLESS

1. **SHARE** your highs and lows of the week one-on-one with another person. Listen carefully and record your friend's thoughts in the space below. Then return to small group and share your friend's highs and lows.

   MY HIGHS + LOWS THIS WEEK WERE:

   ....

   MY FRIEND'S HIGHS + LOWS THIS WEEK WERE:

   ....

2. **READ** and highlight the theme verse in your Bibles. Circle key words and learn the verse in song.

3. **TALK** about how today's verse relates to your highs and lows. Review the art for today, the Quiz Bowl questions, the terms, and the cartoons. Then write a sentence on each of the following:

   ONE NEW THING I LEARNED TODAY:

   ....

   ONE THING I ALREADY KNEW THAT IS WORTH REPEATING:

   ....

   ONE THING I WOULD LIKE TO KNOW MORE ABOUT:

   ....

4. **PRAY** for one another, praising and thanking God for your highs, and asking God to be with you in your lows. Include your friend's highs and lows in your prayers.

   A PRAISING PRAYER: ....

   A THANKING PRAYER: ....

   AN ASKING PRAYER: ....

5. **BLESS** one another using the blessing of the week. (right) Mark each person with the sign of the cross as you bless them.

THIS WEEK'S BLESSING

(NAME), CHILD OF GOD, MAY YOU BE FED AND STRENGTHENED IN WORSHIP, THEN SENT TO SERVE IN JESUS' NAME. AMEN.

THE FAITH5

Read the full devotions using FINKlink
LL27 @ www.faithink.com

WEEK 1

JOURNAL

DAY 1

TODAY'S BIBLE VERSE:

NUMBERS 6:24-26

The Lord bless you and keep you; the Lord make his face to shine upon you, and be gracious to you; the Lord lift up his countenance upon you, and give you peace.

MY HIGH TODAY WAS:

MY LOW TODAY WAS:

MY PRAYER TODAY IS:

DAY 2

TODAY'S BIBLE VERSE:

LUKE 4:8

Worship the Lord your God, and serve only him.

MY HIGH TODAY WAS:

MY LOW TODAY WAS:

MY PRAYER TODAY IS:

DAY 3

TODAY'S BIBLE VERSE:

JAMES 1:27

Religion that is pure and undefiled before God, the Father, is this: to care for orphans and widows in their distress, and to keep oneself unstained by the world.

MY HIGH TODAY WAS:

MY LOW TODAY WAS:

MY PRAYER TODAY IS:

my HIGH today was:

my LOW today was:

my PRAYER today is:

DAY 4

today's bible verse:

I Corinthians 4:1

Think of us in this way, as servants of Christ and stewards of God's mysteries.

my HIGH today was:

my LOW today was:

my PRAYER today is:

DAY 5

today's bible verse:

Isaiah 48:20

Go out from Babylon, flee from Chaldea, declare this with a shout of joy, proclaim it, send it forth to the end of the earth; say, "The Lord has redeemed his servant Jacob!"

my HIGH today was:

my LOW today was:

my PRAYER today is:

DAY 6

today's bible verse:

Matthew 23:11

The greatest among you will be your servant.

my HIGH today was:

my LOW today was:

my PRAYER today is:

DAY 7

this week's blessing

(NAME), child of God, may you be fed and strengthened in worship, then sent to serve in Jesus' name. Amen.

Read the full devotions using FINKlink
LL27 @ www.faithink.com

FAITH journal

WEEK 2

DAY 1

TODAY'S BIBLE VERSE:

JOHN 20:21

Jesus said to them again, "Peace be with you. As the Father has sent me, so I send you."

MY HIGH TODAY WAS:

MY LOW TODAY WAS:

MY PRAYER TODAY IS:

DAY 2

TODAY'S BIBLE VERSE:

Psalm 32:11

Be glad in the Lord and rejoice, O righteous, and shout for joy, all you upright in heart.

MY HIGH TODAY WAS:

MY LOW TODAY WAS:

MY PRAYER TODAY IS:

DAY 3

TODAY'S BIBLE VERSE:

Amos 5:23-24

Take away from me the noise of your songs; I will not listen to the melody of your harps. But let justice roll down like waters, and righteousness like an ever-flowing stream.

MY HIGH TODAY WAS:

MY LOW TODAY WAS:

MY PRAYER TODAY IS:

1. SHARE HIGHS & LOWS OF THE DAY.

2. READ AND HIGHLIGHT THE VERSE OF THE DAY IN YOUR BIBLES.

3. TALK ABOUT HOW TODAY'S VERSE RELATES TO YOUR HIGHS & LOWS.

4. PRAY FOR YOUR HIGHS & LOWS, FOR YOUR FAMILY AND FOR THE WORLD.

5. BLESS ONE ANOTHER USING THIS WEEK'S BLESSING (ON THE PREVIOUS PAGE).

DAY 4

TODAY'S BIBLE VERSE:

JOHN 15:12

This is my commandment, that you love one another as I have loved you.

MY HIGH TODAY WAS:

MY LOW TODAY WAS:

MY PRAYER TODAY IS:

DAY 5

TODAY'S BIBLE VERSE:

PSALM 22:22A

I will tell of your name to my brothers and sisters...

MY HIGH TODAY WAS:

MY LOW TODAY WAS:

MY PRAYER TODAY IS:

DAY 6

TODAY'S BIBLE VERSE:

PSALM 98:4

Make a joyful noise to the Lord, all the earth; break forth into joyous song and sing praises.

MY HIGH TODAY WAS:

MY LOW TODAY WAS:

MY PRAYER TODAY IS:

DUCK CHURCH
SERVICES 8
11:00
INKUBATORS PROVIDED
REV. M.A. LARD PASTOR
EVERY SUNDAY AT DUCK CHURCH THE SAME THING HAPPENS. AFTER THE SERMON HYMN, DUCK PASTOR ASCENDS THE HIGH PULPIT AND PREACHES THE SAME DUCK SERMON
DUCKS! YOU HAVE WINGS!
QUACK QUACK
YOU WERE MADE TO SOAR T
HEAVENS
QUACK! QUACK! QUACK!
YOU CAN DEFY GRAVITY AND SHED THE BONDS OF THE EARTH AND FLY! FLY! FLY!
QUACK! QUACK! QUACK!
AND THEN THEY ALL WADDLE HOME...
GREAT SERMON TODAY, REV!
THANKS
*STORY BY DR. TONY CAMPOLO

S | M | T | W | TH | F | S

THEME IN REVIEW

IF YOU LISTEN TO JESUS CAREFULLY, YOU WORSHIP NOT BY GOING THROUGH THE LITURGY AND JUMPING THROUGH HOOPS. HOW DO YOU WORSHIP? "WHEN DID I SEE YOU HUNGRY AND POOR AND FEED YOU..."

BILL EASUM

DAY 7

MY FAVORITE VERSE FROM THE THEME WAS:

....

....

....

....

....

....

....

....

....

LOOKING BACK ON THESE TWO WEEKS, MY HIGHEST HIGH WAS:

....

MY LOWEST LOW THESE PAST WEEKS WAS:

....

ONE WAY GOD ANSWERED MY PRAYERS WAS:

....

ONE WAY GOD MIGHT USE ME AS A SACRED AGENT TO ANSWER THESE PRAYERS:

....

....

FAMILY COVENANT

We have shared *Highs & Lows* this week, read and highlighted the verses assigned in our Bibles, talked about our lives, prayed for one another's highs and lows, and blessed one another.

....	....	....
Parent's Signature	*Teen's Signature*	*Date*

THE FINKMANIA QUIZ BOWL

Question 1:

After the Invocation, Confession, Absolution, Kyrie, Old Testament, Psalm, New Testament, Gospel and sermon, the next thing that happens in Lutheran worship is:

(A) The Benediction,
(B) The Dismissal,
(C) A hymn, a creed, some prayers and the peace,
(D) Football fans leaving early to catch kick-off

Question 2:

The creed most often used in Lutheran worship after the sermon is:

(A) The Nicene Creed,
(B) The Apostles' Creed,
(C) The Apolo's Creed,
(D) Most often B, but also A

Question 3:

We pass the peace in Lutheran worship to:

(A) Fill the time,
(B) Reconnect and reconcile with our sisters and brothers in Christ,
(C) Witness our oneness in Christ and include all in the family of God,
(D) Both B and C

Question 4:

The "Great Thanksgiving" in Lutheran worship is:

(A) A beautiful and ancient prayer song used to help prepare worshippers for Holy Communion,
(B) A beautiful and ancient prayer poem used to help prepare worshippers for the offering,
(C) The Lord's Prayer
(D) Best sung only by professionals

Question 5:

The Words of Institution are always done before Communion because:

(A) We've always done it that way before,
(B) They help us focus on exactly what Jesus said and did on the night he was betrayed,
(C) God's word with the bread and wine make it a sacrament to Lutherans
(D) C, B and maybe A

Question 6:

"Lord, now let your servant go in peace...":

(A) Is sung following Holy Communion in many Lutheran worship services,
(B) Is called the *Nunc Dimittis* in Latin,
(C) Is a phrase said by an old righteous man named Simeon when he first saw the baby Jesus,
(D) All of the above

Question 7:

The term "benediction" is Latin for:

(A) "Bennie has good diction,"
(B) "Good choice,"
(C) "Good word,"
(D) "Good Lord, get me out of here"

Question 8:

When does the service begin?:

(A) It depends on whether we're on the summer or fall schedule,
(B) Whenever the pastor says so,
(C) When the worship is over the service begins,
(D) Never. We're Lutherans!

Question 9:

The last line in many Lutheran worship services is:

(A) Go in peace, serve the Lord,
(B) Go in peace, serve the pot luck,
(C) Go in peace, serve the pot luck to the pastor,
(D) Thanks be to God!

FINKmania Final Question:

In Numbers 6:24, God instructed Aaron to bless the Children of Israel saying:

(A) "The Lord bless you and keep you,"
(B) "The Lord make his face to shine upon you and be gracious to you,"
(C) "The Lord lift up his countenance upon you,"
(D) All of the above, plus "and give you peace."

Play this online game using **FINKlink**
LL27 @ www.faithink.com

THE WEAKEST FINK

We come to the Hungry feast...

Ray Makeever

TERMS

Write a definition below.

Benediction/Blessing

....

....

Great Thanksgiving

....

....

Holy Communion

....

....

Service

....

....

Words of Institution

....

....

FAITH INKUBATORS

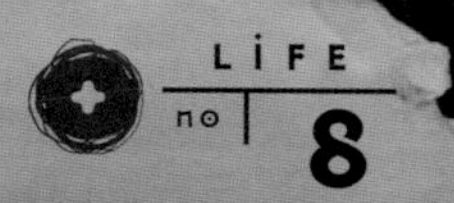

Confessing My Faith

"He is Risen" Copyright © Dr. He Qi www.heqigallery.com

"The word is near you, on your lips and in your heart... because if you confess with your lips that Jesus is Lord and believe in your heart that God raised him from the dead, you will be saved. No one who believes in him will be put to shame."

— Romans 10:8a, 9, 11

Listen to this song using FINKlink
LL28 @ www.faithink.com

Imagine you had just been diagnosed with a terminal illness. Imagine being told you had only a short time to live. How would you spend your last days on earth?

What would you want to do that you normally wouldn't even consider? Would you go parasailing? Sky diving? Bungie jumping? Nascar racing? Swimming with dolphins? Who would you want to see? Where would you want to go?

Think about waking up each morning. Would you jump out of bed with urgency to experience every minute of your remaining time? Or would you pull the covers back over your head and think "why bother?" Would you eat, drink, and be merry, trying to live each moment to the fullest? Or would you find some small chapel on a hillside and sit alone in prayer and thought? If you had only weeks or hours left to live, would the people who annoy you still annoy you? Or would you smile at them, forgive them, and bless them on their way? Would you try to take a quick revenge on those who have done you wrong? Or would you let their insults roll off your back like rain on a Scotch Guard umbrella and forgive them? Would you visit the people whom you had wronged and try to make amends? Would you invest a single minute of that remaining time watching television and playing video games? Or would you try to watch sunsets, play the game of life to the max, and give yourself to others in ways that would be remembered?

Would you give away your favorite possessions to those you loved? Would you hand out all your money to the homeless on the street? Or would you quickly blow it all on lottery tickets, electronic gear, and toys? Would you say "I love you" or "Jesus loves you" to everyone you met? Or would you talk about the weather, sports, and who's dating who at school?

The news was so sudden when I found out I had cancer. I kept asking, "Why me, God?" and "Why did you do this to me?" Then my faith hit me. I realized that God loved me every minute of my life even when I am in heaven.

Alex Lynch
October 17, 1990
- June 15, 2005

What would you do?

Would you sleep your life away or wake and never close your eyes? Would you video tape your life's story to give the world something to remember? Or would you watch someone else's videos? Would you dance? Would you laugh? Would you cry? Would you sing? Would you love?

Maybe you would no longer spend time on anything that didn't ultimately matter.

Maybe you would only invest those fleeting hours in things that would outlast you. Things that mattered. Family. Friends. Love. God. Giving.

Maybe you would finally learn to live before you died.

Order this art print using FINKlink
LL28 | @ www.faithink.com

images in ART

- What do you see in today's painting by Dr. He Qi?
- Where are you in this work of art?
- How do the image and the verse apply to your life today?

So What Does This Mean?

When your time comes to die, be not like those whose hearts are filled with fear of death, so that when their time comes they weep and pray for a little more time to live their lives over again in a different way. Sing your death song, and die like a hero going home.

Tecumseh

Prayer

Holy Jesus, make me live today like it matters. Equip me to live in such a power-filled way that people see Christ in me, know Christ in me, and catch the love of God through all I say and do. I pray in the powerful name of Jesus. Amen.

Confessing My Faith

Guess what. You have a terminal illness. It is called life. It is short and the outcome is certain. No one makes it out of here alive. You may not have the luxury of knowing the day and hour of your death, but you know it is coming. Could you dare—would you dare—to live each moment like it mattered?

The followers of Jesus knew they didn't have time to waste. This uneducated bunch of fishermen, prostitutes, and tax collectors from the back hills of Galilee had seen Jesus live and die. After Easter morning, they swore to their deaths they had seen him raised back to life. Fifty days later, on Pentecost, the Holy Spirit came upon them with power and gave this rag-tag group of followers an urgency they had never known to witness to the world. They went out from that place living like it mattered. They believed in their hearts Jesus was who he said he was—the Son of God. They confessed with their lips that Jesus was Lord. They wanted everyone to know God had raised him from the dead and that God could raise them, too. In the power of the Holy Spirit they made every moment of their lives count. And God gave them the words, wisdom, healing power, boldness, courage and love to transform the world.

That same Holy Spirit from God is available to you. That same living Christ and resurrection power is yours. Pray for the power to confess, believe and live today like it matters.

It does.

Bible Time

Read and highlight the verse of the week, Romans 10:8-11, writing "Confess and Believe" in the margin.

Questions to Ponder

1. What activities do you consider a waste of time? Why? What activities do you consider a wonderful use of time? Why?

2. How would your relationship to God change if you knew you only had a short time to live? How would your relationship with others change if you knew you only had a short time to live?

3. What does the verse of the week mean to you? Why is both confessing and believing essential to salvation?

Small Group

share, read, talk, pray, bless

1. **SHARE** your highs and lows of the week one-on-one with another person. Listen carefully and record your friend's thoughts in the space below. Then return to small group and share your friend's highs and lows.

   MY HIGHS + LOWS THIS WEEK WERE:

   ....

   MY FRIEND'S HIGHS + LOWS THIS WEEK WERE:

   ....

2. **READ** and highlight the theme verse in your Bibles. Circle key words and learn the verse in song.

3. **TALK** about how today's verse relates to your highs and lows. Review the art for today, the Quiz Bowl questions, the terms, and the cartoons. Then write a sentence on each of the following:

   ONE NEW THING I LEARNED TODAY:

   ....

   ONE THING I ALREADY KNEW THAT IS WORTH REPEATING:

   ....

   ONE THING I WOULD LIKE TO KNOW MORE ABOUT:

   ....

4. **PRAY** for one another, praising and thanking God for your highs, and asking God to be with you in your lows. Include your friend's highs and lows in your prayers.

   A PRAISING PRAYER: ....

   A THANKING PRAYER: ....

   AN ASKING PRAYER: ....

5. **BLESS** one another using the blessing of the week. (right) Mark each person with the sign of the cross as you bless them.

THIS WEEK'S BLESSING

(NAME), CHILD OF GOD, MAY YOUR LIFE BE A SONG OF PRAISE AND YOUR DEATH BE A SHOUT OF VICTORY!

THE FAITH 5

Read the full devotions using FINKlink

LL28 @ www.faithink.com

JOURNAL

WEEK 1

DAY 1

TODAY'S BIBLE VERSE:

Romans 10:8a, 9

The word is near you, on your lips and in your heart... because if you confess with your lips that Jesus is Lord and believe in your heart that God raised him from the dead, you will be saved.

MY HIGH TODAY WAS:

MY LOW TODAY WAS:

MY PRAYER TODAY IS:

DAY 2

TODAY'S BIBLE VERSE:

Romans 10:11

No one who believes in him will be put to shame.

MY HIGH TODAY WAS:

MY LOW TODAY WAS:

MY PRAYER TODAY IS:

DAY 3

TODAY'S BIBLE VERSE:

Psalm 27:1

The Lord is my light and my salvation; whom shall I fear? The Lord is the stronghold of my life; of whom shall I be afraid?

MY HIGH TODAY WAS:

MY LOW TODAY WAS:

MY PRAYER TODAY IS:

my HIGH today was:

my LOW today was:

my PRAYER today is:

DAY 4

today's bible verse:

Psalm 18:2

I love you, O Lord, my strength. The Lord is my rock, my fortress, and my deliverer, my God, my rock in whom I take refuge, my shield, and the horn of my salvation, my stronghold.

my HIGH today was:

my LOW today was:

my PRAYER today is:

DAY 5

today's bible verse:

Matthew 10:19-20

When they hand you over, do not worry about how you are to speak or what you are to say; for what you are to say will be given to you at that time; for it is not you who speak, but the Spirit of your Father speaking through you.

my HIGH today was:

my LOW today was:

my PRAYER today is:

DAY 6

today's bible verse:

Psalm 33:5

He loves righteousness and justice; the earth is full of the steadfast love of the Lord.

my HIGH today was:

my LOW today was:

my PRAYER today is:

DAY 7

this week's blessing

(NAME), CHILD OF GOD, MAY YOUR LIFE BE A SONG OF PRAISE AND YOUR DEATH BE A SHOUT OF VICTORY!

Read the full devotions using FINKlink
LL28 @ www.faithink.com

FAITH journal

WEEK 2

DAY 1

TODAY'S BIBLE VERSE:

JEREMIAH 29:11

For surely I know the plans I have for you, says the Lord, plans for your welfare and not for harm, to give you a future with hope.

MY HIGH TODAY WAS:

MY LOW TODAY WAS:

MY PRAYER TODAY IS:

DAY 2

TODAY'S BIBLE VERSE:

Acts 1:8

But you will receive power when the Holy Spirit has come upon you; and you will be my witnesses in Jerusalem, in all Judea and Samaria, and to the ends of the earth.

MY HIGH TODAY WAS:

MY LOW TODAY WAS:

MY PRAYER TODAY IS:

DAY 3

TODAY'S BIBLE VERSE:

Acts 2:38

Peter said to them, "Repent, and be baptized every one of you in the name of Jesus Christ so that your sins may be forgiven; and you will receive the gift of the Holy Spirit."

MY HIGH TODAY WAS:

MY LOW TODAY WAS:

MY PRAYER TODAY IS:

2. READ AND HIGHLIGHT THE VERSE OF THE DAY IN YOUR BIBLES.

3. TALK ABOUT HOW TODAY'S VERSE RELATES TO YOUR HIGHS & LOWS.

4. PRAY FOR YOUR HIGHS & LOWS, FOR YOUR FAMILY AND FOR THE WORLD.

5. BLESS ONE ANOTHER USING THIS WEEK'S BLESSING (ON THE PREVIOUS PAGE).

DAY 4

TODAY'S BIBLE VERSE:

I Corinthians 2:4-5

My speech and my proclamation were not with plausible words of wisdom, but with a demonstration of the Spirit and of power, so that your faith might rest not on human wisdom but on the power of God.

MY HIGH TODAY WAS:

MY LOW TODAY WAS:

MY PRAYER TODAY IS:

DAY 5

TODAY'S BIBLE VERSE:

Ephesians 3:16

I pray that, according to the riches of his glory, he may grant that you may be strengthened in your inner being with power through his Spirit.

MY HIGH TODAY WAS:

MY LOW TODAY WAS:

MY PRAYER TODAY IS:

DAY 6

TODAY'S BIBLE VERSE:

Psalm 119:46

I will also speak of your decrees before kings, and shall not be put to shame.

MY HIGH TODAY WAS:

MY LOW TODAY WAS:

MY PRAYER TODAY IS:

S | M | T | W | TH | F | S

THEME IN REVIEW

WE ARE KNOWN BY THE QUALITY OF OUR INNER LIVES...I MEAN THE QUALITY WHICH MAKES CONTAGIOUS CHRISTIANS, THE QUALITY THAT MAKES PEOPLE CATCH THE LOVE OF GOD FROM YOU.

EVELYN UNDERHILL

DAY 7

MY FAVORITE VERSE FROM THE THEME WAS:

LOOKING BACK ON THESE TWO WEEKS, MY HIGHEST HIGH WAS:

MY LOWEST LOW THESE PAST WEEKS WAS:

ONE WAY GOD ANSWERED MY PRAYERS WAS:

ONE WAY GOD MIGHT USE ME AS A SACRED AGENT TO ANSWER THESE PRAYERS:

FAMILY COVENANT

We have shared *Highs & Lows* this week, read and highlighted the verses assigned in our Bible talked about our lives, prayed for one another's highs and lows, and blessed one another.

Parent's Signature *Teen's Signature* *Date*

THE FINKMANIA QUIZBOWL

QUESTION 1:

If they knew they had only a short time to live, most people would:

(A) Invest more time doing things that really mattered,

(B) Spend more time watching television and playing video games,

(C) Spend more time nagging and complaining about their parents and friends,

(D) Not change a thing

QUESTION 2:

The writer of the letter to the Romans, St. Paul, stressed the importance of:

(A) Confessing Jesus as Lord out loud,

(B) Believing in your heart God raised Jesus from the dead,

(C) Both confessing and believing,

(D) Changing your name if you are going to make it in Hollywood

QUESTION 3:

Why is it important to share your faith in Christ in words?:

(A) Some people need to hear exactly what you believe and why you believe it before they will come to Christ,

(B) It helps you better understand what you believe and why you believe it,

(C) People can't read your mind,

(D) All of the above

QUESTION 4:

The very first Christian creed was:

(A) Jesus is Lord,

(B) One Lord, one faith, one baptism,

(C) I believe in God the Father Almighty, creator of heaven and earth,

(D) Get more

QUESTION 5:

Why is it important to share your faith in Christ through loving actions?:

(A) Faith without works is dead,

(B) Faith without words is dead,

(C) Some people need to see your faith in action before they will come to Christ and faith without works is dead,

(D) All of the above

QUESTION 6:

The word "confession":

(A) Comes from the Latin *con* = with + *fateri* = to admit,

(B) Comes from the Latin *con* = with + *fessioni* = honesty,

(C) Comes from the Latin *con* = with + *pfassioni* = passion,

(D) Comes from the Latin *confusion* = to admit you don't know Latin

QUESTION 7:

What two things do most Lutheran Christians confess every Sunday?:

(A) Sorrow and sins,

(B) Sorrow for sins and their faith

(C) Their sins and their parents sins,

(D) Their need for money and fame

QUESTION 8:

To confess your sins means:

(A) To say you are sorry for them,

(B) To say you are sorry you got caught,

(C) To come clean before God and others,

(D) Both A & C

QUESTION 9:

To confess your faith means:

(A) To say you are sorry for your faith,

(B) To admit what you believe out loud,

(C) To recite a creed whether you believe it or not,

(D) To admit what your parents tell you you're supposed to believe out loud

FINKMANIA FINAL QUESTION:

Romans 10:11 says, "No one who believes in him (Jesus) shall be put...":

(A) To death,

(B) To the test,

(C) To shame,

(D) In any unpleasant situation at any time in the near future

Play this online game using **FINKlink** LL28 @ www.faithink.com

THE WEAKEST FINK

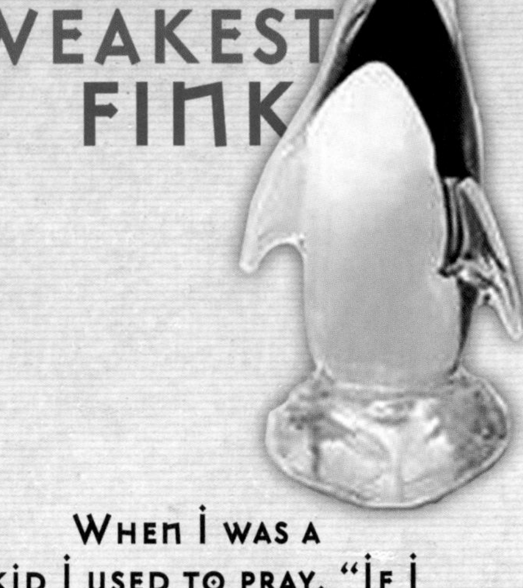

WHEN I WAS A KID I USED TO PRAY, "IF I SHOULD DIE BEFORE I WAKE, I PRAY THE LORD MY SOUL TO TAKE." NOW I PRAY, "IF I SHOULD WAKE BEFORE I DIE..."

RICH MELHEIM

TERMS

WRITE A DEFINITION BELOW.

BELIEVE

CONFESS

SAVE

TERMINAL ILLNESS

WITNESS

"Hear my cry, O God; listen to my prayer. From the end of the earth I call to you, when my heart is faint. Lead me to the rock that is higher than I; for you are my refuge, a strong tower against the enemy. Let me abide in your tent forever, find refuge under the shelter of your wings. For you, O God, have heard my vows; you have given me the heritage of those who fear your name. So I will always sing praises to your name, as I pay my vows day after day."

— Psalm 61: 1-5, 8

Listen to this song using FINKlink

LL29 @ www.faithink.com

1. Jeopardy Category: Currency

Answer: In Asia, the "baht" is the currency of this country. Do you know the question to this answer? Try these:

2. Jeopardy Category: Star Wars

Answer: Boba Fett's father. Question:

3. Jeopardy Category: IM

Answer: ROTFL Question:

4. Jeopardy Category: Idols

Answer: Kelly Clarkson Question:

Jeopardy! is a trivia game covering a variety of topics from history to literature to pop culture. To play, three contestants are presented a clue in the form of an answer. To win, they must give a response phrased in the form of a question. Merv Griffin created this game in his apartment dining room in 1964. Over 12 million viewers still tune in daily to play. (Some say it stalls Alzheimer's!)

5. Jeopardy Category: Eternity

Answer: Jesus Christ Question: *(Key on next page)*

What's the question? Your question to this answer and answer to this question is no trivial matter. Questions and answers about Jesus Christ will have an effect on your life, outlook, and eternal future. Is Jesus who he said he was? Is he the one who loves you? Is he your Lord and your God? Does he guide and direct your decisions? Your thoughts? Your actions? Or is he simply a famous religious figure who said and did some interestingly strange things two thousand years ago and now has no more effect on your life than Buddha, Moses, or Herbert Hoover?

There are a handful of times in life when you stand in the presence of the holy God and make a promise. In Baptism, you may one day stand at a font and make a promise to God on behalf of a child. At a wedding, you may one day stand at an altar and promise faithfulness to your spouse. In court, you may one day be asked to place a hand on a Bible and promise to tell the truth, the whole truth and nothing but the truth. In each of these cases, the promise you make directly involves others. If you break it, they suffer.

In Lutheran confirmation, this promise isn't made primarily for someone else. Hopefully, you are not making it just to keep grandma happy. Others may be involved in your Christian life when you walk down the aisle on confirmation day, but whether you keep the promises or not is a matter between you and God. This is an adult promise with adult consequences. Are you ready for it?

To hold your truth, to believe it with all your heart, to work with all your might, first to make it real to yourself and then to show its preciousness to others, and then—not till then, but then—to leave the questions of when and how and by whom it shall prevail to God: that is the true life of the believer.

Phillips Brooks

Images in Art

- What do you see in today's painting by Dr. He Qi?
- Where are you in this work of art?
- How do the image and the verse apply to your life today?

So What Does This Mean?

HEY HEY GOODBYE
SHANANANANANANA
HEY HEY GOODBYE!
I REALLY LIKE YOUR PLAN FOR THE CONFIRMATION SERVICE, BUT I MUST CONFESS I'M HAVING SOME TROUBLE WITH YOUR CHOICE FOR THE RECESSIONAL HYMN...

From Previous Page:

Question 1:
What is "Thailand?"

Question 2:
Who is "Jango Fett?"

Question 3:
What is "rolling on the floor laughing?"

Question 4:
Who was the first season's winner of the American Idol television show?

Question 5:
Who is my Redeemer and Lord, my Friend and my Savior, my strength when all else fails, the Only Son of the Living God, and the world's first, best, and last hope?

Confirming My Convictions

Some Lutherans call the confirmation service "Affirmation of Baptism." To affirm means to say "yes" to someone or something. In Baptism God says, "yes, this is my child!" In confirmation, you are saying "yes" to the God who first said "yes" to you. In Baptism someone made a promise on your behalf to raise you in the faith and knowledge of Christ. In confirmation, you are making that promise your own. You stand before family and friends to claim the God who claimed you. You now take on the responsibility for your own life of faith. In Baptism you were adopted into God's family. The inheritance was yours. In confirmation, you affirm that adoption and claim it as your own. In Baptism you were grafted into the strong tree of Christ—the church. In confirmation, you are stating to the world that you will continue to be fed and nourished by God's tree, and that you will begin to produce good fruit with the nourishment you have been given.

FINAL JEOPARDY: Answer: Yes!
Question: What's the question?

Bible Time

Read and highlight the theme verses, Psalm 61:1-5, 8, in your Bible, writing "My Vows" in the margin. Next, write out the promises you hear God inviting you to make in the following passages:

Joshua 24:15	I promise to serve...
John 8:31	I promise to continue...
Romans 10: 9	I promise to confess...
Ephesians 6:15	I promise to proclaim...
Hebrews 10:25	I promise to meet...
Revelation 3:20	I promise to open...

Questions to Ponder

1. Look carefully at the promises your parents made for you in Holy Baptism. What did they promise to be and do?

2. Look carefully at the promises you are making on confirmation day. What are you promising to be and do?

3. What will change on confirmation day? What won't change?

Small Group

share, read, talk, pray, bless

1. **SHARE** your highs and lows of the week one-on-one with another person. Listen carefully and record your friend's thoughts in the space below. Then return to small group and share your friend's highs and lows.

   MY HIGHS + LOWS THIS WEEK WERE:

   ....

   MY FRIEND'S HIGHS + LOWS THIS WEEK WERE:

   ....

2. **READ** and highlight the theme verse in your Bibles. Circle key words and learn the verse in song.

3. **TALK** about how today's verse relates to your highs and lows. Review the art for today, the Quiz Bowl questions, the terms, and the cartoons. Then write a sentence on each of the following:

   ONE NEW THING I LEARNED TODAY:

   ....

   ONE THING I ALREADY KNEW THAT IS WORTH REPEATING:

   ....

   ONE THING I WOULD LIKE TO KNOW MORE ABOUT:

   ....

4. **PRAY** for one another, praising and thanking God for your highs, and asking God to be with you in your lows. Include your friend's highs and lows in your prayers.

   A PRAISING PRAYER: ....

   A THANKING PRAYER: ....

   AN ASKING PRAYER: ....

5. **BLESS** one another using the blessing of the week. (right) Mark each person with the sign of the cross as you bless them.

THIS WEEK'S BLESSING

(NAME), MAY GOD GUIDE YOUR LIFE, EMPOWER YOUR SERVING, GIVE YOU PATIENCE IN SUFFERING, AND BRING YOU TO ETERNAL LIFE.

Read the full devotions using FINKlink LL29 @ www.faithink.com

WEEK 1

FAITH JOURNAL

DAY 1

TODAY'S BIBLE VERSE:

Psalm 61:4-5

Let me abide in your tent forever, find refuge under the shelter of your wings. For you, O God, have heard my vows; you have given me the heritage of those who fear your name.

MY HIGH TODAY WAS:

MY LOW TODAY WAS:

MY PRAYER TODAY IS:

DAY 2

TODAY'S BIBLE VERSE:

Psalm 61:8

So I will always sing praises to your name, as I pay my vows day after day.

MY HIGH TODAY WAS:

MY LOW TODAY WAS:

MY PRAYER TODAY IS:

DAY 3

TODAY'S BIBLE VERSE:

Acts 4:12

There is salvation in no one else, for there is no other name under heaven given among mortals by which we must be saved.

MY HIGH TODAY WAS:

MY LOW TODAY WAS:

MY PRAYER TODAY IS:

my HIGH today was:

my LOW today was:

my PRAYER today is:

DAY 4

today's bible verse:

Romans 12:1

I appeal to you therefore, brothers and sisters, by the mercies of God, to present your bodies as a living sacrifice, holy and acceptable to God, which is your spiritual worship.

my HIGH today was:

my LOW today was:

my PRAYER today is:

DAY 5

today's bible verse:

II Corinthians 5:17

So if anyone is in Christ, there is a new creation: everything old has passed away; see, everything has become new!

my HIGH today was:

my LOW today was:

my PRAYER today is:

DAY 6

today's bible verse:

Colossians 2:6-7

As you therefore have received Christ Jesus the Lord, continue to live your lives in him, rooted and built up in him and established in the faith, just as you were taught, abounding in thanksgiving.

my HIGH today was:

my LOW today was:

my PRAYER today is:

DAY 7

this week's blessing

(NAME), MAY GOD GUIDE YOUR LIFE, EMPOWER YOUR SERVING, GIVE YOU PATIENCE IN SUFFERING, AND BRING YOU TO ETERNAL LIFE.

THE FAITH 5

Read the full devotions using FINKlink LL29 @ www.faithink.com

WEEK 2

JOURNAL

DAY 1

TODAY'S BIBLE VERSE:

JOHN 19:5-6

So Jesus came out, wearing the crown of thorns and the purple robe. Pilate said to them, "Here is the man!" When the chief priests and guards saw Jesus they shouted, "Crucify him, crucify him!"

MY HIGH TODAY WAS:

MY LOW TODAY WAS:

MY PRAYER TODAY IS:

DAY 2

TODAY'S BIBLE VERSE:

JOHN 20:31

These are written so that you may come to believe that Jesus is the Messiah, the Son of God. And that through believing you may have life in his name.

MY HIGH TODAY WAS:

MY LOW TODAY WAS:

MY PRAYER TODAY IS:

DAY 3

TODAY'S BIBLE VERSE:

MATTHEW 1:18

Now the birth of Jesus the Messiah took place in this way. When his mother Mary had been engaged to Joseph, but before they lived together, she was found to be with child from the Holy Spirit.

MY HIGH TODAY WAS:

MY LOW TODAY WAS:

MY PRAYER TODAY IS:

1. SHARE HIGHS & LOWS OF THE DAY.

2. READ AND HIGHLIGHT THE VERSE OF THE DAY IN YOUR BIBLES.

3. TALK ABOUT HOW TODAY'S VERSE RELATES TO YOUR HIGHS & LOWS.

4. PRAY FOR YOUR HIGHS & LOWS, FOR YOUR FAMILY AND FOR THE WORLD.

5. BLESS ONE ANOTHER USING THIS WEEK'S BLESSING (ON THE PREVIOUS PAGE).

DAY 4

TODAY'S BIBLE VERSE:

MATTHEW 4:18

As Jesus was walking by the Sea of Galilee, he saw two brothers, Simon (called Peter) and his brother Andrew. They were throwing a net into the sea because they were fishermen.

MY HIGH TODAY WAS:

MY LOW TODAY WAS:

MY PRAYER TODAY IS:

DAY 5

TODAY'S BIBLE VERSE:

MATTHEW 5:6

Blessed are those who hunger and thirst for righteousness: they shall be filled.

MY HIGH TODAY WAS:

MY LOW TODAY WAS:

MY PRAYER TODAY IS:

ME? I'M THE GUY WHO INVENTED LUTHERAN
CONFIRMATION.

DAY 6

TODAY'S BIBLE VERSE:

MATTHEW 28:5B-6

I know you are looking for Jesus, who has been crucified. He is not here. He has risen from the dead as he said he would. Come and see the place where his body was.

MY HIGH TODAY WAS:

MY LOW TODAY WAS:

MY PRAYER TODAY IS:

S | M | T | W | TH | F | S

THEME IN REVIEW

YOUTH IS BY NATURE A TIME OF REBELLION. RATHER THAN TRYING TO SQUELCH THE REBELLION, WHY NOT ENLIST THEM THE JOIN THE CAUSE OF THE GREATEST REBEL OF ALL TIME – JESUS CHRIST?

OUEVELLE

DAY 7

MY FAVORITE VERSE FROM THE THEME WAS:

LOOKING BACK ON THESE TWO WEEKS, MY HIGHEST HIGH WAS:

MY LOWEST LOW THESE PAST WEEKS WAS:

ONE WAY GOD ANSWERED MY PRAYERS WAS:

ONE WAY GOD MIGHT USE ME AS A SACRED AGENT TO ANSWER THESE PRAYERS:

FAMILY COVENANT

We have shared *Highs & Lows* this week, read and highlighted the verses assigned in our Bibles, talked about our lives, prayed for one another's highs and lows, and blessed one another.

Parent's Signature *Teen's Signature* *Date*

THE FINKMANIA QUIZBOWL

Question 1:

The word "confirmation":

(A) Comes from the Latin *con* = with + *firmare* = to strengthen,

(B) Comes from the Latin *con* = with + *fermentus* = to ferment,

(C) Comes from the Latin *con* = with + *fateri* = to admit,

(D) Comes from the Latin *con* = with, + *fermatus*= to make a promise then leave the church

Question 2:

In confirmation we stand in front of an altar and make a promise to God. What other times do we do this?:

(A) Marriage,

(B) Baptism,

(C) Both A & B,

(D) When we smash into the pastor's car

Question 3:

The point of confirmation is:

(A) Affirmation of Baptism,

(B) A serious commitment to a responsible adult faith life in Christ's body, the church,

(C) Both A & B,

(D) A charade followed by a parade, followed by a party, a cake and hopefully big fat checks, from your relatives

Question 4:

Another name for confirmation is:

(A) Constipation,

(B) The Time That Fun Forgot,

(C) Affirmation of Baptism,

(D) The "tick off the pastor" session

Question 5:

In baptism, your parents say "yes" to God for you. In confirmation:

(A) Your parents say "yes" to God again because they are happy you are no longer their responsibility,

(B) You get to say "yes" to God on your own,

(C) You say "yes, I'm done!"

(D) None of the above

Question 6:

How do confirmation and baptism relate?:

(A) They don't,

(B) They are the same thing, but at different times of your life,

(C) Baptism is the beginning and confirmation is the end,

(D) They are both beginnings, but Baptism is a sacrament and confirmation is a rite (not a right)

Question 7:

A sacrament is:

(A) For Lutherans, Baptism, Holy Communion and not confirmation,

(B) A special gift of God's grace commanded by Christ and comes with a physical element attached,

(C) French for "paper or plastic,"

(D) A and B

Question 8:

Which of the following is not promised during confirmation?:

(A) To disappear from the church at the very first opportunity,

(B) To live among God's faithful,

(C) To hear God's word and share Christ's supper,

(D) To serve all people following Christ's example and strive for peace and justice in the world

Question 9:

Which of the following is true about confirmation?:

(A) On that day I will know everything there is to know about the faith,

(B) On that day I will be as close to God as I ever will be in my life,

(C) On that day I will say "yes" to the God who said "yes" to me in Holy Baptism,

(D) I'm out of here!

FINKmania Final Question:

Psalm 61:8 says, "So I will always sing praises to your name, as I pay my vows...":

(A) Once a month,

(B) Once a quarter,

(C) Day after day,

(D) Christmas, Easter and maybe an occasional bar mitzvah

Play this online game using **FINKlink**

LL29 | @ www.faithink.com

THE WEAKEST FINK

A person convinced against their will is not convinced.

LAURENCE J. PETER

TERMS

WRITE A DEFINITION BELOW.

Affirmation of Baptism

Confirmation

Convictions

Covenant

Vow

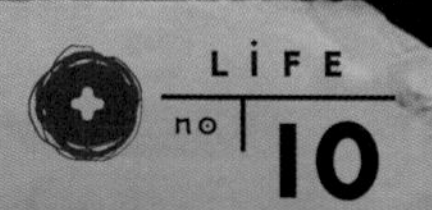

Claiming My Calling

"Esther's Gamble" Copyright © Dr. He Qi www.heqigallery.com.

"Go to the king to make supplication to him and entreat him for her people. Who knows? Perhaps you have come to royal dignity for just such a time as this."

— Esther 4:8b, 14c

Listen to this song using FINKlink LL30 @ www.faithink.com

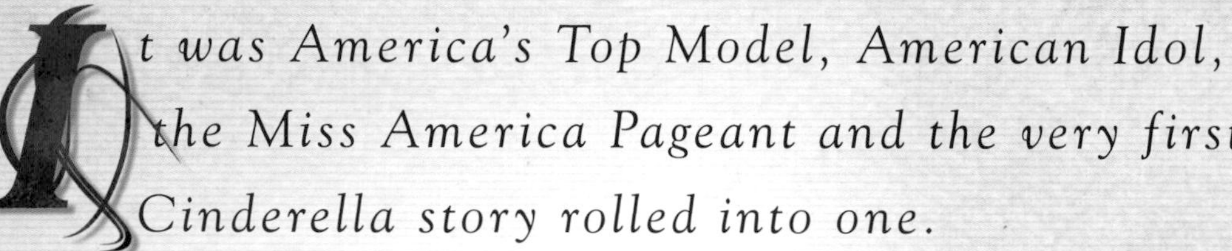

It was America's Top Model, American Idol, the Miss America Pageant and the very first Cinderella story rolled into one.

A young foreign girl was chosen for a beauty contest with the grandest grand prize of all. The winner would become queen of the Empire! Esther was a beauty. No question about that. Chosen for the competition, she was escorted from her home to spend a year in beauty treatments and royal training at the palace. In the end, Esther was hand-picked by the king as winner! But the joy of being number one soon turned into fear and a life-threatening decision. You see, Esther was a Jewish queen in a land that was about to kill all the Jews. When her uncle Mordecai uncovered the plot, he informed her that she had a difficult choice to make: Speak up and risk her life, or remain silent, play it safe, and watch her people die. What did she do? What would you do?

Have you ever felt God calling you to do something risky? Have you ever been compelled to speak up, to speak out, or to act on behalf of someone in trouble? Esther's uncle asked her to consider something: Perhaps there was a reason for her being chosen queen. Perhaps she had come into that royal position at that moment for the very purpose of saving God's people. Perhaps God had set her in that exact right time and place, and was now calling on her to do this great and risky thing. Perhaps the same is true for you, too. Read on.

Calling at the Crossroads

By Bryan Sirchio

What 'cha gonna do when its time to choose?
What 'cha gonna do with your life?
How you gonna use what's been given to you?
How you gonna know what is right?
There are many voices that call to you
And God's voice won't always be loud
But if you want to do what Christ
wants you to
Here's a truth to think about

(Chorus)
Where your greatest source of joy
Intersects with the needs of the world
Go and find that place
And hear the Spirit calling you (calling you)
Where your greatest source of joy
Intersects with the needs of the world
Go and find that place
And hear your calling at the Crossroads

Some are gonna tell you that you
must ask first
Where's the biggest money to be made?
But I will tell you there's no
check that's worth
Pushing what you love away
And some are gonna tell you that growing up
Means saying no to your dreams
But I believe the Spirit wants to
cross your dreams
With a wounded person's needs

(Chorus & Bridge)
You might be a wonderful artist
Your gift flows from deep in your soul
But someone has said there's no market
For what you do, so let it go
But I say give praise to the God who creates
And ask God to show you how
Your artistry can somehow be used
To raise up in a world that puts down

(Chorus)

Order this rocking song on the "Artist's Hand" CD at www.sirchio.com. Tell him FINK sent you.

What do you ABSOLUTELY LOVE to do? That may be part of your CALLING. What are some NEEDS in the world that are clear to you? That may be part of your calling as well.

Is there a way God could use your GIFTS, TALENTS, and PASSIONS to heal the world? That was JESUS' CALLING. Maybe that's the calling of those who call themselves Christ's friends, too.

Images in Art

- What do you see in today's painting by Dr. He Qi?
- Where are you in this work of art?
- How do the image and the verse apply to your life today?

So What Does This Mean?

I THINK GOD IS CALLING YOU TO BE A PASTOR.
I THINK GOD IS CALLING YOU TO BE A COMEDIAN.

Your calling is where your own greatest joy intersects with the needs of the world.

Frederick Buechner

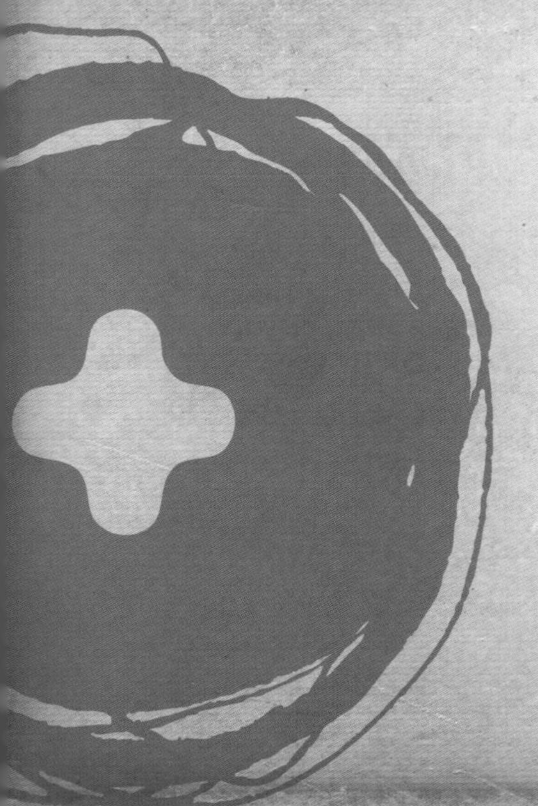

Claiming My Calling

The words vocation and vocal come from the same root word meaning *calling.* Have you ever considered your calling? Not your future job, but your true vocation? God's real purpose for putting you on the earth in the first place? Do you think God has given your life, your gifts, your talents for a specific reason? How can you recognize God's call over all the other calls you hear? How can you even know what God wants you to do with your time, talents and treasures? This is no small question. It could determine your future direction and fulfillment.

Bible Time

Read and highlight Esther 4:14c, writing "Esther's Call" in the margin. Next, look back on these ancestors of faith and see what forms their calls took. How did these individuals respond to their callings? What were the consequences?

I Samuel 3:10

Isaiah 6:5-8

Jeremiah 1:4-8

Luke 1:38

Prayer

Dear God, help me find the place where my greatest source of joy intersects with the needs of this world. May I hear you calling me and gladly answer. Amen.

Questions to Ponder

1. Do you believe God has something specific for you to do in this world? Why or why not?

2. The Latin root of the word of vocation, voca, means voice. Your vocation is God's voice and calling on your life. How does a vocation differ from a job?

3. What are three things you love to do? How might each of these sources of joy be used to touch a need in the world?

Small Group

share, read, talk, pray, bless

1. **SHARE** your highs and lows of the week one-on-one with another person. Listen carefully and record your friend's thoughts in the space below. Then return to small group and share your friend's highs and lows.

   MY HIGHS + LOWS THIS WEEK WERE:

   ....

   MY FRIEND'S HIGHS + LOWS THIS WEEK WERE:

   ....

2. **READ** and highlight the theme verse in your Bibles. Circle key words and learn the verse in song.

3. **TALK** about how today's verse relates to your highs and lows. Review the art for today, the Quiz Bowl questions, the terms, and the cartoons. Then write a sentence on each of the following:

   ONE NEW THING I LEARNED TODAY:

   ....

   ONE THING I ALREADY KNEW THAT IS WORTH REPEATING:

   ....

   ONE THING I WOULD LIKE TO KNOW MORE ABOUT:

   ....

4. **PRAY** for one another, praising and thanking God for your highs, and asking God to be with you in your lows. Include your friend's highs and lows in your prayers.

   A PRAISING PRAYER: ....

   A THANKING PRAYER: ....

   AN ASKING PRAYER: ....

5. **BLESS** one another using the blessing of the week. (right) Mark each person with the sign of the cross as you bless them.

THIS WEEK'S BLESSING

(NAME), CHILD OF GOD, MAY YOU FIND THAT PLACE WHERE YOUR GREATEST SOURCE OF JOY INTERSECTS WITH THE NEEDS OF THE WORLD, AND MAY YOU LIVE GOD'S CALLING. AMEN.

THE FAITH5 JOURNAL

Read the full devotions using FINKlink LL30 @ www.faithink.com

WEEK 1

DAY 1

TODAY'S BIBLE VERSE:

ESTHER 4:8B, 14C

Go to the king to make supplication to him and entreat him for her people. Who knows? Perhaps you have come to royal dignity for just such a time as this.

MY HIGH TODAY WAS:

MY LOW TODAY WAS:

MY PRAYER TODAY IS:

DAY 2

TODAY'S BIBLE VERSE:

ISAIAH 6:8

Then I heard the voice of the Lord saying, "Whom shall I send, and who will go for us?" And I said, "Here am I; send me!"

MY HIGH TODAY WAS:

MY LOW TODAY WAS:

MY PRAYER TODAY IS:

DAY 3

TODAY'S BIBLE VERSE:

1 SAMUEL 3:10

Now the Lord came and stood there, calling as before, "Samuel! Samuel!" And Samuel said, "Speak, for your servant is listening."

MY HIGH TODAY WAS:

MY LOW TODAY WAS:

MY PRAYER TODAY IS:

my HIGH today was:

my LOW today was:

my PRAYER today is:

DAY 4

today's bible verse:

Genesis 6:14

Make yourself an ark of cypress wood; make rooms in the ark, and cover it inside and out with pitch.

my HIGH today was:

my LOW today was:

my PRAYER today is:

DAY 5

today's bible verse:

I Peter 2:9

But you are a chosen race, a royal priesthood, a holy nation, God's own people, in order that you may proclaim the mighty acts of him who called you out of darkness into his marvelous light.

my HIGH today was:

my LOW today was:

my PRAYER today is:

DAY 6

today's bible verse:

Jeremiah 1:5

Before I formed you in the womb I knew you, and before you were born I consecrated you; I appointed you a prophet to the nations.

my HIGH today was:

my LOW today was:

my PRAYER today is:

DAY 7

this week's blessing

(NAME), CHILD OF GOD, MAY YOU FIND THAT PLACE WHERE YOUR GREATEST SOURCE OF JOY INTERSECTS WITH THE NEEDS OF THE WORLD, AND MAY YOU LIVE GOD'S CALLING. AMEN.

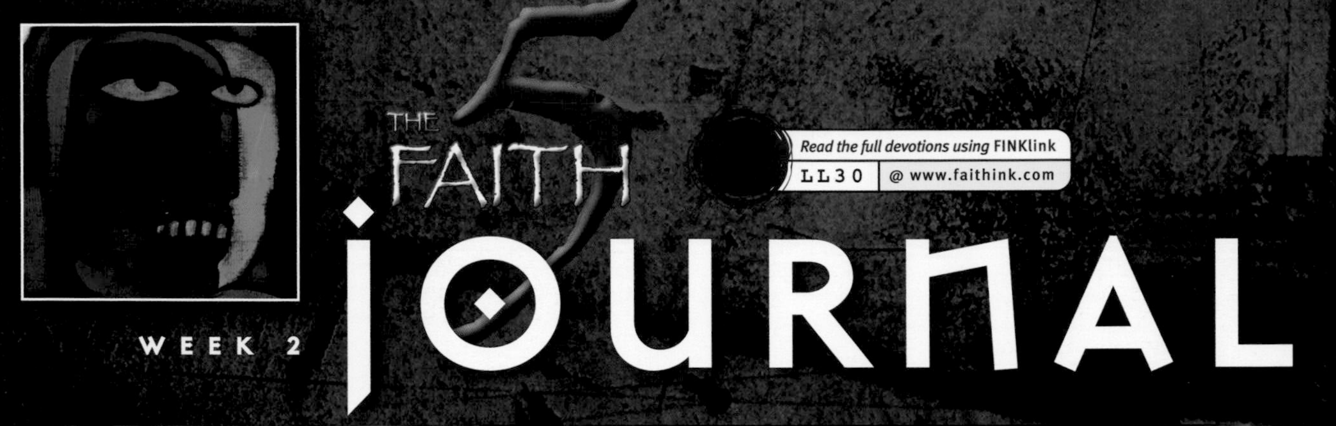

WEEK 2

DAY 1

TODAY'S BIBLE VERSE:

1 Corinthians 12:29-31

Are you all apostles? Are you all prophets? Are you all teachers? Do all work miracles? Do all possess gifts of healing? Do all speak in tongues? Do all interpret? But strive for the greater gifts. And I will show you a still more excellent way.

MY HIGH TODAY WAS:

MY LOW TODAY WAS:

MY PRAYER TODAY IS:

DAY 2

TODAY'S BIBLE VERSE:

Romans 12:2

Do not be conformed to this world, but be transformed by the renewing of your minds, so that you may discern what is the will of God—what is good and acceptable and perfect.

MY HIGH TODAY WAS:

MY LOW TODAY WAS:

MY PRAYER TODAY IS:

DAY 3

TODAY'S BIBLE VERSE:

Mark 1:17

And Jesus said to them, "Follow me and I will make you fish for people."

MY HIGH TODAY WAS:

MY LOW TODAY WAS:

MY PRAYER TODAY IS:

2. READ and highlight the verse of the day in your Bibles.

3. TALK about how today's verse relates to your highs & lows.

4. PRAY for your highs & lows, for your family and for the world.

5. BLESS one another using this week's blessing (on the previous page).

my HIGH today was:

my LOW today was:

my PRAYER today is:

DAY 4

today's Bible verse:

John 15:16

You did not choose me but I chose you. And I appointed you to go and bear fruit, fruit that will last, so that the Father will give you whatever you ask him in my name.

my HIGH today was:

my LOW today was:

my PRAYER today is:

DAY 5

today's Bible verse:

Matthew 28:19-20

Go therefore and make disciples of all nations, baptizing them in the name of the Father and of the Son and of the Holy Spirit, and teaching them to obey everything that I have commanded you.

my HIGH today was:

my LOW today was:

my PRAYER today is:

DAY 6

today's Bible verse:

1 Corinthians 1:8

He will also strengthen you to the end, so that you may be blameless on the day of our Lord Jesus Christ.

S | M | T | W | TH | F | S

THEME IN REVIEW

Don't just make a living. Make a life!

Unknown

WHAT'S THAT?
A OUIJA BOARD.
WHAT'S IT FOR?
I WANT FIND OUT WHAT I SHOULD DO WITH MY LIFE.
I CAN TELL YOU WHAT GOD WANTS YOU TO DO WITH YOUR LIFE.
YOU CAN? WHAT?
GOD WANTS YOU DITCH THE BOARD AND START USING PRAYER TO DISCOVER YOUR CALLING
WOW. COOL.
WHAT ARE YOU DOING NOW?
CALLING MY PSYCHIC FRIEND TO SEE IF IT'S OK.
Melheim

DAY 7

MY FAVORITE VERSE FROM THE THEME WAS:

....

....

....

....

....

....

....

....

LOOKING BACK ON THESE TWO WEEKS, MY HIGHEST HIGH WAS:

....

MY LOWEST LOW THESE PAST WEEKS WAS:

....

ONE WAY GOD ANSWERED MY PRAYERS WAS:

....

ONE WAY GOD MIGHT USE ME AS A SACRED AGENT TO ANSWER THESE PRAYERS:

....

....

Family Covenant

We have shared *Highs & Lows* this week, read and highlighted the verses assigned in our Bibles, talked about our lives, prayed for one another's highs and lows, and blessed one another.

....

Parent's Signature *Teen's Signature* *Date*

THE FINKMANIA QUIZ BOWL

Question 1:

What's more important in the long run: making a living or making a life?:

(A) Making a living,
(B) Making a life,
(C) Neither,
(D) I haven't the foggiest

Question 2:

The root of the word vocation (voca) means:

(A) Coffee,
(B) Voice,
(C) Spirit,
(D) Money

Question 3:

A "vocation" can then be best defined as:

(A) Part-time employment,
(B) A job that can make you some good money,
(C) What the voice of God is calling you to do,
(D) What the voice of your parent, coach, Army Recruiter, or best friend's uncle in the plastic business is telling you to do

Question 4:

To find your true calling you need to:

(A) Ask Jesus,
(B) Go to college,
(C) Find the intersection between your greatest source of joy and the needs of the world,
(D) Find the intersection between your greatest source of joy and the occupation that can make you the most money

Question 5:

What's the difference between God's call for you and a distraction?:

(A) Distractions stop—God's call doesn't,
(B) God's call is louder,
(C) God's call is harder,
(D) Distractions are more fun

Question 6:

In the Bible, beautiful Queen Esther was once called by God to:

(A) Call water from a rock,
(B) Call water from Iraq,
(C) Risk her life to save the Jewish people,
(D) Compete in "Persia's Next Top Model"

Question 7:

Queen Esther chose to:

(A) Speak up, risking her life,
(B) Speak up, risking her social status,
(C) Remain silent, thus condemning her people to death,
(D) Remain silent, thus condemning her people to 20 more weeks of winter

Question 8:

God doesn't only call the gifted, God also:

(A) Gifts the called,
(B) Calls the willing,
(C) Calls the unwilling,
(D) All of the above

Question 9:

How can you know God's calling for your life?:

(A) Search the scriptures,
(B) Pray for God's guidance,
(C) Ask people who love God and love you what they think you should explore,
(D) All of the above and then maybe ask your parents, coaches, Army Recruiters, and best friend's uncles in the plastic business if you have the time

FINKmania Final Question:

Esther 4:14c says, "Who knows? Perhaps you have come to royal dignity for..."

(A) "...just such a time as this,"
(B) "...just such a task as this,"
(C) "...just such a challenge as this,"
(D) "...just such a mistake as you are about to make as this"

Play this online game using FINKlink
LL30 @ www.faithink.com

THE WEAKEST FINK

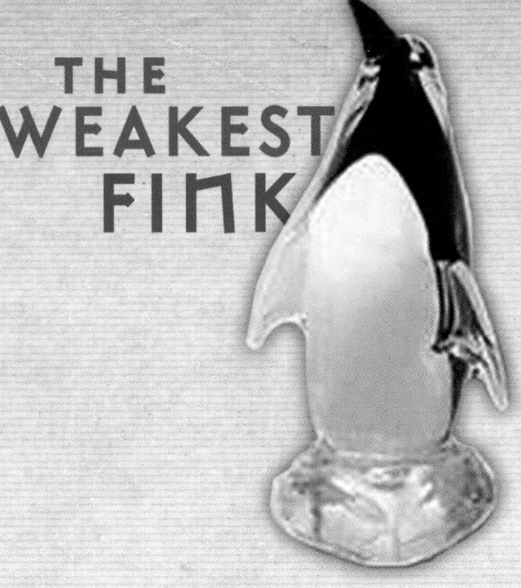

To love what you do and feel it makes a difference—how could anything be more fun!

Kathryn Graham

TERMS

WRITE A DEFINITION BELOW.

Calling

Job

Purpose

Vocation

Voice

THE FAITH 5

FIVE STEPS TO KEEPING YOUR FAMILY TOGETHER IN A WORLD THAT CAN TEAR IT APART

Year in Review

Take a moment to look back on the year and see how you and your friends have changed and grown.

PASTE
End of Year
PHOTO OF YOU
HERE
(MY HOW YOU'VE GROWN)
This is Me

LOOKING BACK ON THE YEAR, MY HIGHEST HIGH WAS:

MY LOWEST LOW THIS YEAR WAS:

THE BIGGEST WAY GOD ANSWERED MY PRAYER THIS YEAR:

ONE WAY I GREW IN MY FAITH THIS YEAR WAS:

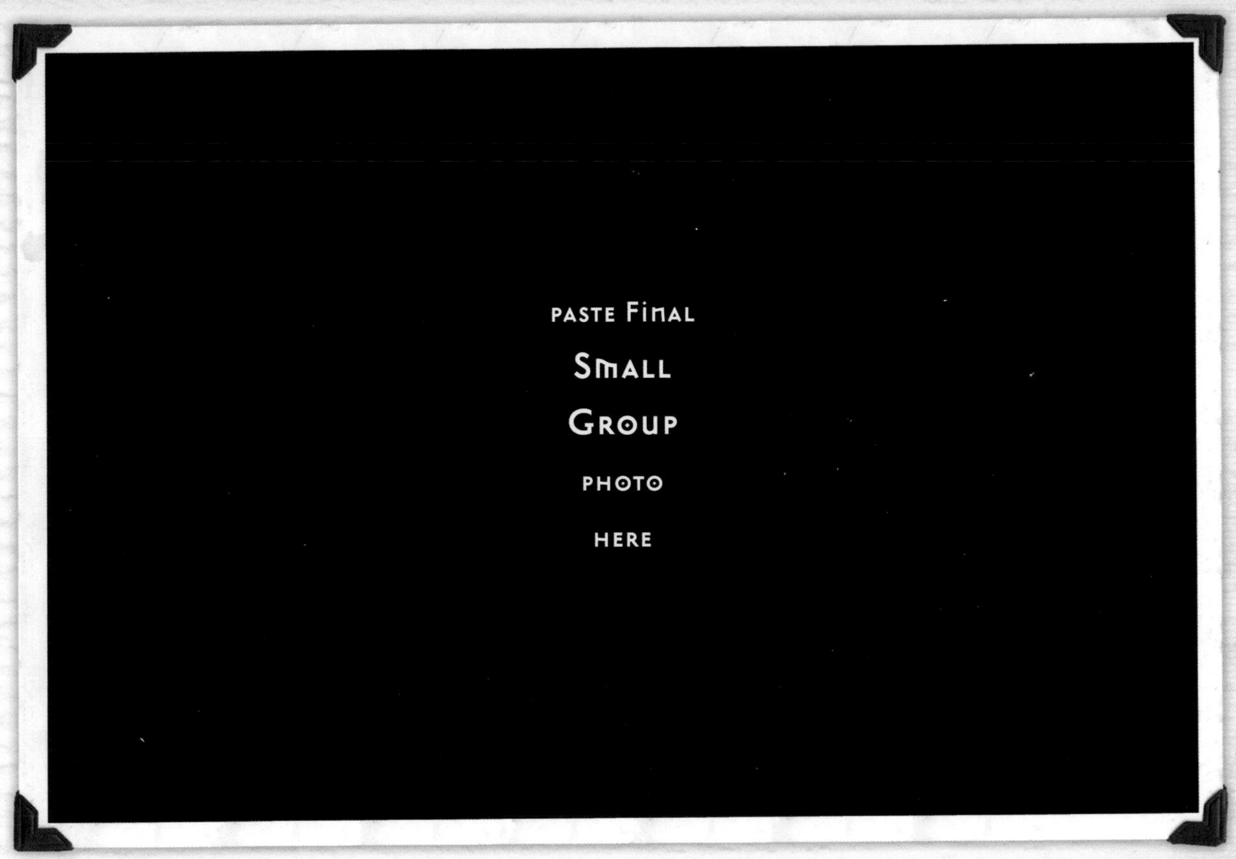
PASTE FINAL
SMALL
GROUP
PHOTO
HERE

This is My Small Group

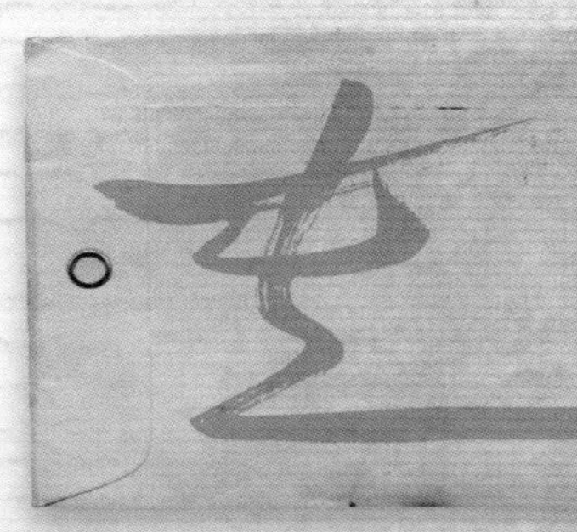

AUTOGRAPHS

PHOTOGRAPHS

& PETROGRAPHS

S,

ALL YOU REALLY NEED FOR AN ASYLUM IS A BIG ROOM AND THE RIGHT KIND OF PEOPLE!

AUTOGRAPHS

PHOTOGRAPHS

& PETROGRAPHS

s,

AUTOGRAPHS

PHOTOGRAPHS

& PETROGRAPHS

s,

OPERATION
SPYGLASS

Sacred agents get ready... It's time to get to know your yearbook. Find each of the 75 items below.

- A Mighty Fortress Sheet Music
- AAA batteries
- Alex Lynch & the Dolphin
- Alien
- Bamboo
- Big Smile
- Black Hawk Helicopter
- Block Letters A, N & Z
- Brass Lion
- Buddah
- Butterfly
- Can of Worms
- Car Keys
- Carved Wooden Soldiers
- CH CH Postit Note
- Christmas Tree
- Circular Slide Viewer
- Coffee Stains
- Coins
- Crystal Penguin
- Do Not Bend (Stamped)
- Elephant
- Faith Inkubators Logo
- Family Symbol in Mandarin
- Feather
- Fire
- Fist Holding Hammer
- Fly
- Four Apostles on a Card
- Girl Eating Ice Cream Cone
- Glasses
- God Symbol in Mandarin
- Graduation Cap
- Grand Cathedral Arches
- He Qi (huh chee) Artist Photo
- Hotel Baggage Cart
- Hurricane Katrina from Space
- Identification Card
- Infant in Womb Sketch by Da Vinci
- Key with Padlock
- Lamb
- Leaf (Red)
- Library Card
- Lightning Warning Sign
- Love Symbol in Mandarin
- Luther's Bible (in his own writing)
- Luther's Seal
- Magister Mundi Sum (i'm King of the Wo
- Match Burning
- Menorah (Seven Candles)
- Messiah (Hebrew) and Christ (Gree
- Mini-Headphone Jack
- Movie Ticket to Admit One
- Old Composition Book
- Old Post Card
- Outreach Chart (Arrow & Os)
- "Past Due" Stamp
- Pirate Ship
- Pocket Watch
- Pope Leo X (Painting)
- Ruler
- Seven-headed Luther Cartoon
- Shushing Angel
- Silentium (Silence) in Latin
- Singing Minstrel Toys (5)
- Space Antennae for Seti Project
- Spike (Iron)
- Spoon, Fork, Knife
- Spy Glass
- Squashed Bug (Aaaargh!)
- Statues atop St. Peter's in Rome
- Teddy Roosevelt Silhouette
- The Black Tower of Wittenberg
- Three-headed Alien
- Trash Can Cartoon